AMERICA AT MID-CENTURY

André Siegfried

AMERICA
AT MID-CENTURY

★ ★
★

TRANSLATED BY MARGARET LEDÉSERT

Harcourt, Brace and Company

NEW YORK

Library of Congress Catalog Card Number: 55-7422

PRINTED IN THE UNITED STATES OF AMERICA

INTRODUCTION

This book is not merely a bringing up to date of one published in 1927 under the title *America Comes of Age*. The last quarter of a century has introduced new perspectives; everything must be changed, including things which once appeared to be changeless. To bring my survey up to date, a completely new book is necessary.

I first visited the United States in 1898 and returned there three times before 1914. I crossed the Atlantic seven times between the two wars and four times since 1945. On the basis of the observations and impressions arising from these contacts I am now attempting, twenty-five years after the publication of *America Comes of Age*, to give a picture of a country which should be of particular interest to us today.

In undertaking this task I have been guided by three essential points of view, which, I believe, must always be kept to the forefront in order to understand post-1914 America.

After the period of economic depression, which lasted from 1929 to 1941, and Roosevelt's New Deal, and World War II, it was impossible for the country to be the same as before, such happenings dig too deeply into the nation's soil. And it must be realized that the consequences of the Depression were probably as far-reaching as those of the war.

In spite of contacts, the differences between Europe and America are increasing; America is more American than it was some years ago, when it could be considered as a daughter of the old European continent who had not yet attained her majority. This gulf which has developed must be considered from a continental rather than a national point of view, for it is in this way that the problems of the United States can more easily be understood.

v

Considering the question from this angle, we come to the realization that we are studying a form of civilization rather than a country. Though both belong to the West, the American civilization is becoming more and more distinct from our traditional European civilization, and, as it takes the lead more and more, the destiny of the whole world is influenced by it.

The distinction varies according to whether the United States is judged from the American or the European standpoint. I am considering it from the European point of view, and this gives rise to certain impressions which might erroneously be taken as critical; they are merely a sign that America is progressing more quickly than we are along the track which is leading Western nations to their destiny.

CONTENTS

vii

PART III

AMERICAN ECONOMY

PART IV

THE SOCIAL BACKGROUND AND THE FORMATION OF PUBLIC OPINION

PART V

POLITICAL LIFE

PART VI

EXTERNAL RELATIONS

CONCLUSION

PART I

THE GEOGRAPHICAL ASPECT

CHAPTER 1

The Personality of the American Continent

★

Continents, like countries, have their individuality, and a country can be understood only when one considers it as forming part of a continent. Countries which together form distinct civilizations are often to be found grouped around a sea or an ocean, but it is the continental unities which bear the more distinctive personalities. It will therefore be essential, when considering the United States, to bear in mind constantly that it is a part of the American continent. The fact that it belongs on the one hand to the Atlantic and on the other hand to the Pacific is indubitably significant, but is, nevertheless, a secondary consideration.

Each of the various continents has its own atmosphere and psychology. There is an American, a European, and an Asiatic way of looking at problems, finding solutions, reacting from the intellectual, sentimental, or political point of view, in brief of conducting one's life. There is, for example, an American temperament. And it is the essentially Asiatic or American outlook which has brought about and which influences the political system of India or the United States.

Moreover, continental differences are so great that, when one passes from one continent to another, one must often change one's ideas of size, perspectives, way of thinking, and, particularly, one's vocabulary. One should not apply European terminology to America, since the sense of the words is often different or even meaningless: such words as socialism, revolution, liberalism, or (politically speaking) left and right, must be used guardedly when applied to America.

The United States obviously forms part of the American conti-

3

nent and therefore it must be considered as part of the New World if errors of judgment are to be avoided; and it is the contrast between Europe and America which impresses itself upon our attention from the beginning of this study.

I

A particularly striking feature of the New World is the vastness of nature. Everything is on a different scale from the European, and has different proportions; whether we are considering the Mississippi, the Rocky Mountains, the Andes, the Brazilian forest, or the limitless plains of the Far West, the geographical concept of the whole is related to that of Asia or Africa rather than to the small European continent. If there are possible points of comparison, they are with Scandinavia or Russia, which geographically do not wholly belong to Europe. The very structure is different: Europe is jointed, diversified, complex; America is massive, simple, unencumbered by man, or by institutions as tangled as the trees of an ancient forest.

This vastness, this lack of common measure, explains the particular relations of the American with nature. It is reflected in agricultural development which is either too easy or too difficult; in some instances the natural resources are there and man has only, so to speak, to harvest them; in other cases the wealth is certainly present in all its magnificence, but only by the means of gigantic enterprises can it be attained. It therefore follows that man has to conquer nature rather than adapt himself to it: he maltreats it because he is too eager to harvest its wealth and, in the operation, he may succeed in devastating it because he treats it not as a living thing but as an industrial raw material. Geoffrey Gorer writes in his book *The American People*: "Significantly often, the terms of mining are applied to agriculture. Crops are extracted, land is mined—the vegetable world is constantly being spoken of, and treated, as though it were a mineral world. Crops are extracted from a piece of land until it is exhausted, after which the land is abandoned, in exactly the same way as metal is extracted from a vein until that is exhausted and the mine abandoned. . . . Instead of mines, farms and forest lands have come to be compared to factories, where the maintenance of the plant is necessary for the production of goods. Land is still a raw material, no more to be loved or identified with than a lump of iron or an oil well under the soil." *

It is, moreover, curious to note that Soviet agriculture indulges in similar tricks of vocabulary. France is proud of her peasants, but the United States boasts of having none: the peasant's outlook is indeed foreign to a country which, having forged ahead, ignores the time factor in production, unless it be to speed up all operations to the maximum without taking into account the necessity of attaining maturity.

This is the sign of the incredible youth of this nation which, apart from the Indians, seems to have started life afresh when crossing the ocean. Europeans, Frenchmen, and above all inhabitants of the Mediterranean shores have two thousand years of history behind them, one might almost say beneath them, and these two thousand years have contributed toward their formation. Most Americans have a tradition of no more than three or four hundred years, sometimes one hundred or even less; they have but a thin keel between them and the ocean of the ages. Wickham Steed once told me of an extraordinarily revealing conversation that he had had with two Californians. "What," he had asked them, "is your oldest historical recollection?" They, after consulting each other, for Americans are always conscientious about their replies, had answered quite simply: "Well, the McKinley Tariff." The McKinley Tariff, which dates back to 1890! Steed, in astonishment, had protested: "But what about the War of Independence?" "Oh! yes, a few Yankees still talk about it." More and more astonished, Steed returned to the charge: "What about the American Civil War? That isn't very far back!" "Oh! that's a matter for a few Negroes in the South."

An astonishing country, where everything is focused on the future! Such youthfulness has serious economic and social implications, which contrast strongly with the maturity and the relative age of Europe. For example, in the New World raw materials are available on the spot in almost unlimited quantities. It follows that, owing to the variety of opportunity, individual success is

* Geoffrey Gorer, *The American People*, New York, W. W. Norton, 1948, pp. 155-56.

possible within the existing framework, and, even if this is no longer completely true, there is a tendency still to believe it to be so. It consequently appears easier to produce than to share, and this has brought about the basic conservatism of the North Americans, so different from the European outlook. In America there has been no struggle for the conquest of fresh territory: is there not already more than enough land to settle in and develop? There is no class struggle, either, and no revolutionary tradition, so that the word "Revolution" written with a capital "R" is meaningless. It is true that the continent itself is growing older, but until now this has hardly been apparent, so that its psychology remains characteristic of a youth that we Europeans have lost.

II

These aspects of his environment have given the American a number of salient psychological characteristics, and those which strike the foreign observer most are his confidence, his good will, and above all his innate optimism. He sincerely believes in progress: American progress—and perhaps it is necessary to qualify it as specifically American—appears to him to be guaranteed, limitless, and almost statutory. He imagines a continually rising tide, which will never cease uplifting the whole American society, its citizens, and their business affairs. I remember the reply of a New Yorker who, when asked to what he attributed his great wealth, said: "It's very simple! When I go downtown in the morning I buy, and when I come uptown in the evening I sell." This confidence in the future is characteristic not only of North Americans but of all Americans; it is to be found in Argentina and Brazil as much as in the United States, but it is nonexistent in any other continent. During the nineteenth century Europe had a similar faith in unlimited progress to be achieved through liberalism: she has lost it.

The American is convinced that man can accomplish anything, and that technical progress can solve any problem. This belief which the Russian has come to hold through indoctrination is with the American a matter of instinctive, spontaneous faith. It is not difficult to find the source of this in the relative ease of everything in this new setting, where there is no lack of space; it arises from the justifiable pride of the pioneer in his work; and again from the almost uninterrupted century of prosperity, particularly in the period since the Spanish-American War. This prosperity was shattered by the crisis of 1929, and cracks appeared in the edifice of satisfaction. The neoprosperity of World War II renewed the former current of optimism, but once optimism has been lost a relapse is always imminent, and the threat of another crisis is always present. This sense of newness and absence of tradition have maintained in the Americans a striking freedom of thought: they are unencumbered by routine and, though they have reason to be conservative, they have no reactionary complexes; they have learned, confronted by the relatively simple problems of an expanding economy, a fact which is not universally true, that as far as they are concerned progress pays. Europe, with its ancient traditions, could not have arrived at such a conclusion. It is, moreover, true to say that this progress is whirling the United States into a cycle of evolution too rapid to be mastered. The nation is not yet stable, not stable geographically, for initial immigration followed by migratory movements within the continent has made the Americans slow to take roots; not stable physically, for the American race, if one can speak of such a thing, has not yet evolved; not stable socially, for the American is still to some extent nomadic, always ready to change either residence or occupation.

America thus has, established in the van of the Western army, the embryo of an individual civilization, which has faith in the possibility of changing the very rhythm of nature. One might almost call it the great American adventure, the end of which is not in sight; for it is problematic whether man can dissociate himself to such an extent from nature.

III

The fundamental unity of the American continent must always be borne in mind when considering the United States. The essential characteristic of the New World is its youth, and this applies equally to North and South America. The geographical differences between the northern and southern land masses are less significant than the points of resemblance between the two; Latins and Anglo-Saxons tread the same soil, breathe the same air, evolve in the same economic climate, with similar problems of production, development, population density, or colonization. Both have similar reactions to international questions and this deep-rooted Pan-Americanism, inasmuch as it is divorced from any vestige of imperialism, is a fundamental reality.

This unity is solely geographical, for historically the differences outweigh the points of resemblance. The two great currents of immigration which peopled the Americas brought mainly Protestant Anglo-Saxons to the North and Catholic Latin races to the South. Thus there appears a historical separatist factor which enters into strong opposition with the unifying tendency of the geographical similarity. There are the two distinct forces. The unifying geographical axis is implanted in the physical structure of the continent.

Baulig writes in his *Géographie Universelle:*

While the relief of the European continent encourages east-west movement, that of North America tends to develop north-south communications: climatic divisions, uneven as far as latitude is concerned, are more marked in the east-west direction, becoming particularly distinct in the mountains of the West. While white settlers have followed the east-west route along the lines of latitude and political frontiers and railway lines have followed this historical development, it is equally true that other currents are appearing, more in keeping with the geographical lay-out of the continent and its fundamental division into East, Center, and West; a division implicit in the physical structure which no technical progress could ever obliterate.*

It is a struggle between latitude and longitude, history and geography. Which of the two must finally dominate? If geography, then Americans, be they Anglo-Saxons or Latins, will become more alike, and Pan-Americanism will become more of a reality. If history, then Europe will continue to influence American destiny. South America will remain more Latin, more Catholic, more specifically American, and North America will become more Anglo-Saxon, more Protestant, and Canada British rather than American. This is the angle from which any American country should be studied, be it Canada or Argentina or, as in this case, the United States.

* Henri Baulig, *Géographie Universelle,* Paris, Armand Colin, Tome XIII, 1935-36, p. 35.

IV

It is, therefore, difficult for a European to understand the United States, and, if he is to pass judgment, it must of necessity be from a European point of view. He is faced with the difference, not between two countries, but between two continents. One European nation can understand another, even if they are separated by violent political differences; are they not in a way tenants of the same block of apartments?

It must be realized, however, that the inhabitants of the United States come almost entirely from European stock; they are a white race, Christians, and belong to Western civilization. They have a history and a tradition, but it has been altered, adapted, assimilated, and often repudiated, and it is almost invariably unrecognizable by virtue of its rebirth in an entirely different continental environment. In order to understand such a country, the European observer must, so to speak, be tuned in. He must acquire the American idea of dimensions, so different from our own, he must accustom himself to its climate, so strange to us, its colors, its flavors, its perfume, its very size; he must come to understand the paradoxical tempo of a society whose rhythm is rapid, but whose members react slowly; he must learn to appreciate a moral background composed of optimism, boldness, pride, weakness, instability, and of youthfulness which can be at times almost childish.

It is at the same time important to take into consideration the wealth of American resources; they are not solely material, and the energy derived from the early Puritans is a striking example of their spiritual wealth.

Finally it must be borne in mind that the atmosphere of the United States is that of a new world and still to a certain extent that of eighteenth-century Europe; that American society is instinctively on the defense against European reaction, be it revolutionary or totalitarian. To be unaware of, to exaggerate, or to underestimate the significance of any one of these essential American characteristics would be to invite misconception, since it would upset the balance between them; for in this country where quantity is of prime significance, a delicate admixture of quality is ever essential.

CHAPTER 2

The Position of the United States in Relation to the American Continent and to the Rest of the World

★

The approximate area of the United States is three million square miles, more than three-quarters the size of Europe, fourteen times the size of France, and about thirty times the size of the United Kingdom. Many of the forty-eight states are comparable in size to European countries: Texas, with 260,000 square miles, is larger than France, and California, with 160,000 square miles, is of similar size to Sweden. The United States from this point of view must be considered as a continent rather than a country; it is not to be compared with France or the United Kingdom, but with Europe itself. This gives a different and clearer significance to American problems.

It is sometimes difficult to realize the distances involved inside the United States unless one crosses the country by road or rail. Then one is aware of the significance of the 3,100 miles which separate New York and San Francisco: one night by aircraft, but three and a half days by rail! One thousand miles divide the Canadian frontier from the Gulf of Mexico, 1,350 miles New York from New Orleans, 750 miles one flank of the Rockies from the other; the country is constructed on a scale unfamiliar to Europe, and the European must become accustomed to this state of affairs which, on this side of the Atlantic, he will find only in Russia. This general impression is increased by the massiveness of North America; on the map it seems rather like a squat chest of drawers

10

with a simplified silhouette, while Europe makes one think of a hand stretched out into the Atlantic. In America nature is revealed on a scale so immense as to be disturbing to man, a continental block not penetrated by any sea, seeming almost dedicated to autonomy. Logically speaking, a distinct type of civilization should evolve there.

II

In this setting the idea of space takes on a new significance. Let us reconsider our idea of scale: everything is larger—mountains, plains, rivers, towns, factories, houses, trains, administrative districts. Sinclair Lewis wrote, speaking of Zenith, Babbitt's home town: It was "a city built—it seemed—for giants." On returning to Europe, everything seems tiny. In the United States, so much space is available that naturally it is wasted; there will always be sufficient space without any limitations. Under these conditions the idea of conquering territory does not appeal to the Americans, and thus they cannot understand how Europeans strive for the possession of a few square miles of land, and they condemn the European colonial policy, for if they wish to conquer or colonize, they can do so at home. This wastage of territory has brought about a remarkable lack of geographical concentration, following the principle that it is always possible to move a little further on. Many states have no natural boundaries but merely frontiers traced arbitrarily, frontiers that could just as conveniently have been placed elsewhere. In a book about the forty-eight states, *These United States,* an author writes as follows about South Dakota, "State without End":

I remember some years ago a friend showed me that every time I went to the post office I crossed latitude forty-five north. I had not been aware of it. He pointed out the exact place, by a tree, and ever afterward I found myself stepping high when I passed over it, bound not to trip. But a State that must depend on these artificial map decorations for its boundaries is unfortunate. How shall it know itself? *

* Hayden Carruth, "South Dakota, State without End," *These United States,* ed. by Ernest Gruening, New York, Boni & Liveright, 1923, 1st series, p. 263.

Towns have a similar propensity to spread over the countryside with open spaces within their confines, and often without any one main focal point.

This failing becomes more marked the further west one advances, for, with the absence of any natural limits, towns tend to spread themselves out without definite form. This is the case with Los Angeles, which may be compared with a rural district completely built up. The widespread use of the private car modifies to a certain extent the effect of distance between interdependent districts; but speed finally works on the side of deconcentration, with the result that a new conception of urban life is born, that of the city set down in the countryside.

The mastery of space on this scale implies a general policy, without which unification of the country would have been impossible, and in this an intensified and efficient system of communications has played an essential role. Rail, road, and air transport have genuinely served the cause of American political solidarity. In South America, man changed his mode of transport from mule directly to aircraft. In the United States railroads, preceding the roads, assisted the growth of the nation, and in spite of crises rail transport still maintains its importance. But the private car has become an equally important personal necessity in a way of life where nobody walks, since distances are too great, with the result that a pedestrian is considered almost suspicious by the traffic police. Even more important is the recently developed role of aircraft, which have succeeded in overcoming today what only yesterday seemed gigantic in the structure of America.

The United States has also been tempted by the idea of loftiness. The skyscraper, a topographical necessity in New York, has spread throughout the country and continent, but it would no more be planned without elevators than would the modern road without motors. Moreover, American genius had created this mechanism before its essential function became apparent: as early as 1861, when he was visiting New York, my father remarked on the presence of "little vertical railways" in the Fifth Avenue Hotel. Here again technical progress has triumphed over space. Telegraph, telephone, radio, and television have all played a similar part, for it is thanks to all these means of communication that rupture between the states has been avoided in spite of geographical remoteness. At the time of the Civil War, according to my father's letters, everyone expected that the country would eventually be divided into two sovereign states: the distances involved, which were really unprecedented for the period, justified to a certain degree such a judgment, and it needed all Lincoln's genius to insist upon the necessity of union. The immense progress achieved in the field of communications has provided a means by which the commerce, industry, and population distribution of this huge area can without reserve be considered as a geographical unit. Now possibilities in this field seem to be unlimited—during the 1952 presidential election experience showed that a political meeting, hastily summoned, could be held equally well at Boston, Saint Louis, or on the Pacific coast.

In spite, however, of all the attempts to overcome them, great distances still exist, and they have certainly influenced American psychology. It must be observed that there is a degree of uniformity about the country which is inclined to produce boredom. American drivers often fall asleep at the wheel on the long, transcontinental roads, and this is the cause of a large number of serious accidents. But although the broad western plains are monotonous, containing little to appeal to the imagination, there is in the United States no question of the Russian *Nitchevo* or the Asiatic *Nirvana*. The American is a Westerner, never lacking in self-control, unable to lose himself like the traditional Russian in the abyss of the immeasurable; he frees himself from the fetters of nature and imposes himself upon her; the influence of his surroundings upon him tends to diminish, and his geographical background to lose much of its significance; the precise location of towns or factories has become purely optional and incidental; since surroundings matter little, migration is natural. This outlook contrasts strongly with that of the traditional European peasant, wedded to his land, attached to his farm by bonds comparable to the roots of a tree. In the United States the farmer buys, sells, or administers his farm just as he would deal in shares on the stock exchange.

The detachment, instability or nomadic nature of the American, which has given rise to so much comment, is to a great extent the natural outcome of his environment. Why should he be tied to any one place when there is an indefinite number of others, equally easy to acquire? The age-old unrest of the white man with his eternal wanderlust has never had greater scope. Nobody settles down permanently.*

Finally, this space must be considered as a source of well-being, the limitation or the loss of which would menace the country's equilibrium. For a country of 160 million inhabitants it is advantageous not to jostle against each other's elbows, and the existence of so many open spaces provides as many possibilities for adventure, initiative, and energy: no enterprise need be considered as decisively lost so long as an alternative remains open. The Americans have maintained a conception of moving west, an idea based on mental outlook rather than on geography, the attitude to what they term "the frontier," that is to say, any open, unexploited space which offers good prospects to unsatisfied ambition. During the crises of the nineteenth century, when a young man could find no outlet in the East he would be told: "Go West, young man!" Such was then the value of this reserve of undeveloped territory, but there are no longer any "frontiers" and the term "West" has very little significance now that the country has been developed right to the Pacific coast. It would seem that the moment when the "frontier" ceased to exist marked the turning of a page, not only in the history of the United States but also in the psychology of the American nation.

III

Are such characteristics sufficient to form a country or, more precisely, a nation? For a whole century the American has come up against no factors to limit his progress, and the vastness of his resources has been such that they can best be described in the words of Pascal, "The imagination wearies sooner in conceiving than nature in supplying." But this very profusion of natural resources, with its lack of cohesion, militated against the creation of a state. Fortunately the geographical structure of the country

* Jules Romains, *Visite aux Américains*, Paris, E. Flammarion, 1937, p. 95.

provided a sound foundation for the development of a well-organized and homogeneous community: the United States consists of a central plain flanked by two mountain systems; it is a continent washed by two oceans, with a river system, rainfall scheme, a sufficient climatic variety, and indeed all the basic elements needed to bring about harmony between a number of complementary regions. The nation was thus developed and unified in a geographical setting which was already stable. In spite of the size of the country it has unshakable unity; this is due less to the physical structure than to the way in which living conditions have been standardized by the practical elimination of the idea of distance. The initial geographical unity has been supplemented by the uniform concept of the famous American way of life, considered by the Americans as a sort of banner.

Because of the transformation brought about by technical progress the country, once so large as to have only escaped being split in two at the time of the Civil War, is not excessively large today. From the twentieth-century standpoint it should, perhaps, be considered as normal for a great power, adapted to the needs and the possibilities of the modern world. The United States has 160 million inhabitants for its three million square miles; the U.S.S.R., still to be regarded as in the giant class, has 200 million people in 8,500,000 square miles. This change in the idea of proportion marks the beginning of a new era.

IV

Since the two World Wars, particularly since the second, the United States has undergone a complete revolution in its world status. The country is still geographically in the same place, but its external relations have been completely transformed.

From the North American standpoint, there is no natural frontier between the United States and Canada, but simply a line drawn arbitrarily on the map: the countries are one economically and socially, and though there is a political frontier it is not a complete barrier, since there is a considerable amount of frontier contact between peoples who do not consider each other as foreigners. The defense line of the United States is not the Canadian frontier but somewhere north of the Arctic Circle; and thus we have a conception of North American unity, comprising a common defense program for a civilization common to both countries. The frontier between the United States and Mexico is equally artificial, and Cuba is very near to Florida. Here contact with the Latin (or Indian) world is very close, not under the aegis of an Anglo-Saxon defense program, but through the outlook common to the American continent. Air transport has for the last fifteen years brought Central and South America into close proximity with New York, Chicago, San Francisco, and more particularly with the southern states, at length recovered from the devastation of the Civil War and undergoing a rapid process of development. By means of the air routes down the west coast to Peru and Chile, and down the east to Brazil and Argentina, the influence of the United States is coming to predominate in a part of the world that until very recently looked toward Europe.

America traditionally prides herself on her isolation from other continents. New York is 3,206 miles from Gibraltar, Quebec 2,625 miles from Liverpool. The distance between Los Angeles and Yokohama is 4,839 miles, between Seattle and Yokohama 4,259 miles. For a long time the only possible routes were by sea; now the air routes pass through the Arctic Circle; the great circle route between Moscow and San Francisco passes through the North Cape, the northern part of Greenland and Alberta; that between Chicago and Calcutta through Edmonton, Alaska, eastern Siberia, and Chungking. Via the North Pole it is only 2,250 miles from Victoria Island in Canada to the Tamir Peninsula in Siberia. Less than 1,500 miles separate Thule, the American outpost in Greenland, and Franz Josef Land, the furthermost Russian base. The air does not offer the same protection as the sea.

Isolation was formerly real enough. The sea journey from Le Havre to New York took twelve to thirteen days in 1880, less than nine at the end of the century, four and a half in the *Normandie* just before World War II, and less than four days today in the *United States*. The distance between Vancouver and Yokohama can now be covered in about twelve days on the fast lines of the Canadian Pacific. Lindbergh's flight across the Atlantic in 1927 caused a sensational upheaval in the existing system of ocean communications. Today the Paris–New York flight takes fourteen hours, but with a jet aircraft this is reduced to seven hours, with the result that transoceanic distances are virtually abolished and there can be no more continental isolation. In the space of a single generation this revolution has been accomplished so rapidly that public opinion, well-informed though it is, has difficulty in realizing it; for even though there is no more isolation, the isolationist spirit survives. The Americans know that they have lost their insular position, but do they really believe it? It is probably impossible to give a single reply to such a question because of the differences between the various regions of America, with their diverse orientation, geographical and political, giving rise to complex relations, amicable or the reverse.

The Atlantic coast as far as the Alleghenies, orientated toward Europe, is aware of the civilization of the Old World and has a personal realization of its actuality as opposed to one merely derived from books; there is the feeling of the existence of another continent at the other side of the street known as the Atlantic Ocean, whose proximity seems almost a physical presence. Orientated toward the Pacific and the Far East, the California coast is equally aware of the Asiatic world; this world has become a source of preoccupation, since the westward orientation is instinctive; and this applies to the whole area west of the Rockies. The Gulf coast, contiguous with the Caribbean world, shares the Caribbean climate, using this word in its broadest sense: it is orientated toward the south. There remains the Center, an area flanked by two chains of mountains and forming an autonomous world, capable of living its own life with a minimum of exterior contact, with little deep-down realization that Europe and the Far East exist. Newspapers may report what is happening in these distant countries, but such outside events have only mild repercussions at home; the Center is like a house with an interior courtyard, built on a grandiose scale, it must be admitted, but with no windows opening onto the street. It is the seat of an isolationism that to all outward appearances has not survived the war, but which is still latent in the form of a persistent provincialism, or rather a sort of continental attitude.

It is easy to understand under these conditions how difficult it is for the United States to have a really international outlook.

There is no stimulus to develop any other than a continental outlook. This is illustrated economically by an instinctive and rudimentary protectionism, which comes from the depths of the national tradition; it is displayed in the nostalgia of the Americans for isolation when they are dragged in spite of themselves into the whirlpool of world conflict. Their attitude toward international affairs is therefore largely based on geographical orientation; the United States is a country in which the two seacoast areas realize essential obligations toward the exterior world, while the Center, although forced to admit that such obligations exist, instinctively puts up an inward resistance to them.

PART II

THE AMERICAN PEOPLE: FORMATION, COMPOSITION, AND PSYCHOLOGY

CHAPTER 3

The Racial Formation of the American People

★

During the nineteenth century and the beginning of the twentieth, forty million men left the Old World to settle across the ocean. Thirty million of them turned toward North America, where they formed a new section of the white race. This immigration tide must be considered as a major historical event, as important as the barbarian invasions of Europe, some of the consequences of which are still apparent. European races of differing origins and from different social strata were flung into a common melting pot, and at the same time they had to make contacts with foreign races new to them, black, yellow, and red. The human elements involved are ancient, even venerable: the result has been the birth of a new nation, in a continental setting which has nothing in common with Europe.

I

The peopling of the United States by European and African immigration was carried out in three phases, as it were three tides, each of which has left, like a geological formation, a distinct stratum of population.

The first influx in the seventeenth to the nineteenth centuries populated the thirteen original colonies with elements almost solely English and Protestant, but three parallel waves of immigration can be distinguished, directed toward New England, the Center, and the South. In New England the colonists were mainly Puritan dissenters who had left their mother country to escape the domination of the established church. They formed an egalitarian

21

democracy of simple, independent people, governing themselves
according to the tradition of their religious communities and organized with autonomous congregations: a serious, moralizing,
well-educated society, whose strong personality, characterized by
initiative and energy, left an indelible imprint upon American life
which is still visible today. It is almost impossible to understand
even twentieth-century America without reference to that Puritanism, the fundamental source of the magnificent work accomplished by the elite of the pioneers.

The second group, established in the New York and Philadelphia regions, comprised, in addition to Anglo-Scottish settlers,
Irish Protestants, German Lutheran peasants, Dutchmen, and
French Huguenots: this group of colonists, though less well-educated, was richer and more commercial-minded, and already displayed a more characteristically American desire for comfort and
wealth. The colonies were in each case settled by people of the
same racial origin, equal among themselves, who carried out all
the tasks necessary to the community, down to the hardest and
most humble.

The situation was very different in the five southern colonies
where, in a climate already subtropical, rich planters, generally
Anglicans, cultivated sugar, tobacco, or cotton with convict labor
and, from the eighteenth century onward, with Negro slaves trans-
ported from Africa. The regime was that of a colony administered
by planters, divided into various social strata, a community where
the white man who was not a slaveowner was reduced by the
force of circumstances to the humiliating status of "poor white."
The way to the Civil War was paved by this antidemocratic constitution, contrasting strongly with the main current of North
American society.

It should be noted that immediately after the War of Independence the country was colonized only as far as the Alleghenies, and
that in 1790 it had only 3,929,000 inhabitants. Nevertheless, a few
outstanding characteristics had been implanted so firmly in the
American people that the trace of them is still apparent: whether
they were Yankees, egalitarians and democrats, or gentlemen of
the South, aristocrats and conservatives, they were all Brititsh by
tradition and Protestant by religion, and even when they became

politically independent they remained culturally English. This origin must never be overlooked, however deeply it may appear to be buried beneath the alluvium of subsequent waves of immigration.

It was from 1840 onward that Europe began to overflow into America in considerable proportions. Since the Declaration of Independence there had been barely a million immigrants, but between 1840 and 1880 there was an influx of nearly ten million men into the United States, nine-tenths of whom were European. Famine in Ireland, revolutions, the appeal of a country with virgin soil awaiting development, the hope of finding in America an atmosphere of liberty too often absent from the old continent of Europe, were all causes of this large-scale population movement. Central and northwest Europe provided, between 1870 and 1880, 92% of the immigrants, the Slav and Latin elements being still negligible: 26% were German, 20% English or Scottish, 15% Irish, and 7.5% Scandinavian. The Germans, Englishmen, Scots, and Scandinavians were excellent colonists, who formed, together with the Puritans of New England, an excellent army of pioneers in the migration toward the West. As for the Irish, they settled mainly in the large towns, which they soon succeeded in dominating. Thus, during the nineteenth century the United States, while remaining essentially Anglo-Saxon, became less exclusively English. An Irish spirit invaded the country, working like a leaven and counterbalancing the Puritan atmosphere with its phantasy, its sense of humor, and its somewhat uncontrolled vitality. A Germanic element, also, was introduced by the German and Scandinavian settlers, which to this day impregnates the American character with a taste for systematic and conscientious research, a didactic spirit, and a love of regulations. The United States ceased henceforth to be exclusively Protestant; the Irish and many of the Germans were Catholics, and at the same time considerable numbers of Jews were making their presence felt. Through this second wave of immigration America had become by the end of the nineteenth century Anglo-Germano-Irish. I myself made the acquaintance of this earlier America before the third wave of immigrants had cast up on its shores its considerable Slav and Latin element.

Between 1880 and 1914 a real tidal wave of immigration swept the Atlantic coast; there were nearly twenty-two million immigrants, including 1,218,000 in the year 1914 alone. But their racial composition was entirely different from that of the preceding wave, since between 1900 and 1910 the Nordic element accounted for only 23% (British 6%, Germans 4%), while Slavs and Latins made up the remaining 77% (Austro-Hungarians 26%, Italians 23%, Russians 18%). During this period the immigrants were of a lower social status, they were mainly poor people, driven from the Old World because of overpopulation, attracted by the higher wages paid in America, and largely recruited by agents of the maritime companies. These newcomers settled in the poorer quarters of the great cities of the East, in national groups which were not easily assimilated, for most of them were Catholics or members of the Orthodox Church, whose traditions had nothing in common with the colonists of the first or even the second period of immigration. It was at that period that the problem of assimililation appeared, and that doubts arose as to what the eventual character of the American people would become. Would it remain Anglo-Saxon and Protestant? Would it become Slavo-Latin and Catholic? Or would it correspond to a completely new national type, freed from its European origins to become finally and wholly American? This new problem of assimilation marked the approaching end of an immigration period which had lasted for several centuries.

The 1914 war ended the long initial period of foreign immigration. After 1918 Europe would still have a surplus population to pour into the United States, but the Americans, already frightened by the overforeign element among the immigrants and particularly by the suspicion of Bolshevik tendencies among them, passed from an open-door policy to a policy of defense. The vital laws of 1921 and 1924, which limited immigration under the new quota system, reduced the number of entries in 1925 to 294,000; this figure continued to diminish and immigration ceased almost entirely from the time of the Great Depression of 1929. Between 1901 and 1910 there had been 8,795,386 immigrants, between 1911 and 1920 5,735,811, but only 4,107,209 between 1921 and 1930, with a further reduction to 528,431 in the period 1931 to 1940.

Though limited immigration reappeared immediately after World War II, the settlers largely consisted of several thousand displaced persons who were allowed to enter the country under the Displaced Persons Act, 1948-1950. In 1950 there were 249,187 entries, 17% from the American continent and 79% from Europe, mainly from central Europe. Thus since 1914 another page of American history has been completed: the United States no longer receives immigrants and has no wish to do so.

II

The table below shows the evolution of the population of the United States in its main stages:

Year	Population	
1790	3,929,000	
1860	31,443,000	Civil War
1890	62,947,000	McKinley Tariff
1920	105,710,000	World War I
1945	139,586,000	World War II
1950	150,697,000	Last Census
1955	163,930,000	Latest Estimate

This population of over 160 million inhabitants makes the United States the fourth largest country in the world, coming after China, India, and the U.S.S.R. In comparison with the whole of Asia and even with Europe this is not a very large population, but it counts for more than all the Asiatic peoples put together, for an American, by reason of his superior equipment and his mobility, is worth several Indians or Chinamen. From this, one may conclude that apart from mere numbers of inhabitants, for which the United States by no means sets a record, the American civilization is, more than that of any other nation, a mass civilization. Emphasis must also be placed on the role played in American economy by the progressive population increase; a regular, statutory increase, corresponding to an increase in purchasing power which resembles an ever-rising tide and creates the optimism referred to earlier, which is a distinctive feature of the atmosphere of the New World.

At the same time the population of the United States, though large numerically, is not large compared with the size of the territory; the population density was only about fifty inhabitants per square mile in 1950, which is very small when compared with certain European and Asiatic countries. North America is scantily peopled, and it is doubtful whether it will ever attain the population density of the older continents. The American civilization is characterized by a small number of efficient men occupying a large territory; here again we have this notion of space which seems typical of the American continent.

CHAPTER 4

The Racial Composition of the American People and the Immigration Policy

★

The American people are essentially diverse in origin. In spite of an intensive attempt at adaptation, the composing elements have a tendency to remain distinct over long periods. The cessation of immigration since World War I has had the result of speeding up unification, but the general effect is still far from homogeneous. This has resulted in a somewhat exotic impression as compared with the European nations racially blended at an earlier date.

I

If the United States is not wholly a white country, the white races form a decisive majority; in the census of 1950 they accounted for 135,215,000 out of a total population of 150,697,361, *i.e.*, 89.6%, while the black population was 15,042,286 or 9.9%, and the Indians and the yellow races 588,000 or 0.5%. These percentages show little change from the 1940 census, the relative number of Negroes having increased by only 1%. The place occupied by the Chinese, the Japanese, and the Indians is practically negligible, though the presence of some Puerto Ricans and a large number of Mexicans is not insignificant; but the Negro bloc is substantial and in no way diminishing and has given rise to the tragic color problem of the United States, for which no solution can be foreseen.

The 1950 census revealed that approximately 90% of the white population were born in the United States and 10% abroad as compared with 89% and 11% in 1940, which suggests that the popu-

27

lation is becoming increasingly American but that progress in this direction is extremely slow. The foreign element is not limited to this 10%, for in 1950 15.7% of the Americans born in the United States were the children of either one or two foreign parents, as against 21% in 1930. Adding this 15.7% to the 10% born abroad one sees that in 1950 25.7% of the population was either foreign-born or first-generation American. This proportion, which was 30% in 1940, is decreasing regularly but slowly, with the result that a foreign element remains an essential feature of American psychology.

In the 124-year period from 1820 to 1943 the countries which contributed most toward American immigration were as follows:

Country	Number of Immigrants	Year of Maximum Immigration
Germany	6,028,377	1882
Italy	4,719,825	1907
Ireland	4,592,525	1851
Great Britain	4,264,728	1888
Austria-Hungary	4,144,366	1907
Russia	3,343,480	1913
Canada and Newfoundland	3,037,561	1924
Scandinavia	2,359,049	1882

According to the census of 1950 Americans born abroad were divided according to the following nationalities:

Italians	1,427,000
Germans	984,000
Canadians	995,000
Russians	895,000
Poles	861,000
Englishmen	585,000
Irishmen	505,000

The importance of the Germano-Irish and Slavo-Latin elements is immediately obvious, and without the introduction of immigration restrictions it is possible that the latter would finally have dominated. Although checked, the Slavo-Latin group makes its presence felt more and more through the success achieved by a number of its members; the increasing frequency of Slav and

Latin names among holders of important positions is an unde-
niable proof of this. The Jewish population of five million, including 2,100,000 in the New York agglomeration alone, must also be
taken into account. In the years which preceded World War II
Jews formed a considerable proportion of the immigrants, though
immigration, it is true, was on a greatly reduced scale during this
period. These entrants were the direct result of persecutions
under the Hitler regime, and since the war a large percentage of
the displaced persons who have emigrated to the United States
have been of Jewish origin. The Jews, with the Irish, form a kind
of leaven of unexpectedness and passion in a national psychology
which is dangerously conformist.

There can scarcely be any racial unity in a nation that has been
formed in this way, and one feels justified in speculating upon
what an American really is. Sinclair Lewis in *Arrowsmith* suggests the following: "Martin was, like most inhabitants of Elk
Mills before the Slavo-Italian immigration, a Typical Pure-bred
Anglo-Saxon American, which means that he was a union of German, French, Scotch, Irish, perhaps a little Spanish, conceivably
a little of the strains lumped together as 'Jewish,' and a great deal
of English, which is itself a combination of Primitive Britain,
Celt, Phoenician, Roman, German, Dane, and Swede." It is in the
same spirit that Saint Cloud, Minnesota, which may have provided some of the background for Sinclair Lewis's small towns,
was described by its mayor as "a city with a French name,
founded by Swedes, administered by Irishmen, though the population is half-German, and with a Polish Mayor, though the Poles
form only a small minority of its inhabitants."

Similar racial admixtures are common throughout the United
States and give rise to the impression of a nation still in the stage
of formation. Adaptation to American customs may have been
rapid, but racial differences remain in evidence, particularly in
the large cities where streets retain a foreign character just like
those of certain French Mediterranean ports. The evolution continues or rather it has restarted with the Slavo-Latin intrusion, for
the country during the nineteenth century was more or less stabil-
ized and Germano-British in essence, a characteristic which it no
longer retains today. The old-established Anglo-Saxon families are

to be found essentially in the South, where 95% of the population is American-born of American parents (in the Carolinas the figure is almost 100%); immigrants were naturally repelled by a region where Negro labor dominated. The inland areas, the upstate of the eastern states, are similar in character; the immigrants, especially those of the Slavo-Latin period, settled in the coastal urban agglomerations, but in the countryside and in the small townships of the interior, in spite of some groups of Italians, Russians, or Canadians, the general atmosphere is Protestant and Republican. It should also be noted that the influential or monied people of the western cities are equally Anglo-Saxon: a perusal of *Who's Who* would confirm this.

On the other hand the main groups of inhabitants of foreign origin are to be found in the large cities of the Atlantic coast north of Washington, and generally speaking in all the important industrial centers. As a consequence of Irish, Italian, Russian, Portuguese, and Polish immigration (the list of nations could be prolonged almost indefinitely) new elements, very diverse in nature, have transformed areas hitherto Anglo-Saxon and Protestant into Slavo-Latin Catholic strongholds, where the old American element is scarcely to be discerned. The states which in 1950 had the highest percentage of white foreign-born inhabitants belong to this part of the country: New York had 17%, Massachusetts 15%, Rhode Island 14%, Connecticut 15%, New Jersey 13%. In Massachusetts, out of a total of 713,699 foreign-born, there were 192,514 Canadians, 101,548 Italians, 81,214 Irishmen, 46,597 Poles, 46,193 Englishmen, 52,353 Russians, and 21,333 Swedes. In Boston, the American Geneva, the old-established English Protestant element is now no more than a fortress assailed by a wave of foreigners; the German or Irish prelate and the Irish mayor are dominating personalities in the city. New York is, if possible, more cosmopolitan. In 1950 1,784,206 or 23% of a population of 7,891,957 inhabitants were foreign-born, and 2,659,935 or 34% of foreign parentage, so that, without counting either Negroes or Puerto Ricans, nearly two-thirds of the population was of foreign origin. In this setting the Jew flourishes and Italians, Irishmen, Russians, Germans, Poles, Austrians, Negroes, and Puerto Ricans jostle one another in the streets, and the racial mixture is as varied as in any city of the eastern Mediterranean, but yet this city of foreigners is as typically American as any other. Just as it is not necessary to be French to be a Parisian, it is not necesasry to be American to be a typical New Yorker. The mayors of New York, once traditionally Irish, are now more often Italian, and a party ticket is more likely to be adopted if it is headed by an Irishman, an Italian, and a Jew.

A second and similar racial group is to be found in the Middle West and Northwest. It consists principally of Germans in Ohio, Illinois, and Wisconsin, and Scandinavians in Minnesota and the Dakotas; not forgetting the extraordinary national mixture of Chicago, with its Italians, Poles, and practically all the races of the Mediterranean and of eastern Europe. Finally, there is in California a group no less foreign but more essentially Latin and Mediterranean consisting of Italians, Spaniards, Mexicans, French, Chinese, and Japanese. The racial atmosphere of the Far West is more Mediterranean, either because of the Spanish and Mexican element in its history, or because of the bluer sky, almost African in shade, which makes the southern Frenchman, for example, feel more at home.

According to the 1950 census, there was a total of 10,161,168 foreign-born inhabitants, of whom 78% were domiciled in the East and Center, 14.5% in the Rockies and along the Pacific coast, but only 7.6% in the South. Rapid assimilation tends to decrease the significance of these foreign groups, though the recent influx of displaced persons, small in number but powerful in influence, appears to have given them a new stimulus. Neither American politics, particularly local politics, nor the American way of life as a whole can be understood without taking this foreign element into account. The problem of Marseilles, not unlike that of Chicago, perhaps provides a French equivalent of the issues involved.

II

What was the purpose of the American restrictive legislation on immigration? The desire to become a homogeneous nation rather than one great numerically. One sees in this attitude a result of the growth of technology combined, immediately after World

War I, with the Malthusianism which laid emphasis not on the
total size of a population but on its efficiency.

Until the beginning of the twentieth century the United States
had been a country which definitely welcomed immigrants, confident in its boundless capacity to assimilate even the most diverse
foreign elements. But when immigration became no longer essentially Anglo-Saxon and Protestant, while at the same time the
more recent immigrants showed themselves to have a higher birth
rate than their predecessors, an instinctive fear arose that the
country might lose its traditional character. The theory of the
melting pot of the nations, universally accepted until then, laid
emphasis on the importance of environment as against heredity;
nobody doubted that authentic American Anglo-Saxons would be
produced whatever the mixture of nationalities of the immigrants.
During the nineteenth century and up to 1914 the immigration
policy, therefore, consisted of the selection of individuals; apart
from members of the yellow race, immigrants were accepted or
refused on a basis of personal merit, irrespective of national or
racial origin. Under this policy tens of millions of Europeans were
able, without serious restriction, to settle in North America.

The presence of this increasing influx of foreigners gave rise to
doubts about the racial melting pot, and greater credence was
given to the Mendelian doctrine, according to which heredity is
the decisive factor. In 1917 this new theory was definitely affirmed
and the principle of racial discrimination was admitted, with the
consequence that immigrants from Asia or the Pacific islands were
on principle refused as being unassimilable. The restriction was
frankly racial, and similar principles governed the legislation of
1921-1924, which opposed mass immigration of Europeans. The
reasons for this reversal of policy were complex, but at the same
time convergent. After the war, the old-established Anglo-Saxons
feared a mass Slavo-Italian invasion, the effect of which they
could, in some measure, judge; the Protestants feared a Catholic
invasion, having had for some time past the example of the Irish
and Italian immigrants before them; the working classes feared
the possibility of a decrease in wages, and were thus opposed to
the mass entry of workers with a low standard of living; employers feared a Communist intrusion; finally the eugenists, bas-

ing themselves on Mendel, emphasized the importance of maintaining the purity of the race and advised the exclusion of all those whom they picturesquely described as "cacogenic." All these arguments converged, and the unprecedented concord of employers and workers, Protestants, nationalists, racial theorists, and doctrinaires in demanding an American defense policy brought about a complete revision of the immigration laws which had existed for the last century.

Under the new legislation the immigrant was admitted or rejected in the first instance not on personal merit but according to racial origin, within the limits of strictly controlled contingents. Only races considered as assimilable were accepted, and among them the Nordic races had preference over the Slavo-Latin, being considered as more adaptable to assimilation with the Anglo-Saxon type. Thus differential discrimination was applied to immigration according to geographical origin; Asiatics were purely and simply excluded; Canadians, Mexicans, and South Americans were accepted without quotas under a policy of continental solidarity, though individuals might be refused after police scrutiny; Europeans, Africans, and the inhabitants of the Near East were admitted under an annual quota, each country having the right to send 2% of the total that its national group represented in the population of the United States in 1890. From 1929 onward the total annual quota was fixed at 150,000, the percentage to which each nation was entitled being proportionate to its contribution toward the formation of the American nation. Within the framework of the quotas individual selection was made by means of interrogations, which provoked much irony on the part of the Europeans, but which might have very serious consequences. "Are you an anarchist?" "Do you hold any opinions against the government?" "Have you committed bigamy?" (More recently I was merely asked, "Are you polygamous?") "Does the money in your pocket belong to you?" "Has your father ever been an inmate of a lunatic asylum?" "Are you in good moral and physical spirits?" "Are you dumb?" (I once heard an inspector repeat with insistence, "I want to hear your voice," to a woman who was so terrified that she could not utter a single sound.) But, whatever the circumstances, the authorities, represented either by the immigration officer at the port of entry or by the consul issuing the visa, might refuse their consent and the door might at any time be closed to the would-be immigrant.

This legislation produced the effect desired. Under the annual immigration quota of 150,000 established in 1929 the United Kingdom has a right to 65,721 entries, Germany 25,957, Ireland 17,853, Italy only 5,799, and Poland 6,524. The English, Germans, Irish, Dutch, and Scandinavians are allowed 79% of the total, while Italian immigration, which had been on an average 195,000 per annum between 1900 and 1910, is drastically reduced. Quotas not taken up may not be transferred, so that, since the Nordic races do not always use theirs fully, the number of admissions is often reduced. Total annual immigration, which had been 1,218,480 in 1914 and 706,896 in 1924, fell to 294,314 in 1925 and to below 100,000 after the 1929 crisis. It must therefore now be considered that the great wave of European immigration which peopled the United States from the seventeenth century onward, and in particular during the nineteenth century, has subsided. This fact is of primary significance in world history. It is almost equally significant in the history of the United States, for this suppression of immigration, added to a traditional protectionist policy in industry, marks a new phase in Pan-Americanism.

III

The immigration policy of 1921-1924 was a result of World War I, but neither the Depression nor World War II have changed the outlook on this subject. Mention should, of course, be made of the special conditions which have applied to displaced persons since 1945: in 1945 they had priority for 42,000 entries out of the total quota, in 1948 205,000 refugees were admitted, and in 1950 the quota was raised to 400,744; in 1953 admission was granted over three years to 214,000 refugees over and above the quota. Apart from these special admissions, total immigration has remained very low: 108,721 in 1946, 147,292 in 1947, 170,570 in 1948, 188,317 in 1949, 249,187 in 1950. The United States no longer wishes to encourage immigration.

Particularly since the beginning of the Korean War there has been an increase of anti-Communism, which has led to an almost pathological fear of foreign invasion. The state of mind which, after World War I, led to the legislation of 1921-1924, reappeared in the guise of an instinctive suspicion of anything that appeared to be totalitarian, fascist, or more particularly Communist, and in general the "radical" outlook; "radical" in the American vocabulary has retained its original significance of extremist or revolutionary in a derogatory sense, which no longer applies in England or France.

This attitude of mind has given rise to new legislation, strengthening and outdistancing the former, and Europe is not alone in judging this to be unhealthy. The Internal Security Act of 1951 excludes, even for a brief visit, Communists, anarchists, members of totalitarian organizations, or persons favoring "overthrowing the government by violence." Consuls are under instructions to · refuse visas to all those whom they know or believe to be engaged in activities against the public interest or which would endanger the prosperity, safety, or security of the United States. This law, as applied by timid subordinates, might finally lead to the arbitrary refusal of visas to people most suited to be granted them. Terrorized by Senator McCarthy, consuls apply the letter of the law and arrive at the most absurd and shocking refusals, and often ambassadors dare not intervene, believing, not wholly unjustifiably, that they would risk losing their positions. The Internal Security Act shocks liberal-minded Americans, but it continues to exist.

No less important is the McCarran-Walter Immigration Act of 1952, an omnibus bill of three hundred pages, which codifies all former legislation directed against immigration, strengthening rather than modifying it. The new policy maintains the quota system, but applies it more strictly; the annual quota corresponds to one-seventh of 1% of the 1920 population of the United States. This represents only one-tenth of 1% of the 1950 population, and, if one takes into account quotas not taken up, one-fifteenth of 1%. In order to appease Asiatic susceptibility and to give the illusion of suppressing racial discrimination, the law is extended to include Asiatics, but their quota is absurdly small, permitting, for example, the entry of only 185 Japanese. The maximum number of immigrants is fixed at 154,000.

It would be foolish to deny that this legislation corresponds to basic American opinion. It doubtless inflamed opposition in liberal circles, particularly in states with a high percentage of inhabitants of foreign origin, and it was vetoed by President Truman. "Such a concept," he wrote, "is absolutely unworthy of our traditions and our ideals and it violates the great political doctrine of the Declaration of Independence, that 'all men are created equal.' It is a step backward," he concluded. But his veto was annulled by the two-thirds majority constitutionally required in the two Houses of Congress, and the President was not even backed by the whole of his party; in the Senate 57 votes (32 Republican and 25 Democratic) confirmed the law against 26 votes, composed of 18 Democrats and 8 Republicans; Senator Patrick McCarran, who gave his name to the bill, was himself a Democrat. It cannot be denied that public opinion as a whole approves this policy, which echoes the tendencies, not only of openly nationalist circles, such as the Daughters of the American Revolution or the Huguenot Societies Federation, but also of the Government departments concerned, the State Department, the Immigration and Naturalization Service, and the Department of Justice. McCarran was indubitably speaking for the majority of the population when he described the Act as "essential to the preservation of our way of life." It is significant to observe that the amendments, suggesting that unfulfilled quotas might be held over and that the admission of displaced persons should not be counted in the quota, were defeated.

In 1953 President Eisenhower had to use his most insistent powers of persuasion to obtain from Congress the approval of a law admitting exceptionally 207,000 refugees. This was granted only after considerable bargaining and it manifestly ran contrary to the true opinions held in the House of Representatives and the Senate. It even appears to have been conceded only in return for the assurance (given by whom?) that no revision of the McCarran Act should be discussed before 1956. We may therefore conclude that the change of attitude vis-à-vis immigration which followed World War I represented fundamental public opinion. World War II has confirmed this; the American people intend henceforth to reserve their continent for themselves alone.

CHAPTER 5

Assimilation and Its Problems

★

Is this great influx of diverse human elements becoming assimilated? Is the famous melting pot of the nations working efficiently? Has it not been given an excessively difficult task?

What, in fact, is assimilation? To what must all these foreigners be assimilated? The old-established Americans consider that immigrants, of whatever origin, should be assimilated to an Anglo-Saxon type similar to their own. There is, however, an alternative, which consists in mingling the nations to create a new racial type, not narrowly Anglo-Saxon, but, from a different standpoint, American. This was the almost mystical hope expressed by Israel Zangwill when he wrote in prophetic strain half a century ago: "America is God's crucible, the great melting-pot where all the races of Europe are melting and re-forming. . . . The real American has not yet arrived. He is only in the crucible. I tell you—he will be the fusion of all races, perhaps the coming Superman." The second of these two conceptions has by the very force of circumstances a tendency to override the first, but the first corresponds to a deep-seated instinct, which has become increasingly nostalgic, of the descendants of the first immigrants.

In the process of assimilation, which consists in transforming foreigners into Americans, foreigners do not all react in the same way in the melting pot. Some easily undergo the process of fusion, as it were at a low temperature, some achieve fusion only at a high temperature and with difficulty, while others find fusion impossible to attain. The English, the Scots, and, in general, the Protestants of northern Europe are quickly and easily assimilated because, to some extent, of a certain common factor of race and

37

language and a similar religious and social tradition; they have the same protestant conception of the rights of the individual, the same civic sense deriving from Calvinist tradition, but it is to be observed that, although they speak English, the Irish retain their individuality for a longer period because they are Catholics, and possibly also just because they are Irish.

In a second category of immigrants who become assimilated more slowly, there are those who are not Anglo-Saxon and who are generally Catholics, holding a different conception of the family, the state, and the role of the clergy; they are to be found particularly in the large cities, where they remain separate entities for a considerable period, grouped together under the leadership of their priests. They belong to civilizations where the family or clan plays a preponderant role, and where saving is traditional; they are peasants or artisans in origin, with a sense of the importance of individual effort, so that they initially feel homesick in a country where labor is highly mechanized and collectively organized. Among these are the immigrants from the Mediterranean countries, the Slavs, and, in general, most of the immigrants who arrived after 1880.

American society has such a capacity for absorption that finally all Europeans succeed in becoming integrated into the system. It is only in the case of races other than the white that complete assimilation is impossible. Negroes are by their customs truly American, often more American than many of the recent immigrants, but their color prevents them from passing muster. The few descendants of the Redskins, living on their reservations, maintain their individuality with passive determination; and the Mexicans, also Indians, remain foreigners. The yellow races would be capable of complete adaptation to the life of the United States, but here again the color bar proves an insurmountable obstacle.

In all these cases two diametrically opposed factors enter into the situation: the geographical background speeds up assimilation while heredity retards it. History is thrown into the geographical melting pot, but finally geography triumphs. The influence of environment, particularly in the New World, is extremely powerful. Immigrants, especially those of the third cycle, arrived bowed down with the cares of centuries upon their shoulders; the East, often the East of the Bible, was flung without transition into twentieth-century America, to find an astonishing and miraculous rebirth. The newcomer, who had generally suffered greatly in Europe, shook the dust of the Old World from his feet and repudiated his past tradition, setting off toward a new life in a new continental environment; he was asked for nothing but a pair of strong hands and energy to work—at least that was so before the nationalist reaction of 1918—and he discovered the new and unaccustomed dignity of a man who earns his living free and unfettered. He conceived for the country which welcomed him in this way a deep-seated gratitude, having found there both independence and a higher standard of living.

The great explorer Henry M. Stanley, himself one of these immigrants, paints in his autobiography a striking picture of this attitude of mind:

> But, within a few weeks of arriving in America, I had become different in temper and spirit. . . . My new feeling of dignity made me stretch myself to my full height, and revel luxuriously in fond ideas. . . . The two-feet square of the street I occupied were mine for the time being, and no living man could budge me except at his peril. . . . Neither poverty nor youth was degrading, nor was it liable to abuse from wealth or age. . . . There were proud thoughts. I respired more freely, my shoulders rose considerably, my back straightened, my strides became longer, as my mind comprehended this new feeling of independence. . . . Many years of travel have not extinguished my early faith, but it would require ages to eradicate my affection for the city which first taught me that a boy may become a man.*

In a similar vein Adlai Stevenson, Governor of Illinois, could say in July, 1952, in his speech to the Democratic convention in Chicago which was to nominate him as candidate for the presidency:

> . . . until four years ago the people of Illinois had chosen but three Democratic governors in a hundred years. One was John Peter Altgeld, the Eagle Forgotten, an immigrant; one was Edward F. Dunne, whose parents came from Ireland; and the last was Henry Horner, but one generation removed from Germany. John Peter Altgeld was a Protestant; Governor Dunne was a Catholic and Henry Horner was a Jew.

* *The Autobiography of Sir Henry Morton Stanley*, ed. by his wife, Dorothy Stanley, Boston, Houghton Mifflin, 1909, pp. 95-96.

That, my friends, is the American story, written here on the prairies of Illinois, in the heartland of the nation.

These quotations illustrate the immense confidence of the American in his country, his fundamental optimism and his conviction that the New World, henceforward his own, represents something that is really new on this earth; this is the American mentality, though its welcoming attitude has become a thing of the past in a society where immigration has been made almost impossible.

The rhythm of assimilation follows an almost physiological law. The first generation usually remains foreign, immigrants of the same nationality grouping together in certain districts of a city and retaining their customs, their language, and their mode of dress: in certain streets of New York even today one could almost believe oneself to be in Naples, Lisbon, or Odessa. By means of the all-powerful influence of environment and the educational system, the second generation adapts itself with extraordinary facility; the children refuse to speak their hereditary language and are often ashamed of their parents, whose bearded faces and accent they despise—a state that often gives rise to painful and truly pathetic scenes. Nevertheless, these young Germano-Americans or Italo-Americans are aware of their racial origin, still evident in their names, their physique, even their memories; if they have repudiated Europe, if they systematically endeavor to forget it, they retain an instinctive bond with the country from which their family came. No trace of foreign origin is visible by the third generation; they are 100% American, they have finally changed their name—Troudeau to Waterhole or Sbarboro to Barber—and sometimes their religion; they generally retain to a large extent their physical type and this would appear to support the partisans of the theory of heredity.

This same rhythm exists wherever there is immigration, for example, in Argentina, Brazil, or France, and the process cannot be speeded up any more than a chemical experiment can be. But to what extent is there real assimilation? There are things which can be acquired speedily and without effort: the language, which the second generation will speak without accent; the mode of dress and the haircut—only the old men will retain their unkempt beards; the American way of life, which is considered almost as a religion; and above all the American attitude to life, which is expressed in striving after success, raising the standard of living, and disregarding the past. The immigrant who is advancing toward assimilation will have shed, when crossing the ocean, his ancestral tradition, which the American ideology would shatter uncompromisingly and which he, moreover, is the first to repudiate, and his old-fashioned European reactions, better adapted to the smaller scale of the Old World. He is completely uprooted and has quite cut himself adrift, for there are some European characteristics which can never cross the Atlantic. But at the same time, though this uprooted European takes root again in the American soil, he does not entirely belong to it, he has not acquired the moral background of the Puritan, the Protestant outlook which is fundamentally American; he has easily acquired the outward veneer but he can easily remain fundamentally a foreigner. Is the Italian Methodist or the Anglican Jew who has adopted the name of Smith a real American who would pass muster with the Fathers of the Constitution? As Nietzsche wrote in *Also sprach Zarathustra:* "It is not easy to understand if one is of foreign blood; each nation has its language of good and evil; the foreigner does not comprehend it."

There are thus problems the existence of which the United States had not realized before the middle of the nineteenth century, and they furnish an obvious point of comparison with the palimpsest, where an older text shows through one of more recent date, just as the foreign mental attitude can often be seen beneath the uniform American mask. "Tents pitched by nomads each night in a new country," wrote Barrès, "have not the stable character of ancient hereditary dwellings, but how great is the joy felt by the wanderers who mingle with the natives to sing the morning hymn, while, to beautify it, their memory secretly mingles the song learned the day before in a foreign land."

The main essence of the American nation has been formed from self-denial, with the consequent creative energy which is characteristic of the Puritans, and the civic spirit which to me appears to be the hallmark of complete adaptation. Later immigrants, arriving in time to profit rather than to create, have adopted the materialistic outlook of their new environment with its striving after success and its higher standard of living, an outlook not wholly in keeping with the traditional Puritan ideal. Consequently currents of good and evil mingle curiously in the great river formed from these diverse immigration streams; there are currents of English or Scandinavian civic spirit, of German solidarity, of Dutch seriousness, but in this main stream there also flow the unstable geniality of the Irish, typically Jewish reactions, and oriental influences and customs which belong to the Mediterranean lands. This is clearly visible in the swindles carried out by gangsters or the political machinery sometimes associated with them, but germs of the same outlook exist among men who would most strongly repudiate them. The latest arrival is often the most aggressively American, full of scorn for Europeans, one of whom he was until only yesterday. In *La case de l'Oncle Sam* Henri Troyat wittily portrays a patronizing attitude of this nature on the part of one of his Russian friends recently arrived in the States:

"Here," said Boris, "everyone is brought up with a sense of responsibility toward his neighbor, a kind of civic good manners."

"Aren't you looking at America through rose-colored spectacles?"

"Oh, no," said Boris, "I hate these civic good manners, but what can you do about it—it's in our blood."

"In your blood? I thought you were of Russian descent."

"I took the examination to become an American citizen three years ago," replied Boris indignantly.

I dared not contradict him.

II

The Anglo-Saxon element has been unable completely to digest the mass of immigrants. Immigration has practically ceased for the last quarter of a century; nevertheless there are certain groups of people who have not become integrated and a foreign impression remains latent, perhaps more today than fifty years ago. In essentially foreign circles marriage is largely restricted to the national group; for example not more than 10% of the Jews or 15% of the Italians of the Atlantic coastal area contract mixed marriages, and it is, therefore, not astonishing that unions between the black or yellow races and the white should be negligible.

Under these circumstances the mingling of the different national elements is a long process, with the result that there is a continuous struggle between two streams. The older continues to provide the ruling force, deriving its power from its long-established British tradition and its puritanical moral principles. It is of these people that Nietzsche might have said, "They did not aim at happiness." But the characteristics of the Americans descended from the nineteenth-century immigrants, and particularly from the Slavs or Latin peoples who entered the country from 1880 or 1890 onward, are completely different. Gobineau's theory, which was very popular in the United States at the time of World War I, had convinced the Protestant Anglo-Saxons that these newcomers were of an inferior race. Experience has proved, however, that Slavs or the Latin races are often more gifted, more alert, more resourceful, and finally more creative artistically or scientifically than the Nordic peoples. The recent attainments of numerous Italians, Poles, and Russians illustrate this. The influence of this section of the population has increased accordingly, bringing with it a corresponding increase in Catholicism, and the United States has become enriched to an extent which would have been impossible had its tradition remained purely Anglo-Saxon. American society has for some time been influenced by an outlook completely foreign to that of New England, characterized by a taste for material ease, enjoyment, and profit acquired without excessive hampering by conscience. If, as Saint Just said in 1793, "happiness is an idea new to Europe," it is certainly in relatively recent times that this idea of happiness has come to express the aim of Americans, and it is an aim which must have appealed particularly to the recent immigrants who, like the poor people despised by Zarathustra, "abandoned those countries where very existence was difficult."

Even when he is Dutch or Scandinavian rather than English, the traditional American is always Protestant and British in outlook. From England he has derived his language, his culture, his literature, his social code, his legislation, and a great number of his institutions, and he is, therefore, undoubtedly a member of the Anglo-American family. It is he who is the leader, not so much politically (especially as far as local government is concerned) as socially; following an unwritten law, certain confidential posts in the universities, the churches, and even in business, are conferred upon him as a kind of privilege; one has only to consult the list of social leaders appearing in *Who's Who* to be convinced of this. It is, as it were, an implicit choice, by virtue of which, according to the saying of a seventeenth-century divine, "God has sifted a whole nation so that He might sow in the desert a chosen seed"; a healthy heredity confirmed by healthy tradition. Among the Americans listed in *Who's Who* 56% state that they are members of a church, but only 5% of these are Catholics. Among the thirty-three American Presidents from Washington to Eisenhower, twenty-eight were British in origin and thirty Protestants; Jefferson, Lincoln, and Hayes alone declared that they were members of no church, though they came from Protestant families. Nearer to this British tradition than either the Slavs or the Latin races are the Germans, and in the course of my travels in the United States I do not recall ever having encountered an Italian or Russian president of a university.

The non-Nordic foreigner has very different characteristics. This is immediately noticeable in his name, when he has not changed it, for it is often necessary in this connection to ask people the name under which they were born; when he has not been converted he is distinguished by his religion, Catholic, Jewish, or Orthodox. His brilliant and frequently genial character and his personal gifts are also striking; displaced persons have provided atomic research not only with some of its most brilliant scientists but also with spies. But his qualities are personal rather than collective and he possesses neither a civic sense nor a Calvinist tradition. If he achieves an important position, it is owing to personal merit and even, like the adventurer, by devious ways. He is preeminent in the arts, the theater, literature, and also in local politics and those commercial activities which, though they may finally attain important status, have their source in oriental bargaining rather than in Western economic organization. Giannini, the founder of the largest joint-stock bank in the United States and probably in the world, whom I came to know in San Francisco, was a rough and simple peasant from the mountains of northern Italy. In 1925 I amused myself by examining the list of the players in the New York Symphony Orchestra; they all seemed to have names ending in ski, vich, or ino, and not one of them was named Smith. The exclusion of Slavs and Latins from positions of influence is rapidly diminishing, though certain prejudices still exist. If the report of July 9, 1953, in the New York *Times* is to be believed, it is more difficult for Jews or Catholic Italians to gain admittance to the medical schools than it is for Protestants. It must, however, be admitted that though barriers still exist they are now sometimes overcome, and that Catholic influence is now to be felt in much higher strata of American society than it was some years ago, though the new elements which have enriched this society have in no way increased its moral unity. It must, however, be realized that the foreigner has no other alternative than to integrate himself into this Anglo-Saxon background, which is a heritage of the past. This integration, which gives rise to conformism, is the test of an Americanization that he wants to acquire at all costs, even to the point of trying to reach it by all kinds of outward show, like a recent convert. From this point of view, although it has lost its initial purity, the Anglo-Saxon concept remains dominant in spite of everything.

III

There is, then, properly speaking, no American race, any more than there is a French race, and no country has less call than the United States to be race conscious, but nobody can deny the existence of an American people. There is no definite physical type, but the authentic American is recognizable by his general outlook, his reactions, his feelings, and his bearing. The type is still in the process of evolution, but it is developing within the fixed framework of the English language and Protestant-inspired political and civic institutions; immigrants and their descendants must adjust themselves to this general conception.

It must be emphasized that the nation has severed its connections with Europe and has for a long time been 100% American. The newcomer has immigrated with the idea of forgetting the past and developing this 100% American outlook. The gulf separating the American and the European civilizations is rapidly widening; the New World has lost all sense of reality of contact with Greco-Roman culture, and, if it remains fundamentally

Christian, it is in the Jewish rather than the Greek sense, following the testimony of the Bible rather than critical argument. Tens of millions of immigrants have been Americanized, they have not become old-type Anglo-Saxons with close links with England, but rather a new generation of Americans, not far removed from Zangwill's conception. Geography has triumphed over history, environment over heredity.

CHAPTER 6

The Geographical Distribution of the Population of the United States

★

The population of the United States, originally augmented by immigration, now increases almost solely by the natural excess of births over deaths. At first the immigrants settled in the Atlantic coastal belt only, but subsequently migrations toward the interior gradually transferred a proportion of the population westward, until the whole continent was settled.

The colonization of the western states took place after the War of Independence and more particularly after the Civil War. The western trend was more or less completed by about 1890, the "frontier" having receded farther and farther. The idea of where the "West" begins is a matter of outlook rather than of geography. I recall having heard people exclaim with satisfaction just after having crossed the Alleghenies, "We are getting west!" But others in Saint Paul, Minnesota, are able to speak with equal conviction of "way down east in Chicago." The Pacific coast had been settled ever since the discovery of gold in 1848, but the first prospectors arrived by way of Panama, and the first transcontinental railroad, the Union Pacific, dates back no further than 1869. The development of the whole country did not mark the end of population transfers, for World War II gave rise to one of the largest-scale redistributions, which considerably modified the center of population of the country.

I

During the nineteenth century there were two principal migratory currents. The first was west from New England via the southern end of the Great Lakes, through Ohio, Indiana, Illinois, Iowa, Missouri, and Kansas, transplanting as it moved a chosen group of pioneers whose influence and leadership are still felt today. This movement may be compared with the way in which the Scottish Presbyterians from the Maritime provinces colonized western Canada. Farther south a parallel movement, originating from Virginia and Tennessee, settled in the southern part of these states. These migrants were also Protestants but poorer and less resolute, often belonging to the category known as "poor whites." Abraham Lincoln came from this stock.

This double migratory movement is significant in that it maintained in the West the two original types of American, the Republican in the North and the Democrat in the South; even today in such states as Illinois and Missouri the distribution of votes in an election depends much on the ancestry of the voters. The Middle West outlook, which has become more typically American than that of a New England invaded by Irishmen, Canadians, and Italians, is explained to a great extent by the presence in the very center of the continent of these outposts of Puritanism which have directed economic development. The initial internal migrations were followed by westward trends to the Pacific coast, by the Santa Fe trail toward southern California and Texas, and finally by a movement toward Montana and Oregon; and these migrations established a Republican tradition in the Northwest and a Democratic tradition in the Southwest.

The principal movements followed the lines of latitude, but another important influx from the North in the second half of the nineteenth century peopled New England with a million French Canadians who supplied labor for the textile industry. The Catholic religion and a somewhat corrupt form of the French language were thus transplanted into the most typical Anglo-Protestant stronghold of the country, and did much to change its initial purity.

These major population trends belong to the period before World War I, and even before 1900, but there have been subsequent movements, the importance of which must not be under-estimated; the poorer sections of the community were drawn toward regions where the standard of living was higher, those who had made money toward the areas of pleasanter climate. Since World War I a considerable proportion of the Negroes of the South have migrated toward the large cities of the North where there were openings in industry and where they hoped to receive better treatment from a social point of view. There are now 776,000 Negroes in New York and more than 500,000 in Chicago.

The northward trend is not confined to Negroes. It is estimated that in 1950 there were 350,000 Puerto Ricans in New York, forming alongside the Negro district of Harlem a mob element which could not be excluded, since Puerto Rico is an American possession and no immigration visa is required for its citizens. The penetration of Mexicans into the West, Southwest, and California is on a much larger scale. They are attracted by wages which, though much higher than in Mexico, constitute from an American standpoint starvation level. Permanent agricultural labor is tending to disappear because of increasing mechanization, and farmers are glad to employ these energetic if rough seasonal workers. Moreover, employers need have little consideration for them because they have usually crossed the frontier fraudulently, generally by swimming the Rio Grande, from which they get their nickname of "wetbacks." Six hundred policemen employed on a frontier 1,600 miles long are obviously insufficient to prevent them from passing. It is estimated that in 1950 the border patrol seized 127,000 "wetbacks," while 230,000 were caught in California alone. The western states do not wish any decisive action to be taken to stop this foreign influx, which has come to be an accepted part of the economy of the states west of the Mississippi. They would be unwilling to relinquish the labor thus provided for harvesting and work in the mines.

The fact is that, as the United States has for the past generation systematically cut down regulation immigration from Europe, the country is seriously short of heavy labor because Americans refuse more and more to undertake work which they consider fit only for "colonials," while the latter are drawn northward by the difference in the standard of living.

Crosscurrents have attracted the poorer people toward the North and the wealthy, particularly those whose wealth is of recent origin, toward the South. The general aspect of the population of Florida has been greatly modified by the wealthy people who pass their winters or summers there, introducing a Republican element into this former Democratic stronghold. Following on the agricultural prosperity of World War I, southern California has been invaded by farmers from Iowa and Kansas, seeking a milder climate on the Pacific coast. In Los Angeles they form a group apart among the retired people, bringing an indefinable Middle West Protestant influence into this Latin community. One should also mention the migration to the mountains and cloudless skies of New Mexico and Arizona of selected groups of invalids and convalescents, and the colony of painters, poets, and writers established there: Santa Fe and Taos are literary and artistic centers where the memory of D. H. Lawrence is ever present.

The traditional migration linked with the development of the country's resources was made not only in a westerly but also in a southerly direction. Until World War I the South, still smarting under its defeat in the Civil War, remained sleepy and undeveloped, an area apart. After 1918 came the transfer of the textile industry from the Northeast to North Carolina, Georgia, and Alabama, and now three-quarters of the industry is carried on in these states. Then, during the boom which followed World War II, Texas underwent sensational development and the states of the Missouri-Mississippi basin are now becoming industrialized with astonishing rapidity. This dual development is but an outcome of the prodigious industrial activity occasioned by the war, when the state took over the whole of the national production and directed, organized, and orientated it to speed final victory. About eight million men were involved in labor transfers. This has appreciably affected population distribution, for, though many of the transfers were temporary, a considerable number of the families involved found the new areas more to their taste and remained there.

The general movement was westward, and in the period 1940-1950 the population of the western states increased by 40.9%, compared with a national average of 14.5%. The population of the Pacific coast increased by 48.8%, that of the Rockies by 22.3%, the southeast Atlantic coast by 18.8%. The states with the greatest percentage increases were: California 53.3%, Arizona, 50.1%, Nevada 45.2%, Oregon 39.6%, Washington 37.0%, and Florida 46.1%. In contrast to this, Oklahoma lost 4.4% of its population, North Dakota 3.5%, Arkansas 2.0%, Mississippi 0.2%, while in Iowa, Kentucky, South Dakota, and Nebraska the population has remained at almost stagnation level.

While after World War I migration was toward the center, it is now toward the periphery. Manufacturing industry, no longer dominated by coal, is not today associated with particular rock formations, and the fear of bombings militates against too great a concentration in the North and East; moreover, as the asceticism of the early pioneers has given way to a need for greater comfort, people are becoming less and less resigned to the severe climates which contented their ancestors. The twentieth century refuses to bow to the dictates of nature as the nineteenth century did.

II

The numerical aspect of the population of the different regions has been greatly modified in the interval between the last two censuses (1940 and 1950). In 1940 the ten states with the largest populations were New York, Pennsylvania, Illinois, Ohio, California, Texas, Michigan, Massachusetts, New Jersey, and Missouri. In 1950 the order had changed to: New York, California, Pennsylvania, Illinois, Ohio, Texas, Michigan, New Jersey, Massachusetts, and North Carolina. The three first-named are monster states with more than ten million inhabitants each. California has passed from fifth to second place and now has a larger population than Pennsylvania, Illinois, or Ohio. The East remains the most densely populated region, but the Far West is beginning to counterbalance it.

This change in the population distribution has its political repercussion in the geographical distribution of the 531 electoral votes (435 seats in the House of Representatives allocated according to population and 96 seats in the Senate on the basis of two per state). New York has 45 votes, California and Pennsylvania 32 each, while four more states have at least 20 each: Illinois (27), Ohio (25),

Texas (24), and Michigan (20). The East remains the main voting center, but the three Pacific coast states have 47 votes as compared with 35 in 1940, and the South Atlantic states 76 instead of 70. California has 32 votes instead of 22, Washington has increased from 8 to 9, Florida from 7 to 10, and Texas from 23 to 24; in contrast to this, New York has dropped from 47 to 45, Pennsylvania from 36 to 32, and Illinois from 29 to 27. These figures underline the population changes shown in the 1950 census.

On October 18, 1951, the Bureau of the Census officially announced over the radio that the center of population of the United States in 1950 was situated eight miles northwest of Olney in southeast Illinois, near its frontier with Indiana. This calculation is made on the assumption that the national territory is a plane surface and that each inhabitant is of equal weight! If a pivot were placed under the surface, the center of population would be where the surface was in perfect equilibrium in relation to the pivot; thus each inhabitant can influence this equilibrium by the place in which he lives, so that this center of population gives, in the most accurate way possible, the population movements at each ten-year census.

Since 1790, when the first calculation of this type was made, a movement of 644 miles toward the west has been observed, the original center being twenty-three miles east of Baltimore. The general direction of movement has been west along the thirty-ninth parallel with a slight tendency to drift toward the south; it had passed Ohio in 1890 and was in the west of Indiana in 1940. This change in position of the center of population corresponds to the progress of the economic development of the continent, a development that was most striking in its intensity from 1850 onward. The center of population moved eighty-one miles in the decade 1850-1860, from West Virginia to Ohio. Between 1940 and 1950 the movement was forty-two miles westward and seven and six-tenths miles southward, and in 1950 it reached the most southerly point which it has attained in the history of the United States.

The industrial map of the country has undergone a rapid transformation; there is no longer an area of industrial monopoly, but on the contrary manufacturing centers are to be found throughout the country. Technical progress in the field of agriculture has permitted the development of new areas with a small labor force, and regions previously neglected, such as the South, have been the object of what might be termed a policy of colonization. During World War II, industries such as aviation, shipbuilding, and automobile production gravitated toward the West.

The first World War had not the same effect as the second; between 1910 and 1920 the center of population moved only ten miles west; war industries were concentrated principally in the East and Middle West, and attracted a considerable black labor force northward. Only after 1918 was there substantial movement toward the Pacific coast; but this was on a large scale because of the policy of decentralizing industry for political, strategic, or productivity reasons. This is the explanation of the increased economic and political importance of the West, Far West, and South. The widespread underestimation of the importance of the Pacific coast on the part of travelers has now become almost unpardonable.

This purely theoretical idea of the country's center of population does not, of course, give a true picture of the infinitely complex social and economic conditions of the different groups, but its consistent movement westward is significant. Between the two wars the main seat of industrial power had passed to the region of the Great Lakes, in the very heart of the continent. The present tendency is one of movement toward the periphery; the states which have made most progress in the last fifteen years are not those of the center but those of the Pacific and Gulf coasts. The latest industrial development that has taken place has been in Texas and the lower Mississippi basin. The opening of the Panama Canal, which allowed Pacific states, such as California, to communicate directly with the Atlantic coast and with Europe, and thus to develop their industry, probably contributed in no small measure to the modification of the general equilibrium. From this point of view the central states are handicapped in relation to states with a seacoast, this disadvantage being aggravated by the fact that the iron ore of the Lake Superior area is becoming exhausted. But all this does not imply a decline of the importance of the East, the zone of capital and industrial and financial tradition, or the Middle West, which remains the area typical of American economic power, though the simplified picture of the industry and finance of the East contrasted with the agriculture and mining of the West is certainly no longer true.

CHAPTER 7

General Population Tendencies of the American People

★

The increase of population in the United States has been constant since the Declaration of Independence, and the total number of inhabitants has now passed the 160-million mark.

The ten-year increases have become progressively greater, as the following statistics show:

Period	Increase
1800-1810	1,931,398
1850-1860	8,251,445
1890-1900	13,046,861
1900-1910	15,977,691
1920-1930	17,064,426
1930-1940	8,894,229
1940-1950	19,028,086

The effect of the Depression is very marked in the decade 1930-1940, but it is to be noted that generally speaking the percentage increase has fallen; it remained above 30% until 1870 and above 20% until 1920, but has not reached such high figures at any time since, as the figures below demonstrate:

Period	% Increase
1910-1920	14.9
1920-1930	16.1
1930-1940	7.2
1940-1950	14.5

The general result, however, is that the United States is numerically the fourth greatest country in the world and is indubitably the first from the point of view of productivity and of power.

The immigration factor has been important but not decisive in this development. Between 1820 and 1950 immigration accounted for 39,325,482 inhabitants out of a total 150,697,361, *i.e.*, 27%. The percentage has varied according to the periods: 20% between 1820 and 1880, 22% between 1880 and 1910, 30% between 1920 and 1930, and 9% between 1930 and 1950. It is now practically negligible, so that the population curve depends only on the relation between the birth and death rates. The figures relating to the period 1940-1950, with its "baby boom," show that even without immigration population increases can be sensational.

Since the second half of the nineteenth century there had been a constant decrease in the birth rate. It dropped from 30 per thousand inhabitants to 25.0 in 1915 and 16.7 in 1936. According to contemporary thought this tendency appeared irreversible. The United States was par excellence a country of small families, strictly limited by deliberate nationwide birth control, with an outlook openly—not hypocritically—Malthusian. The machine age had banished faith in the importance of numerical superiority, and large families were ridiculed almost to the point of appearing shocking. If the birth rate remained relatively high as compared with certain European countries, this was largely because of the higher birth rate among recent immigrants, farmers in the West, and poor whites in the South, all sections of the community which lag somewhat behind the general trend.

The increase in the birth rate from 1940, and more especially from 1945 onward, was completely unexpected; the rate rose from 21.5 per thousand in 1943 to 25.8 in 1947 and was still at 23.5 in 1950; the total annual number of births, which was from two to two and a half million per annum between 1935 and 1942, exceeded three million in 1946 and three and a half million from 1947 onward. The main reason for this reversal in tendency was doubtless the war; marriages were put forward because of impending draft and, when the husbands returned after discharge, a spate of births resulted. Furthermore Americans were granted draft deferment if their wives were pregnant. These conditions were renewed in 1950 by the Korean War. But these circumstances are insufficient to explain what would appear to be a more permanent change in the nation's customs; for several generations small families had been fashionable and indeed they were often limited to a single child, but now it appears that three or even four are acceptable. In 1940 18.6% of women had two children, but this had increased to over 30% by 1950. Far from ridiculing the large family, the American now appears to consider it as a proof of the virility of his race. In searching for an explanation of this the old Scandinavian saying comes to mind: "The tree of Ygdrasil blossoms or withers according to laws too profound to bear examination." This increase in the birth rate may be only temporary, but the "baby boom" is, nevertheless, an important demographic feature, the effects of which will be felt over a long period.

Its consequences will be all the more marked by reason of the decline in the death rate, which has been steadily diminishing since the beginning of the century; it was 17.2 per thousand inhabitants in 1900, 13 in 1920, and 9.6 in 1950, the war not having affected this tendency in any way. This decrease is due mainly to outstanding progress in hygiene in a new civilization where efficient sanitary laws are properly observed, but immigration and the increase of the birth rate have also played their part by raising the percentage of young people in the nation. The survival rate is high (13.9 per thousand in 1950), and the population is increasing on an average between three and four million annually.

On the eve of World War II the experts were of the opinion that a continued decrease in the birth rate would bring about a higher death rate because of the raising of the average age of the population; therefore, since immigration was no longer an important factor, there would be a decline in the rate of increase of the population as a whole. It was estimated that the total population would rise very gradually to about 180 million and remain static at that figure. From these calculations and their meaning emerged a whole social philosophy, that of scorn of large numbers in a highly mechanized society, a philosophy that was in keeping with, or even based on, Malthusianism. Thus, in international conferences on population problems, bitter and insoluble conflicts arose between the champions of large families and the American partisans of birth control, and in this matter American Catholics, opposed to birth control by religious principle, stood out as a foreign element in their own country.

Population forecasts are now completely different. With four million births per annum and a minimum death rate it would appear reasonable to expect the number of inhabitants to increase by between thirty and forty million within the next twenty-five years, even allowing for some decrease in the birth rate and for a consequent increase in the death rate by reason of the higher average age of the population; under these conditions the two hundred million mark will be reached in about 1975. The general outlook has therefore changed and, like other nations, the United States finds attraction in the prestige of numerical superiority; the high birth rate has become a matter for pride, demonstrating the virility and power of the nation.

II

The American nation has passed through the youthful stage to a certain measure of demographic maturity, but it still continues to evolve and with disconcerting rapidity. It has changed since yesterday, it will be different again tomorrow, and these changes bring about corresponding changes in psychological outlook. There is in the nation a curious mixture of age with some features characteristic of extreme youth.

Increasing maturity is shown in the relative decrease in the male population. At the beginning of the century the important wave of Slavo-Latin immigration brought, naturally enough, more men than women to the American shores. In 1900 there were 104.4 men for every 100 women in the United States. The same phenomenon had been observed during the colonization of the Far West in the nineteenth century, particularly in California where, at the time of the Gold Rush, the early settlements contained practically no female element. The consequences of this state of affairs have been far-reaching since, following the economic law of supply and demand, scarcity created for woman the essentially privileged position that she holds in American society. With the passage of years and the decline in immigration, a tendency toward equilibrium between the sexes was naturally established; in 1940 there were 98.6 men for every 100 women, and in 1950 only 94.6.

These figures are only national averages. In the East and South there are more women than men, but in the West there are more men than women, particularly in the Pacific coast area. Statistics for the different states are interesting. Montana has 115 men for 100 women, Washington 109, but there has been a recent proportional increase in the number of women in some of the states; in Illinois there are now (1950 census) 98.3 men for 100 women compared with 100.4 in 1940, in California 100.1 in 1950 compared with 103.7 in 1940. The difference is explained by the fact that the population of California has increased considerably in recent years through migration, while Illinois has experienced only natural population increase.

Under these conditions one may wonder whether the supremacy of woman, which formerly seemed to be a permanent characteristic of the American nation, has not reached or even passed its peak. It is woman who reigns in the United States, she is always sought after and has but to choose from among a number of aspirants only too willing to escort her. By tomorrow this position may have undergone reversal, and it may even be that, as in England, advances will not come exclusively from the male. A recent enquiry has revealed that an exceptional woman in the East has less matrimonial opportunities than an average woman in Texas, and if it is true that men remain in awe of the exceptional woman, there is equally no doubt about the fact that the numerical relation between the sexes has a direct and important influence on their personal relations. The United States is thus confronting a long-term development of great social significance, which marks the end of the youth, demographically speaking, of the nation.

This is one aspect of the general tendency toward an increase in the average age of the population which from 17 years in 1826 rose to 30 in 1950. There is a larger percentage of old people; the over-65 age group increased by 36% between 1940 and 1950, the 45-64 group by 16.7%. Although 25% of the over-65's are still capable of earning their own living, the remainder have to live on savings, pensions, or family help, and new problems have therefore arisen which affect an increasing number of Americans.

The psychology of the nation up to the present time has been one characteristic of youth, thinking neither of death nor old age, confident in a capacity to work and a certitude of finding employment, though the latter was somewhat shaken by the years of depression. Anxiety about security has now made itself felt, age counts for a great deal in this, but there is also the threat of unemployment. The American traditionally shows foresight in the matter of insurance, but the Great Depression made security problems a national rather than a personal affair, and the New Deal ushered in a new stage in social policy. Dr. Townsend's campaign on behalf of old people gained immediate success, several states granted pensions, and even in the demands of the trade unions social security measures have at times assumed more importance than wage increases. This certainly marks a psychology no longer essentially youthful.

The "baby boom" stemmed the flow of the current that was aging the American nation. Between 1940 and 1950 the group under 10 years increased by 39.3%, while the total population increase of the country was 14.5%. The general atmosphere is modified by this increase in the younger age groups, even if it is only temporary. Fifteen years ago the main items of social service discussed were hospitals, homes for the aged, small cars, and pensions. Now the country must be equipped for this unexpected rise in her population by the recruitment of teachers, the building of schools, an intensified housing program, and greater emphasis on the manufacture of school equipment, playthings, and everything a child needs. And because this is America there is already talk of a new boom in business. The country is back in its element; for it was hardly recognizable as the United States when all conversation tended toward the Depression, restrictions, social security, and pensions. For the nation to feel really itself, everything must show a persistent upward movement.

In spite of this rejuvenation, the country is progressing toward maturity. Considerations of defense arise as well as problems of expansion, and this situation cannot fail to make its imprint on the American character. European influence, formerly preponderant because of immigration, is diminishing, leaving environment alone to mold the nation—in which way has not yet become apparent.

A new race is gradually being formed, biologically different from that of the European peoples. The American's vitality is linked with nervous instability, his attention is easily distracted, his enthusiasm for action results in overwork leading to nervous breakdowns, his infatuation easily turns to hatred, and in the long run the perfection of modern machinery will engender in him a certain mental sloth because of his excessive respect for technical achievements and the opinion of experts. He is a new type of man, the product of an industrial civilization which has been permitted to develop fully in the New World.

CHAPTER 8

The Negro Problem: Legacy of the Past

★

There are in the United States three important minorities which are not yet completely assimilated—the Catholics, the Jews, and the Negroes. The Negroes, unlike the other two groups, cannot in the foreseeable future be assimilated and this has brought about the extreme gravity of the color problem in the United States.

According to the 1950 census there are 15,042,286 Negroes, or 9.9% of the total population, compared with 12,865,518 (9.8%) in 1940. They form a bloc that is increasing numerically if not proportionately to the total population, and remain as a homogeneous group, so that a Negro problem will always exist. The definition of a Negro varies in the different states; generally speaking the term applies to anyone who has one-eighth Negro blood, that is to say, anyone who had one black great-grandparent, but it is often sufficient to have any Negro blood—a single drop is enough. It is an idea that is neither legal nor racially accurate, but one that arouses passionate feelings. Before 1914 almost all Negroes lived in the South, but since World War I several million have been drawn toward the North, from the southeast Atlantic coastal area to Pennsylvania, New York, and New England, and from the lower Mississippi basin to Ohio, Michigan, Indiana, and Illinois; there were openings for them as industrial workers and they hoped to receive better treatment than in the South. In 1947, 9,530,000 of them, or 64%, were still established in the thirteen southern states, there were 4,600,000, or 30%, in the central and eastern states, while 892,000, or 6%, had recently migrated to the southwestern states and the Pacific coast. The southern states now have the greatest proportion of Negro inhabitants: Mississippi 45%,

South Carolina 39%, Alabama 32%, Georgia 31%, Florida 22%, Arkansas 22%, Virginia 22%, and Negroes also form almost one-third of the population of the District of Columbia. The cities that have the greatest number of Negroes are situated in the East and Center: New York 776,000, Chicago 509,437, Philadelphia 378,968, Detroit 303,721, Washington, D. C., 284,031; these numbers are increasing rapidly. In the northern states 90% of the Negroes live in the towns, but in the South the range is from 40% to 60%, and there are frequently areas in which the Negro population dominates. Fear of the Negro invasion, not at all justified statistically, has arisen in those communities where the white population represents a small and decreasing minority.

II

The origin of the Negroes in the United States is well known. They are the descendants of slaves imported from Africa during the colonial period by the planters of the South, who required foreign labor adapted to a subtropical climate. This need was not felt in the North and therefore slavery did not develop there. The slave trade, however, experienced a new stimulus during the eighteenth century when the invention of a cotton-sorting machine gave an impetus to the cultivation of cotton in the southern states, thus creating a new demand for labor. When the slave trade was abolished in 1808, Virginia and Maryland developed what one might almost describe as a Negro breeding center, in order to sell Negroes to the southern states where, though the trade in slaves had ceased, slavery still persisted. In 1820 the northern states had 5,090,237 white inhabitants, the South had 2,776,560 and 1,642,672 Negroes, while of the 1,772,000 Negroes in the country 1,538,000 were slaves.

Reactions toward slavery were different in the different parts of the country. The North considered it scandalous, but to the South it was a normal institution which in no way contravened religious principles. Nobody wished to raise the question of the existence of slavery in those states where it was established, but the problem arose as to what the law should be in the new states that were developing in the West. Should they be free states or slave states? According to the conclusion reached there would arise two entirely different conceptions of work and ways of living in general. This problem constituted a threat to the unity of the country, for, on a question of such paramount importance, it was clear that the compromise of half-slave and half-free, to use Lincoln's famous phrase, could not continue indefinitely. A crisis was inevitable, though the half-measures adopted deferred it for a certain time. By the Missouri Compromise slavery was excluded north of a latitude of 36° 30', and by the Compromise of 1850 each state organized from the territory acquired from Mexico could decide whether slavery should be recognized or forbidden. These were not solutions, for the North was bearing, with growing impatience, a system which it condemned, while the South feared that the majority of the states would finally be in favor of freeing the slaves and would attempt to impose their will upon the whole country.

Thus the problem came gradually to take first place in all federal discussion. Politicians, anxious to maintain the Union, were ready to admit the existence in the South of an institution of which they themselves disapproved, but, in 1832, a society for the abolition of slavery was formed in Boston and this society made a point of considering the problem from a moral angle: it was against humanity and the dictates of Christian conscience to tolerate any longer a system incompatible with the principles on which the very unity of the nation should rest. The South, now beginning to realize all the implications of the situation, admitted that it put the maintenance of slavery before union. Lincoln, partisan of the moralists as far as his ideals were concerned, but on the side of the politicians in his profound desire to maintain the Union, agreed to tolerate slavery in the South, but declared that it should not be legal in any new state. This policy gained him the presidency of the republic in 1860. Then came the secession of the South, bringing about a war that lasted until 1865 and ended in a complete victory for the North.

The victorious North abolished slavery (Thirteenth Amendment to the Constitution) and conferred upon the Negroes the rights of citizenship (Fourteenth Amendment), imposing forcibly upon the vanquished South the detested "Reconstruction" regime, with its saturnalia of freed Negroes and carpetbaggers. The memory of this lingers today with a bitterness that time has been powerless to heal. The South, moreover, did not submit. With obstinate local resistance groups, the whites regained, little by little, control of the government in the states where cliques of Negroes and politicians had installed themselves, and the freed Negroes were again reduced, by unconstitutional legislation, to a sort of serfdom. Thus the North, victorious in arms, had not won a moral victory over the South, which still remains a region apart in the United States.

In the matter of the relations between the two races, slavery, though a bad solution, was a solution. The Negro had his place in the social hierarchy, and, in spite of serious abuses, he was to a certain extent a member of the family and could often exert a considerable influence over his master. But what was to be the position of the freed slave? Was absolute equality, as affirmed by the Thirteenth and Fourteenth Amendments, wholly acceptable? Was it not necessary, rather, to keep the Negro in his place, as was so often said in the South? The first solution would eventually bring about the integration of the Negro element into the nation, the second meant immediate segregation. The problem could not be avoided in view of the size of the Negro community, either in the South where it was obviously urgent, or even in the North where it had become impossible to ignore it. It was a problem of daily life rather than a problem for the legislators, and it affected the attitude of the individual citizen toward the Union. Should the Constitution, based on a conception of equal rights for all, be applied to Negroes? The Negroes themselves demanded it as a right implicit in the principles laid down in the eighteenth century. But then . . . ?

III

The South never changed its fundamental opinion. The question was one that affected the South alone and could be solved adequately only by the South; the North had no right to interfere. The black race is inferior to the white and should be kept at the bottom of the social ladder, in its natural place. In this way the Negro can be a useful subordinate in a society where he will not be treated as a foreigner. It is not even exaggerating to say that in contrast to the Northerners, whose kindly attitude was theoretical and distant, the Southerners tended to show affection for the Negro as long as he recognized his subordinate position. "We alone," they said, "know how to command with the natural authority of the superior race, we alone know how to talk with him, treat his familiarly and joke with him without losing the sense of our position. . . . But if he is given complete liberty all is lost, for he will consider every concession as a sign of weakness, will become impossible and nothing more nor less than a dangerous beast, and finally will have to be shot down like a mad dog. The North is playing with fire, for to them it is a question only of secondary importance, while to the South, if it is to remain a white man's country, it is a question of life and death."

In spite of notable concessions, particularly since the recent economic revival, I do not believe that the South has at heart completely abandoned this point of view.

After the excesses of the Reconstruction had subsided, the Negroes of the South, citizens in theory, found themselves ostracized under a regime that is now undergoing some modifications but that still exists in its essentials. According to this system, which the policy of civil rights is attempting to break down, the Negro is denied the right to vote, he is prevented from registering himself or presenting himself at the polling booth, and if he does it is at the peril of his life. For example, as recently as 1948 a Negro from Georgia, Isaiah Nixon, was assassinated for penetrating into a voting booth and refusing to leave. This exclusion is carried on without any explanation, either through mere spite or in virtue of state legislation. Thus certain states (Alabama, Arkansas, Mississippi, South Carolina, Tennessee, Texas, and Virginia) have imposed a poll tax on voters, but this is a two-edged weapon, since the Negro, when he has the means, pays, while a number of poor whites are prevented from voting. In some areas the Grandfather Clause was used to exclude from voting all persons whose grandfathers were not on the voting rolls. Sometimes the subterfuge of an examination on the Constitution is resorted to, and frequently the Negro does not pass. Under these conditions only a very small percentage of black men succeeds in voting in the South; in 1940 it was estimated that the total did not exceed 250,000.

By means of the "Jim Crow" laws of segregation, the colored population is forced to live in certain districts of the towns, where the upkeep of the roads and drainage system is of a most rudimentary nature, all the worse owing to the fact that the inhabitants are not represented on the municipal councils; the districts are overcrowded and the houses neglected, contrasting strongly with the cleanliness of the streets occupied by white inhabitants. Negroes are excluded from theaters, hotels, and restaurants considered suitable for white customers, and in buses and on the railroads they can travel only in the special compartments marked "For Negroes"; they would not be admitted to a sleeping car. Even the churches apply racial discrimination, and in the South the segregation of the races in the schools has become a matter of principle, though now vetoed by law. Thus the Negro is systematically treated as an inferior. Even when he is educated the Southerners appear to find some difficulty in calling him "Mr."; they prefer to call him John or Joseph and expect him to reply with cordial politeness, Sir, Boss, or Captain. It is said that Theodore Roosevelt avoided the difficulty when he received Booker T. Washington by calling him Professor, but this mode of address is not without a slight trace of irony. It is evident that under such a system there is no justice for the oppressed race; the white assassin of a Negro is not always pursued, or if he stands trial he is sometimes acquitted by a deliberately lenient jury. There is the same discrimination in sexual crimes; a Negro would risk being lynched, but a colored victim could not complain of a wrong done by a white man without personal risk. A permanently scandalous state of affairs would appear to exist, tempting one to quote Shakespeare: "Something is rotten in the state of Denmark" (*Hamlet,* I, iv).

A curious feature about this racial hatred is that it is most violent among the working classes. Before the Civil War, the slave-owners, who possessed their own labor, did not employ free workers, and therefore there arose a class of "poor whites," chronically unemployed, reduced to living on public assistance, taking refuge in the mountains, or enlisting in the army. These conditions lasted for some time after the abolition of slavery, since Negroes provided cheaper and more docile labor and prevented the white worker from raising his standard of living. The latter was particularly apprehensive of being grouped with the inferior race, to which he was nearer from an economic viewpoint. Moreover, there reigns in the South a sort of sacred union founded on race, which traditionally serves the interests of the employer class: leaders such as Huey Long, who appeal to the class consciousness of the poor whites, remain exceptions in it. This part of the country has long been right wing and reactionary; this effect is achieved anywhere by the presence of a colored population, and it would be incorrect to attribute this obstinate attitude of the whites principally to economic causes. Although the greater part of the population of the South is white, this fear of the Negroes, numerically greater in certain localities, must not be ignored. It has become a kind of obsession which a Frenchman, if he has had no experience of colonial affairs, finds difficult to understand. The white population is haunted unreasonably but insidiously by a fear of the decline that would result from a mixing of the two races, by an almost physical fear of the Negro population, with whom contact, nevertheless, remains inevitable. It is a confused feeling, curiously emphasized as far as relations between the sexes are concerned, for though mixed marriages are prohibited, there are often sexual relations between the two races, more frequently, of course, between a white man and a black woman. It is not infrequent for a man to have a black mistress, and in spite of the physical repulsion openly avowed it cannot be denied that in the United States colored women have sex appeal. Relations of this order were common during the slavery period and have not ceased to exist. It is estimated that between seven and eight million white people have some black blood and an equal number of Negroes have white blood; it is, moreover, sufficient to look at the Negroes to realize that they are a mixed race, different from the pure African Negro.

This question of the physical defense of the race seems so deep-rooted in the South that anything appears permissible in order to maintain it—threats, violence, lynching; no principles are effective against this instinctive reaction, which can be terrifying when it is mass-produced. Such uncontrolled scenes are associated in France only with revolutions. The South seceded in 1860-1861 to preserve its unity, and deep down its attitude has not changed, but if it has not progressed the world around it has been transformed, and the South can no longer resist the constant pressure from outside.

IV

The attitude of the North contrasts strongly to this. The problem is traditionally theoretical, as it is for Europeans, because there were few Negroes in the cities of the East and Center before World War I. Negroes were almost unknown to Northerners before that, but they wished them well because they had emancipated them. Now important migrations have established colonies of Negroes in Chicago, Detroit, Philadelphia, New York, and other northern cities, and this has created, though in a different way, the same problems that are to be found in the South.

The North, faithful to the principles of the Constitution, recognizes the Negro's rights as a citizen. He may therefore vote, stand as a candidate, send his children to school, travel freely in trains or buses, work in factories side by side with white men, be employed as a skilled worker, contract a mixed marriage, and, in principle, live without segregation. The law has done everything possible, but the problem has not been solved. Customs run contrary to it. The Negro is excluded from hotels, restaurants, and clubs, which are in fact, if not in principle, reserved for white men. If he attempts to settle in a district inhabited by white people, he may be chased away violently. If he bathes, at Chicago for example, on a beach where he would be considered an interloper, he may provoke a riot, as has happened more than once. Jealousy is shown toward colored workers, whether they occupy skilled posts or continue to work when some white men are unemployed. There is peace, but everywhere the seeds of civil war are visible.

The Negro cannot, any more than he can in the South, become assimilated into a population that remains foreign and fundamentally hostile to him. But he adapts himself to city life and to that Western civilization which to a large extent becomes his own, so that he can claim to a greater degree than his brother on the Gulf coast to have integrated himself into a society that repels him. The problem is different but equally insoluble.

And what is the Negro attitude to all this, in the South and in the North?

CHAPTER 9

The Negro Problem: Present and Future

★

Persecuted, bullied, or merely tolerated, the freed slave could at least attempt to defend himself. But does he?

The southern Negro is essentially a parasite, instinctively gravitating toward the white man as toward a natural patron whose racial superiority he acknowledges. He would rather adapt himself than resist, but the weight of his slave tradition bears heavily upon him, and he is discouraged by the treatment which he receives and the contempt with which he is treated. Indeed, Negroes who have migrated to the North remember their childhood in the South as a kind of hell. Nevertheless, as they mingle to a fair degree of intimacy in white society, they can appreciate finely enough the standing of white people; they can judge them keenly, and are ironical about the *nouveaux riches,* for they can recall the aristocracy of the past in the South and are disdainful of the poor whites, who are often more wretched materially than they are.

In the North the attitude of the Negroes changes rapidly, for they are essentially an urban population and assimilation with the customs around them is easier. Apart from the color question, the Negro can become Americanized more quickly and often more completely than many European immigrants. Moreover, has he not three centuries of American tradition? He has forgotten his African ancestry and wishes to associate himself only with the traditions of the New World. In the less personal environment of the great urban agglomerations of the East or Center he is certainly better treated than his brother in the South, but inasmuch as he has evolved more he suffers more from the discriminating attitude taken toward him, and the fact that he has civil rights makes him resent all the more bitterly that he is refused social ones.

Under these conditions he is no longer obsequious according to the accepted idea of the submissive Negro, and tends to put forward his claims and often to become even insolent. Feeling himself less and less different in his way of life from the people around him, he is impatient of an ostracism which is a constant reminder of the fact that the color of his skin has not changed.

In the North as in the South, the attitude of Negroes toward each other is typical of the idea that they have of themselves and of their status. They consider their slave heredity as humiliating, and the descendants of free men are loath to mingle with the others, but they retain, nevertheless, traces of the atmosphere and the hierarchy of their slavery; like English butlers in the nineteenth century, the grandchildren of slaves in the households of the most aristocratic planters retain a kind of pride of position. They seem to continue to judge everything from the standpoint of the dominant race, including the color of their skins, the lighter in color the more highly esteemed it *is*, and Negroes themselves distinguish an incredible number of shades. Here is the color range according to Mencken's *American Mercury:* black, brown, deep brown, yellow, reddish-brown, deep yellow, dark-brown, chocolate, gingerbread, fair, light brown, red, pink, tan, olive, copper-color, blue, cream, pale black, dead black, bronze, banana. A Negress prefers to marry a man whose skin is lighter than her own. On the other hand, a preacher or an agitator will have more influence if he is very black, doubtless because he would never "pass."

To "pass," when one's skin is light in color, means to succeed in passing oneself off as a white man. This can be achieved in several ways. It is possible to "pass" exceptionally for a short period by slipping into a restaurant or theater without being noticed, but there is also the Negro who changes his racial status and who generally does so without any intention of turning back. The practice is quite frequent, and it is estimated that every year about 20,000 or 30,000 Negroes merge into the ocean of the white race. Negroes themselves seem to be sympathetic to those of their numbers who desert in this way; they know too well the handicap under which they are living to be unable to understand anyone seeking to escape from it. It nevertheless happens that sometimes colored men who have deserted their race are seized with scruples and return voluntarily. A man whom I met in Atlanta and whom I took to be white, subsequently told me that he was a Negro who had "passed" and then come back to his own race, fired with a desire to serve it.

The black race as such has aspirations beyond those of the individual, varying greatly according to social status. The majority of Negroes are in a position so inferior to that of the white race, having no contact with them other than that of employee or servant, that their one concern is to live as well as they can. Their idea of the destiny of their race is based on humiliation and century-old suffering. There is something pathetic in this sentiment, which has given rise to artistic expression, as the Negro spirituals testify. But, apart from opportunities from which the individual Negro may profit, the general outlook is one of passiveness and resignation.

But there is an elite, becoming increasingly numerous and educated, which is capable of conceiving a plan of campaign and carrying it out. It includes the group of men who have achieved material distinction and who, even from the white standpoint, may be considered as wealthy; then there are also those who have gained success in the professions, who are well educated, may have university degrees, and are often very cultured: in 1950 an estimated 3,769 doctors, 1,650 dentists, 1,367 lawyers, 9,000 nurses. Finally there are the artists and writers, who are numerous in a race which has such gifts for music, dancing, and the theater; many of them are famous throughout the world and occupy an important place in the artistic life of the United States. The ambitions of these Negroes have developed with the years. The plan formerly put forward by Marcus Garvey of a return to Africa must not be taken seriously. Whether the Negroes of the New World feel any racial solidarity with the Africans or not, they have no wish whatever to return to their continent of origin, and I think that they probably feel a sort of disdainful pity for their African brothers with their lower standard of living; they are American in their way of tending to look down upon anything outside their

continent, even including Europeans. Indeed, is not the standard
of living of a Negro from New York or Chicago superior to that
of many Europeans?

At the end of the nineteenth century Booker T. Washington, the
founder of the Negro university at Tuskegee, Alabama, attempted
to raise the level of his compatriots through education, though in
an attitude of deference toward the white race, and not without a
certain inferiority complex. Then, at the beginning of the present
century, William Edward Burghardt Du Bois, a descendant of free
Negroes of the West Indies and a man of great physical and intellectual distinction, founded the periodical *Crisis,* whose object
was the raising of the status of the Negro by the Negro. Following his example, a large number of newspapers and periodicals
are now addressed to the black population and discuss racial problems, stimulating pride in Negro achievement, which is often outstanding.

It seems to me, however, in the light of a number of conversations that I have had with Negro leaders in Chicago and New
York, that they are seeking something unattainable. They are aiming at integration into white society, and this is not a recent development, for I had already received a similar impression thirty
years before. "Are we not men like the other inhabitants of the
United States? Are we not Americans, proud of our citizenship,
ready to claim our rights under the Constitution? We ask to be
treated as human beings and as Americans. We are of a different
color, you say, but is that not a secondary consideration?" They
never speak of themselves as American Negroes, but always as
Americans. From this point of view their feelings toward the
country that has treated them so badly show perfect loyalty. Just
as Jews persecuted by the Germans could not succeed in hating
the German people, so Negroes, who, nevertheless, have so much
to complain of, never have a bad word for the United States, nor
do they appear to think unkindly of it.

Ralph Johnson Bunche, the Negro who was awarded a Nobel
Prize in 1950, wrote:

I am a native-born American, as were my ancestors as far back as I
can trace ancestry. This is my country. I have, to be sure, suffered
racial rebuffs and indignities and encountered racial obstacles here,

some of which I have surmounted and others not. But I have also enjoyed many and great profits. I understand my country and I am
devoted to it. I am deeply conscious of my obligations and my solemn
responsibilities as a citizen. I believe in my country and in its democratic
way of life. I like the freedom, the rights and dignity of the individual,
and the principle of equality of peoples for which it stands. I know
of few Negroes who would not share these views.*

Thus civil rights, as legally recognized in the North, are insufficient, for social equality is equally essential. What does this
mean? Not only that hotels, restaurants, theaters, and the homes
of white men should be open to Negroes, but also that inter-
marriage should be possible without any humiliating restrictions.
The Negro elite appear to me to be claiming this rather than any
recognition of their status as colored people. Doubtless most Negroes, particularly the more evolved, shaking off the burdens of
their race, would willingly "pass" if they could.

What is the reply of the white race to these aspirations? The
elite of the Americans have indubitably progressed toward a certain liberalism and have made an effort to improve relations between the two races; Roosevelt and Truman openly declared themselves in favor of civil rights. But in spite of a designedly more
kindly outlook there is still an instinctive defensive attitude in the
South and even to a certain extent in the North. World War II
brought about an improvement in the treatment of Negroes, but
it did not ease the solution of the problem, since, when they
fought in the Western armies in Europe, they found across the
Atlantic a better attitude toward them, and those who were pro-
moted to be officers found it more difficult to bear the daily hu-
miliations to which they were still subjected. They had, moreover,
learned, especially since the New Deal, the importance of their
vote, not only in obtaining legal recognition of their rights but
in the application of them. The problem is, therefore, posed on a
more and more general basis.

II

Negroes have to their credit many important achievements. In the
scholastic field they have founded a number of establishments,

* *Survey,* March, 1951.

among them Atlanta University, Fisk University, Hampton Institute, Howard University, Lincoln University, Tuskegee Institute, Xavier University. Ninety per cent of Negroes in 1865 were illiterate; this proportion had fallen to 11% in 1947, though it is only 1.8% for the white race. At the end of the Civil War there were not more than about twenty Negro graduates, but there are now more than 8,000 a year and around 80,000 Negroes are studying in colleges. Despite this fact there is still reluctance on the part of certain universities in the South to admit Negro students, although by a recent Supreme Court decision segregation is no longer legal anywhere. Particularly since World War I a very important Negro press has developed: *Defender* and *Crisis* are high-grade papers and periodicals, typically American in presentation, which endeavor to develop in an intelligent fashion the Negro contribution to civilization, particularly to the civilization of the United States, in literature, art, and sport. The National Negro Business League, on its side, together with other similar institutions, looks after the economic interests of the race, an increasingly important consideration in view of the spread of Negro success in business. The cohesion of all these movements is accentuated by the role of the Negro churches, especially the Baptist and the Methodist, whose activity and conviction are incontestable, though they may not always be associated with high educational value. The Negro minority has, in short, realized for some time that it must work out its own salvation.

But this cannot succeed without the consent and the help of the white race. The Protestant churches of the North show sincere good will in this respect, but common worship between the races has not yet been achieved. Some of the most passionate opponents of the liberation of Negroes are to be found in the Protestant churches of the South; the white Baptist pastor receives particular attention from the Ku Klux Klan.*

Mention must be made of the efforts of many chambers of commerce to achieve collaboration between the races; on the other hand, the political parties have let much time elapse without making any useful or efficient contribution to the problem. The traditional policy of the Democrats, based on the "Solid South," is

* On the Ku Klux Klan see pages 243-245.

the defense of the white race. The Republicans, in principle partisans of the Negroes, have no practical policy in this matter. Moreover, in the South there are really no Republicans, and therefore the racial minority is not represented politically. A complete reversal of this position was brought about when the Democrats were returned with Roosevelt in 1933; because the party on principle defended the nonassimilated immigrants, and particularly because, since the number of Negroes in the North with a right to vote had increased, the black population was included in the group of minorities that came under Democratic protection. This provoked a series of secessions in the South, the main one of which was the Dixiecrats, who in 1948 refused to support the candidature of Truman, partisan of civil rights. Thus the color question has come increasingly into the political arena.

From the beginning of World War II, Roosevelt abolished racial discrimination in the army, and in 1948 President Truman presented to Congress a complete program of civil rights: the creation of a Civil Rights Division of the Department of Justice and a permanent Commission of Civil Rights assuring equality of legal treatment, federal protection against lynching, abolition of poll taxes and a guaranteed right to vote, suppression of discrimination in industry and transport, and special protection of Negroes in the District of Columbia. It is not surprising that the South protested violently and that, with the support of various Republican elements, it succeeded in preventing this bill from being adopted. But Negro opinion, on the alert and finding itself supported for once, reacted by means of unrest and parliamentary agitation, ably led by the National Association for the Advancement of Colored People. And what were the results?

III

Negro franchise, recognized in the North, is not in the South, but growing external pressure is beginning to force its adoption in spite of unwillingness on the part of election officials to enroll Negroes. It seems probable that, in future, the Negro vote will be of increasing significance in the elections in the South. These elections, as the result of the monopoly of the Democrats, are in effect carried out in the primaries, where the white voters claim to stand alone, as in a closed club, but here again the door is slowly opening: in 1944 the Supreme Court decided that Negroes should be admitted. This decision has yet to be applied, but resistance is weakening all along the line. The Negro vote now counts in several Southern towns as well as in all the Northern ones, sometimes to the point of giving the deciding vote, and it is no longer exceptional for elective posts to be allotted to Negroes.

Segregation still persists almost everywhere, in spite of increasing legislation against it. In the field of transport, it was admitted by the Supreme Court in 1896, though in 1946 a judgment declared it to be illegal for journeys that involved crossing a state boundary; but up to the present the Court has not condemned a practice which, south of a certain line, remains the general rule. Even in the North a Negro is rarely seen in a Pullman. The problem is no nearer solution where housing is concerned. Segregation is legal everywhere in the South, but elsewhere it is applied in practice if not by law. In Chicago and New York a Negro can legally live wherever he wishes, and in 1948, after a number of different decisions, a verdict of the Supreme Court annulled all contracts forbidding the renting of a dwelling to a Negro or a Jew. In practice, however, if a colored tenant settles in a block, the white tenants either leave the building, thus greatly diminishing its value to the owner, or else use violence to prevent the Negro from moving in. Sinclair Lewis has described such a case in *Kingsblood Royal*, but the riot provoked in the Cicero district of Chicago in 1951 is only one example among many incidents of this nature; custom refuses to permit contact between the two races.

Incidents of the same sort happen in connection with hotels, restaurants, theaters, and places of amusement in general. If a Negro tries to book a hotel room, he will be refused in Chicago just as much as in New Orleans. If he wants to dine in a restaurant, there is never a table free. The fact that the law is on his side makes very little difference, even for a cultured man holding an important position. At the time of the conference of Episcopalian bishops in New Orleans, one of them, a Negro, had booked a room at the largest hotel in the town, where I myself was staying, but he was unable to remain there because the white domestic staff refused to serve him and threatened to strike. When European delegations that include colored men arrive in New York, they have the greatest difficulty in accommodating their colored members along with the rest. But the presence in the United States of foreign delegations more and more mixed racially has brought about a certain relaxation of severity; it is possible to say that the situation has become easier, at least in the North, and in broad-minded circles it does occasionally happen that Negroes receive invitations. A Negro intellectual, not very dark-skinned I must admit, invited me to lunch in a large restaurant in New York whose management, he assured me, would shut their eyes to his presence; nothing embarrassing happened, but the meal made me think of La Fontaine's town rat and country rat. Here again the problem, though less acute than in former times, is moving no nearer to a solution.

If any real progress is to be observed, it is in the army, where segregation, condemned by Roosevelt, is being gradually eliminated in the sea and air forces, though less quickly in the land army. There has also been some progress in industry, where Executive Order No. 8802 of 1941 forbade any discrimination in factories working for the war effort. This Order is now extended to all Government enterprises and to those working on federal contracts. In the North and East it has long been the custom for black and white workers to work side by side in factories. Negroes are admitted to skilled posts and have the same rights as other workers, except for the fact that they are more readily demoted, and in times of crisis they are the first to be dismissed. While they have been admitted to the Congress of Industrial Organizations, the American Federation of Labor has for a long time barred them from its unions. Steps have, however, been made in the direction of equality of treatment, and the movement is now extending toward the South, where the present rapid industrialization is often carried out by vast enterprises from the North, which have no racial prejudices. About ten states, all in the North, have laws forbidding racial discrimination in industry, but the project for a federal law on this subject did not succeed in passing Congress owing to opposition from the South.

Finally, it is on the question of segregation in schools that feelings seem to run highest. This is considered not to exist in the North, where the presence of black children in public schools is generally accepted, and where the admittance of colored students to universities is becoming more widespread, at least as far as individual applications and limited numbers are concerned. But until May 17, 1954, when the Supreme Court declared segregation in schools illegal and unconstitutional, seventeen states accepted it in their legislation (Alabama, Arkansas, Delaware, Florida, Mississippi, Missouri, North Carolina, Oklahoma, Georgia, Kentucky, Louisiana, Maryland, South Carolina, Tennessee, Texas, Virginia, and West Virginia); and in four other states it was on occasion permissible. This system is now legally condemned. The justification which had hitherto been given was based on a Supreme Court decision of 1896, which admitted that segregation in schools, though clearly contrary to the Fourteenth Amendment, could be tolerated, provided that, in their separate schools, black children had scholastic opportunities equal to those of the white. This was the doctrine of "separate but equal." If there was not this equality, and the contrary was more often true, then the more recent decisions insisted on the admission, on a sufficiently generous scale, of black children into ordinary public schools. The Court's jurisprudence was moving toward a general condemnation of the principle of segregation, in keeping with the tendency shown toward other aspects of the Negro problem. The decision of May 17, 1954, which may be described as of historical significance is a fact of prime importance in the evolution of the status of the Negro; but in this as in other matters there arises the question of theory as opposed to practice. In several Southern border states where schools have been forced to accept colored children, parents of white children have withdrawn them in large numbers, and there have been actual riots over this question, as at Cairo, Illinois, in 1952. The Deep South will doubtless show the greatest amount of ill will toward the new decision of the Supreme Court. In the most unwilling states, such as South Carolina or Georgia, it is possible that resistance will take the form of abandoning public schools in favor of private schools, in which segregation would not be unconstitutional. It is clear that a long and painful period of adaptation lies ahead, while segregation in schools is being abolished.

IV

By considering the development of the Negro question in this way, it is easy to see why it is practically insoluble. The Negroes have become more highly civilized, especially in the North, and international opinion, which has affected the United States much more since the establishment of the United Nations, favors a liberal racial policy. But there are at the same time irreconcilable differences between the two races, now apparent in the North as well as the South because of the large Negro population recently established there.

Given these conditions, no solution appears satisfactory or even possible. The South would indubitably prefer to keep the Negro in his place in the South African manner, but this policy has finally been demonstrated to be just as impossible from the practical point of view as the maintenance of slavery was a hundred years ago, and the South has begun to realize it. The mixing of the races, which produced for the Portuguese freedom from ethnical problems, has had in Brazil the effect of gradually absorbing the colored element in the population, but the Americans seem to fear more than anything else the effect of a similar infiltration of alien blood. Segregation on terms of equality and without loss of dignity would appear to be the best solution for both whites and Negroes, but it seems impossible to achieve. The Negro, so recently treated as an inferior, still feels humiliation in the fact that he is not treated as an equal, even though he realizes that he is different.

Therefore, although progress has been made in the relations between the two races, any solution acceptable to both sides seems to disappear like a mirage as one gets nearer to it. Thanks to their voting power, Negroes will establish a place for themselves in American society, guaranteed by law, and finally, in the main, respected. Through international pressure, and also because they have come to merit it more and more by their personal achievements, the more distinguished of the Negroes will be treated with greater courtesy, and even admitted to important posts. But it is doubtful whether a colored man will ever be treated as an equal, except so far as his legal position is concerned, nor will he receive that recognition of his social dignity without which he will never feel fully satisfied. It was said ironically in Austria-Hungary, under the old regime, that no man below the rank of a baron need be considered as a man. In the United States, is the Negro really considered as a man? The American message to the world is thus weakened by not being entirely humane.

CHAPTER 10

The Religious Factor in the American Make-up

★

In order to understand a nation it is always important to consider its attitude toward God. As far as the Americans are concerned this is essential. Western Christianity is divided among three main religious conceptions which influence spiritual development and social behavior and thus the formation of the national outlook. The three main religious traditions are those of Luther, of Calvin, and of the Catholic church. To which of these does the United States belong?

According to Luther nature is fundamentally evil; the world of politics is ruled by force, and the laws of the Scriptures cannot, therefore, be applied in worldly affairs. The Christian must endeavor to maintain the purity of his spiritual life, but in his contacts with the outside world he must obey the laws of the sovereign permitted to reign by the will of God, and whose existence is therefore justified. It is a conception that is pessimistic from the point of view of the world, but which leads to a spiritual idealism that allows no compromise.

The Calvinist tradition does not admit that there can be two moral attitudes, one on spiritual questions and one on political matters, for the Christian ideal must be applied to everyday life and not only to the inner life of the soul. Regenerated through grace, the elect will collaborate in performing the will of God on this earth, which means that they will exert a moralizing influence on society and the state. Salvation is not to be acquired through good works, but he who has freely received divine grace must bear witness by acting in accordance with the divine law; he must

82

be a man of action, deriving a practical optimism from his faith, for the Kingdom of God can come upon the earth.

Finally, from the Catholic point of view, the church constitutes a distinct spiritual society in a wicked world. The individual can live as a spiritual entity only insofar as he is a member of this great family, in terms of this church which, although established on the earth, does not live for it; the church gives its spiritual blessing in the form of the Holy Sacrament, which the priest alone can administer. Man's main interests are not in this world; apart from that, the outlook of the church is optimistic.

The American is essentially Protestant and Calvinist, and it is important to bear this in mind in order to understand American society. There are Lutheran and Catholic minorities of some importance, but they are not typically American, and one might almost say that the Catholic element runs counter to American tradition.

I

Three phases of evolution may be distinguished in the religious development of the American people.

The initial tradition, which still remains the strongest element, is that of the English Puritans of the seventeenth century. They were nonconformists who refused to submit to the dictates of the established state church, authentic Calvinist Protestants, Presbyterian by constitution. Their Christianity, therefore, followed the tradition of belief in divine election, by which the elect were charged as missionaries to reform the world. With this conception of the link between spiritual and everyday life, there could be no question of retiring to a life of contemplative worship, and it was believed that God would cause the affairs of those who served Him to prosper. The American nation has always felt the moral impetus given to it by the conviction of these early colonists. Today as yesterday the American Protestant is an evangelist, whether he be Eisenhower or Billy Sunday, the revivalist, whether he preaches the truth of the Bible, the American way of life, or technical progress. It would be wrong to neglect the religious source of American social reform, all the more so because there is nothing to go against the faith in this transposition from the spiritual to the social plane, since observance of the moral law leads by its very nature to material success.

The New England Puritan was ascetic and considered worldly pleasure a sin; he taught that man was a sinner, saved from eternal damnation only by the grace of God. But he had the task of colonizing and developing a continent; therefore his virtue must be in action, not in contemplation; thus, in the eighteenth century, in the democratic atmosphere of the New World, there was an ideal environment for the development of an optimism that was to become one of the salient characteristics of American psychology. It is on the far side of the ocean that Rousseau's influence, which is still felt, had greater repercussions on society than it had in Europe. Franklin, Jefferson, and most of their compatriots believed that men, freed from the social injustice of the old regime, would live wise and virtuous lives. This strange rationalization of Puritanism produced a combination, the remarkable efficiency of which is still characteristic of the American outlook; for the ascetic energy of the Puritan, far from being incompatible with social achievement, serves its cause admirably, while the discipline of the Presbyterian community, used to self-government, is the best preparation for democracy and civic life. There will never be in the United States any conflict between Protestantism and civic life, because both sides have the layman's attitude; this, of course, could never be true where the Catholic church is concerned.

During the nineteenth century, which represents the third phase of a long evolution, there was an attempt to bridge the gap between the tradition of the eighteenth century and that of the seventeenth. Into the asceticism of the Puritans merged gradually the idea of acceptance of the good things of this world, and the belief in original sin gave way to a faith in the natural goodness of man. The American, with his pessimistic Calvinist tradition, became an optimist and a disciple of Jean Jacques Rousseau. This brought about a change in doctrine. While it was still believed that man was born evil, it was considered that with regeneration he became essentially good; confidence in his energy, his possibilities, and his power was affirmed in all good faith. The Devil insinuated into the United States the dangerous temptation of success. Was not working to increase output working for God?

Quietism, mysticism, and contemplation are not condemned as such, but they encounter fundamental disapproval. Action above all is to be advocated as something healthy and almost holy. Experience does not always prove this, but the dangerous optimism that claimed to reconcile success and moral worth was preferred to the realism typified by La Rochefoucauld.

It is important to emphasize that this Protestant attitude does not constitute, properly speaking, a church, in the sense of the Catholic church, but a democratic individual religion, following the nonconformist tradition rather than the established church. The individual is responsible to his conscience without any intermediary between God and himself. The sacrament, following the doctrines of Zwingli, Calvin, and, to a certain extent, Luther, is not like the Catholic sacrament, in that it does not entail the existence of a priesthood in the strict sense of the term. The conception of a sacramental and hierarchical priesthood is foreign to the American outlook, to be regarded with some sort of suspicion as un-American. The pastor is a popular leader as much as a priest. Thus religion penetrates into daily life, into society or even politics, but its continuous presence in no way introduces a clerical element into American society. The churches are constitutionally separate from the state, but religion does not stand apart from society, and this explains the preponderant place of Protestantism in this nation which is Protestant by design.

11

According to the *Yearbook of American Churches* the total number of Americans in 1951 who declared that they belonged to a church was 88,673,000, 58% of the population. There were 252 religious bodies and 284,592 places of worship. Protestants numbered 52,162,000 or 59% of the total, and Catholics 29,242,000 or 32%. There is a slight increase noticeable in the number of people affiliated with a church, but the majority of nonadherents are indifferent rather than hostile and, if a strong anti-Catholic feeling is shown at times, there is practically no antireligious sentiment. According to an inquiry made by the *Catholic Digest* on the prevalence of the belief in God, 87% of the population, Catholics and Protestants alike, are *absolutely sure* of their faith, 10% *fairly sure,* and 2% *not quite sure,* so that only 1% of the population must be atheist, the proportion being in approximately the same proportions whatever the religious denomination of the people questioned. According to the same source, 25% of the Protestants are regular worshipers, 43% irregular, while 32% never attend a place of worship; among Catholics the proportions were respectively 62%, 20%, and 18%. It must be observed that the statistics of church membership are in a way misleading as to the relative importance of the Catholic and Protestant churches; most of the nonmembers of a church are of Protestant descent, so that it may be concluded that, in spite of a strong Catholic minority, the United States is essentially a Protestant country, probably about 80% Protestant.

There are 250 Protestant denominations registered in the United States, 97% of the churches belong to fifty of them and 80% to the eight main groups; the minor sects listed correspond then to only 3% of the total, though there are many that have not been included. This variety, as long as it does not make itself ridiculous by excesses, is not unhealthy from the Protestant point of view; it represents the fundamental spirit of the Reformation, and present-day movements toward union cannot entirely be considered as signs of increasing faith. There are only about eight denominations that are really significant; in 1951 the Baptists had 17,156,000 members, the Methodists 11,159,000, the Lutherans 6,257,000, the Presbyterians 3,438,000, the Episcopalians (Anglicans) 2,417,000, the Disciples of Christ 1,793,000, the Congregationalists 1,241,000, and the Churches of Christ 1,000,000. These are really main divisions, for there were twenty-four distinct types of Baptist church, twenty-three Methodist, twenty-one Lutheran, and ten Presbyterian, but they are all clearly characterized religious groups. The Episcopalians and Lutherans, representing English and German tradition, are relatively small in numbers. The general outlook is nonconformist, and the Baptists and Methodists provide the largest groups; but the Presbyterians and Congregationalists are also of considerable significance. Negroes are mainly Baptists or Methodists.

Members of churches other than the reformed churches included 29,242,000 Catholics, 5,000,000 Jews, 1,859,000 members of the

Greek Orthodox church, 337,000 dissident Catholics, and 73,000 Buddhists. The only important minorities, then, are the Catholics and the Jews. The Catholics form a disciplined, compact minority, constantly on the increase, and this, in relation to the political and moral equilibrium of the country, raises a delicate problem, which could become acute at any moment. Contrary to popular belief there is no marked increase in the number of Catholics in relation to Protestants; between 1926 and 1951 the number of Catholics increased by 57% compared with 65% for the Protestants; Catholics in 1951 represented 19% of the population as against 16% in 1926; Protestants 34% as against 27% in 1926. Conversions to Catholicism are spectacular and publicized in accordance with the best American tradition, but it is evident that the country is not becoming Catholic.

III

It is of interest to study the geographical location of the different churches. Protestants of the first or second period of immigration are to be found particularly in the inland districts of the eastern states, in the South, Middle West, Northwest, and Southwest, in fact throughout the country. The churches which derive from the original Puritans, that is, the Presbyterians, Congregationalists, and Unitarians, are found mainly in New England; the Quakers in Pennsylvania; the Baptists in the South, but also to a certain extent in New England; the Methodists in the Middle West and South and in New England; the Lutherans, whether German or Scandinavian, in the Middle West (Ohio, Illinois, Wisconsin), also in the Northwest; the Episcopalians in the East, in California, and, generally speaking, in the fashionable districts of the great cities. As for the Catholics, who belong to the second and third periods of immigration, they are to be found principally in the large urban centers of the Atlantic coast and the Middle West and in San Francisco, though there are Catholic communities in Louisiana and the extreme Southwest which are French, Spanish, or Mexican in origin.

The division of church membership according to social status is no less significant. The higher strata are mainly Presbyterians, Congregationalists, Unitarians, or Episcopalians. The first-named, in the East and more particularly in New England, belong to the old-established wealthy families of cultural background, who are members of a rather closed society that has considerable worldly prestige. The Episcopalians are to be found in the large cities in wealthy and often snobbish circles, which are inclined to be Anglophile. This church is to a certain extent frequented by the *nouveaux riches,* who are seeking social advancement; a converted Jew will readily become an Episcopalian. The Methodists are, generally speaking, represented by the middle classes; they form a powerful church which is influential politically but which has lost much of its dissident character and now shelters large numbers of comfortable and satisfied citizens, wealthy or in fairly comfortable positions, businessmen, and members of the teaching profession. Finally the lower middle classes and working classes— if that term is applicable in the United States—are essentially Baptists, Catholics, or members of the miscellaneous sects. The Catholics were originally recruited from the Irish, Italians, and Europeans of the third immigration period, and for a considerable time represented only the lower strata of the population, viewed by the long-established Protestants with condescension; but this is no longer true by reason of the social progress of the immigrants and recent conversions to Catholicism among the upper strata of society. The miscellaneous sects prosper especially among the humbler people, as they do in the south of France; their members are less prosperous people who have a narrow, Biblical tradition, and who find what almost amounts to a source of relaxation in these various sects.

From this point of view a perusal of *Who's Who* is most instructive, as expressive of a social hierarchy, almost a caste system, which is curiously linked with church membership; and this, moreover, in a country vowed to equality. The distinctions are now less rigorous than they used to be but, between the two wars, out of one hundred people appearing in *Who's Who* and stating that they were church members, twenty-one were Episcopalians, twenty-one Presbyterians, fourteen Methodists, and eleven Congregationalists, but only nine were Baptists and five Catholics. If I were drawing up a guide to the religious attitude most suitable to adopt in order to gain social distinction in the United States, I should state that a Presbyterian would find no advantage in becoming an Episcopalian, but that a wealthy Methodist or an important Jew might well consider it. Thirty years ago I would have said that there was no worldly advantage in becoming a Catholic, rather the reverse, but I would not say the same today, since experience has shown that there is no serious social disadvantage attaching to it.

CHAPTER 11

Religious Tendencies and Reactions
in the United States

★

Three tendencies, corresponding to three types of religious temperament, are traditional in American Protestantism. Orthodoxy or fundamentalism is derived either from the seventeenth-century English Puritans, or from the eighteenth-century romantic Methodists, and the initial impulse, handed down to the nineteenth century, has been preserved in the twentieth century, stimulated from time to time by revivals. Liberalism or the moderate tendency, a legacy of the eighteenth century, aims at adapting religion to the needs of contemporary development. The imaginative religion of the minor sects, prophetical, mystical, or fanciful, has perpetuated a Biblical tradition in the New World, in the main based on the Old Testament, but ready when necessary to use all the resources of modern technique.

American orthodoxy is founded on the literal interpretation of the Bible, the Good Book, the source of all truth. Americans of the old school consider it above all as the "Book of our fathers," thus belonging to national tradition, to a point where they appear at times to forget that it is a Jewish book, and one which belongs, also, to other nations. They believe without any reasoning that everything in it is true, down to the most extraordinary of miracles. In 1925, in the case about the teaching of the theory of evolution at Dayton, Tennessee, which remains famous to this day, William Jennings Bryan, former Secretary of State and leader of the fundamentalists, replied as follows to the questions of Clarence Darrow, the counsel for the defense:

Darrow: Do you claim that everything in the Bible should be literally
interpreted?

Bryan: I believe everything in the Bible should be accepted as it is
given there. . . .

Darrow: But when you read that Jonah swallowed the whale—or that
the whale swallowed Jonah—excuse me please—how do you literally
interpret that? . . . But do you believe . . . that He made such
a fish and that it was big enough to swallow Jonah?

Bryan: Yes, Sir. Let me add: One miracle is just as easy to believe as
another. . . .

Darrow: Perfectly easy to believe that Jonah swallowed the whale?

Bryan: If the Bible said so. . . .

A humorist suggested that the liberal is the man who believes
that the whale swallowed Jonah, while the fundamentalist believes
that Jonah swallowed the whale; but it must be realized that
Bryan gave his testimony in all seriousness. The uncompromising
nature of this orthodoxy set up and maintained a moral bulwark
which condemned the looseness of the moral code imported from
the Babylons of Europe, but which also repudiated any scientific
doctrine that might have the effect of shaking the faith. And it
must not be thought that this attitude is now old-fashioned; it is
maintained not only in old-established American circles and among
the humbler people of the Bible Belt, but also among wealthy
and powerful businessmen who respect tradition and are the
pillars and bankers of their churches. The American national outlook finds its most solid base in this fundamentalism.

Liberalism, on the contrary, is an outlook that attempts to free
itself from restrictive dogma, from narrow and literally interpreted
religion, to concentrate on seeking the spirit rather than the letter,
and engaging in moral and social reform. It shows a tendency to
pass from transcendence to immanence, since its humanism is indispensable to spiritual preoccupation. In this it is linked to the
liberal movement in Europe in the nineteenth century, but it is
distinguished from it by an almost childish anxiety, also to be
found in fundamentalism, to modernize religion by a systematic
use of the most up-to-date technical equipment and vocabulary,
as little ecclesiastic as possible. Some of its pastors are assisted by
psychoanalysts: and after all why should not God use modern
methods?

Robert S. Lynd reports in *Middletown* the following words of a minister in a working-class church some time after a high-school baskbetball game:

"I have been asked, 'Is it right to pray for the Bearcats to win?' by one of you who tells me he no longer believes in prayer because he prayed as hard as he could for the Bearcats and they lost. I believe that prayer should be used only in cases where a moral or spiritual issue is at stake. God *could* favor the weaker team, but that would be unsportsmanlike of God." *

The European has a tendency to laugh at this, if he is not a trifle shocked, but the familiarity underlining the practical character which religion must needs have in the modern world is quite acceptable to the Americans. Is there not a religious agency that advertises its most efficient prayer department? But, though one feels obliged to quote these excesses, one should not lose sight of the fact that, with its liberation from dogmatic narrowness of outlook, this modernization remains essentially religious, with a fundamentally spiritual outlook, though unable to distinguish spiritual life from everyday action, and particularly from social reform. At the risk of losing its foundation of positive faith, the church therefore sometimes tends to become primarily an instrument for achieving social progress, with promises, reports, and orders of the day similar to those issued by the political parties.

As for the minor sects in the United States, they represent the spontaneous and sporadic gushing forth of springs which never run dry. They are generally based on a particular interpretation of a certain verse of the Bible, on the revelation of a member of a religious community, on some superstition finding its proof in the Scriptures, on some particular rite, or on the stressing of some puritanical rule. They are infinitely diverse, generally exclusive, often microscopic in size, sometimes grotesque. The Primitive Friends had in 1926 only twenty-five members and the Bullockite Free Will Baptists thirty-six. Half of the sects have no more than 7,000 members. Some of them remain completely unknown and almost impossible to identify, such as the Predestinarian Baptists, the Pillars of Fire, the House of Prayer, and the Church Trium-

* Robert S. Lynd and Helen Merrell Lynd, *Middletown*, New York, Harcourt, Brace, 1929, p. 377.

phant. The Church of God and Saints of Christ owes its formation to the testimony of a Negro cook on the Santa Fe Railroad; according to the Church of the Living God, Job, David, and Jesus were all Negroes; the Amish Mennonites consider buttons to be sinful. But Jehovah's Witnesses, who are to be found in all the five continents, gathered together 82,861 adherents on July 19, 1953, in Yankee Stadium at New York. The development of strange religious sects is not an American monopoly, however, as examples in England, Germany, Switzerland, and the Cévennes region of France show, but the United States appears to have a soil particularly favorable to their growth and blossoming. They are the refuge of the unwanted, and take advantage of the credulity of uneducated people who are moved by prophecy and attracted by the illusion of a return to the primitive church, and ready to accept any testimony whatever. If I said that I was Elijah come to life again, there would be Americans who would believe me!

The revivals, founded on emotion and conducted according to the Calvinist Methodist tradition of sudden conversion, must be grouped with the minor sects; leaders with a deep knowledge of crowd psychology and religious publicity ably sway the emotions of their congregations. These revivals attract and succeed in moving huge crowds, who, taken in hand by evangelists who are sincere and widely experienced, become converted; they soon fall back into their old ways . . . but are again moved by subsequent revivals. In *Elmer Gantry* by Sinclair Lewis there is a scene where a professional revivalist has a long discussion on whether it is ethical to count as two conversions the same man who has been twice converted.

Fundamentalism and modernism are now no longer really controversial points. On the whole, modernism has conquered, although it is not considered good to describe oneself as liberal, this term being considered derogatory and of leftist tendency; but at the same time the fundamentalist tradition, still very active, especially in the South and Middle West, has maintained in the United States a strong sense of attachment to the church and the religious life of the parish, and to the Protestant conception of religion as a source of inspiration in everyday life. There are thus certain characteristic tendencies that belong in common to all

American Protestants, notably, in spite of belief in original sin, the confidence in man, regenerated man if you will, who typifies the American conception of energy, easily degraded into striving after success. Religion, therefore, must construct and organize; it is a concept less of meditation than of action, of action in the social field, man's moral dignity becoming at times confused with his standard of living.

Thus Christ, although still the central figure of the faith, tends to be not so much the Christ of sacrifice and redemption as Christ the superman, a model for the ideal life, but, as we have said above, an essentially modern life, adapted to all present needs. American literature is particularly fond of painting a picture of Jesus living in our own times, giving an example of perfect holiness, associated at the same time with a completely modern setting. The classic example of this is Charles Monroe Sheldon's book, *In His Steps*. It does not appear unseemly to picture Christ as a Boy Scout, a member of a Rotary Club, or a member of a chamber of commerce. The most extraordinary picture is that given by Bruce Barton in *The Man Nobody Knows*. He represents Christ as the founder of the biggest organization the world has ever known; as a business executive and leader (Chapter I), the founder of modern business (Chapter VI), knowing how to make the best use of publicity, in no way weak physically (would He have been able to chase the traders from the Temple?), or a killjoy (the most popular dinner guest in Jerusalem). When I first read this book I thought that it was a humorous story, but I have since discovered that the author was perfectly serious.

I would not wish by these humorous allusions to appear to disparage American Protestantism, which is essentially sincere in its search after a higher spiritual life associated with a better social position. It is impossible, at the same time, to avoid remarking that religion thus conceived reflects American life, rather than it indicates an independent spiritual force. Under these conditions many churches tend to become social clubs rather than places of worship, in which sports meetings for the young and Sunday suppers occupy an important place alongside the liturgy or the sermon. The pastor is expected to be stimulating, a good mixer, and an efficient leader of his community, which he will have to defend against the competition of rival congregations. Religious citizenship thus conceived is characteristic of American Protestants—"Follow Christ in the market place, the factory, the banking house, and the halls of government"—for the nation must be religious and it is the duty of the Christian to watch over it. Thus Protestants, clergy or laymen, intervene as such in the political struggle, trying to give urgent moral needs the force of law, fighting for social reforms and clean government. There is a danger that, in order to attain worldly success, the Christian may adopt some of the world's methods; for example, the way in which prohibition was defended cannot be described as wholly pure. When speaking as a popular leader, the pastor must display the qualities of a political candidate, but he then runs the risk of contracting a candidate's weaknesses. Though these criticisms are often made, this program of moralizing the state nonetheless does credit to American Protestants.

II

The Protestant faith thus conceived has not failed to invite a certain measure of reproach as a religion for the Anglo-Saxons, proud of their respectability, gentlemen of principle and prosperity, who relegate foreigners and immigrants to a sort of secondary status from the religious, moral, and social standpoint. It has also been suggested that, in this orientation toward action, the essential elements of religion are apt to be lost; the ever-present preoccupation about results or, one might almost say, human output, does not allow for the significance of the divine transcendence and the spirit of selfless worship; moreover, the desire for being up-to-date has given certain evangelists a sort of cordial vulgarity which does much harm to the poetry of religion, sometimes even to its essential dignity. Religious-minded people eventually feel that something is lacking. Catholicism has to some extent benefited from these objections, but they have on the rebound brought about certain Protestant reforms that are not without significance.

Catholicism in the United States has always been under a handicap. It is considered a religion for foreigners, aliens even, giving that word its derogatory significance. It is the church of the immigrants, the unassimilated, consequently the humble people low down in the social scale; when the son of a Protestant magnate married a Catholic—what a scandal!—his mother would remark, when she went on that occasion to the little local Catholic church, on the fact that she had never set foot in it before, except for the weddings or funerals of her servants. It is no exaggeration to say that the pomp of the Roman church, the splendor of its ritual, the brilliance of its ecclesiastical vestments, and the magnificence of its processions before which the faithful kneel, give to the old-fashioned American the uncomfortable impression of something too exotic for a Protestant country. This impression is reinforced by the fact that the members of the Catholic church belong to national groups not easily assimilated into the American background; besides the traditionally dominant Irish group, there are Italians, Germans, Poles, and French Canadians.

Feeling itself to be kept on the fringe, outside the main axis of society, when its wish is to take part in the national life on an equal footing, American Catholicism is, above all, anxious to become Americanized. Great prelates, such as Monsignor Ireland or Monsignor Gibbons, were on the way toward carrying out this program at the end of the last century; and though the immigration of Slav and Latin peoples has retarded this assimilation, it is nonetheless making progress, particularly as the newcomers show extraordinary eagerness to adopt the customs of the New World. If this is carried on, it is with a clear wish to integrate Catholicism in its entirety into American society. It is already a church that has adapted itself to the national environment; it is proud of its wealth, of the size of the churches it has built, of the modernity and comfort of its schools and convents. Its priests, well-fed, living in well-heated houses, accustomed to travel by sleeping car, must feel a sort of condescending pity for their poor European colleagues. Their contribution to the religious thought of the world is negligible, but they have a feeling of power which, moreover, does not fail to cause some anxiety in Protestant circles, long accustomed to having the monopoly of influence.

Catholic action in the United States, therefore, belongs to the national environment, but, though essentially American, it has its own particular moral and religious aspect. Catholicism is particularly active in the defense of family life, far more so than the

Protestant faith. It is un-American in the firm stand that it takes against birth control and sterilization. It also runs counter to American policy on the subject of separate schools, claiming for its educational establishments subsidies that are surely contrary to the constitutional principle of separation of church and state. The existence of a religious minority that receives orders from a foreign pope, and, moreover, an Italian, is more and more a source of annoyance to the Protestants, who, faced with an indubitable increase in Catholicism, are taking up the anticlerical arguments so familiar in France. But in the United States the attitude is anti-Catholic rather than anticlerical.

If such anxiety is arising, it is because Catholicism has made progress since World War I. The general level of social standing among Catholics has risen, but there have also been numerous conversions from Protestantism. To what are these due? The austerity of the Protestant form of worship draws some Americans away from the severity of the reformed church to the more poetic ritual, in which the mystical side of religion is more fully developed. According to Sinclair Lewis, the monotony of the daily life of the little townships of the West is broken only by two events which open its windows toward a conception of the infinite: the passage of the train and the Catholic Mass. As everywhere in the world, the dispersed nature of the Protestant church makes men eager for discipline, ready to appreciate the strength of a church founded on authority. I believe that the Catholic church has made progress in the United States because of its excellent organization, the efficiency of its particularly active clergy, its indefatigable propaganda, and the intelligent pressure that it brings to bear upon politicians. It must be added that the higher birth rate among Catholics naturally swells their numbers.

Statistics indeed show a considerable increase in the number of Catholics, which will soon be more than thirty million, but there has been no increase in the proportion of Catholics as compared with total population. The growth of their influence cannot, however, be denied, and this influence marks a new phase in the history of the country. They form a substantial minority, ready to make its voice heard and to put forward ideas that cannot be said to be in line with the basic doctrines of the United States.

A religion founded on authority, which refuses to recognize the exclusion of religion from public schools and is not resigned to the principle of separation of church and state, forms what is virtually a foreign element in the national life. There is no question of not recognizing its place in the community, but this recognition creates difficult adjustments and grave political differences.

This does not mean that the patriotism of the Catholics is in any way inferior to that of their older-established or assimilated fellow citizens. The patriotism of the latter is Anglo-Saxon—and naturally Protestant—in concept. That of the Catholics amounts to a loyal and even passionate attachment to the American way of life and a sincere feeling of gratitude to the country that has made this life possible. The nationalism of the United States was formerly exclusively Protestant, like that of the Ku Klux Klan, but it is now possible for a Catholic nationalism to exist, no less exclusive, but possessing other lines of defense: one has only to think of Senator McCarthy.

III

The ever-growing claims of the Catholic minority have aroused a new spirit of anti-Catholicism among the Protestants. All the arguments of French anticlericalism have reappeared, with a freshness of approach which they have now lost in France. The pope is a foreign sovereign, and it is scandalous that Americans should follow his dictates when they vote. The Roman hierarchy is incompatible with the American Constitution; Rome has not abandoned the idea of conquering America: *Caveant Consules!* When in 1951 President Truman wished to appoint an ambassador to the Vatican, he met with Protestant opposition of astonishing violence; pastors denounced the measure from their pulpits as an intolerable scandal, an insult to the Protestant character of the nation, and innumerable lists of signatures confirmed their protests. The depth of this reaction must not be misunderstood; it represented instinctive defense on the part of a religious monopoly which has ceased to exist.

Catholic thought has nevertheless exercised its influence in the very heart of the Protestant world. The Catholic ritual exerts evident attraction, not only in High Church Episcopalian circles, where the churches positively overflow with stained glass, crosses, incense, candelabras, candles, and sumptuous priestly vestments, but also in the churches of the reformed tradition, where today there is an esthetic preoccupation which contrasts strangely with their early asceticism: the Baptist church entrusted by Rockefeller to Harry Emerson Fosdick is partly based on Chartres Cathedral, with chapels commemorating great men such as Lincoln and Pasteur; and a desire for elegance is widespread among most of the denominations. But this must not be mistaken for a return to Catholic practices, for the intention is exclusively esthetic without any bearing on the form of worship, except in the case of the Episcopalians. There are, however, signs of a more strictly religious conception of religion, an indefinable weariness of a form of Christianity so practical as to become matter of fact, and the reintroduction into worship of the spirit of adoration, with emphasis on the altar rather than exclusively on the pulpit. The Federal Council of the Churches of Christ has instituted a "section of worship." The idea of divine transcendence, long eclipsed by the eighteenth-century idea of God pervading the universe, reappeared under the influence of Karl Barth, and, though his influence is now somewhat on the wane, there is definitely a greater interest taken in theology. These tendencies, reflecting the influence of analogous European movements, mark also an infiltration of Catholicism which does not, however, penetrate down to the roots of the Protestant faith.

On the contrary, the Protestants, who consider themselves threatened by Catholic competition and unity, have felt the need for concentration and organization. Faced on one side by Communist atheism and on the other by Roman propaganda, disputes on matters of doctrine between their different denominations seem rather out of place, and the union of the churches has become a primary consideration. Insistence is placed on the fact that the points of similarity between the Protestant churches outweigh the differences which separate them, and, since America is a country where rationalization is the order of the day, it can be pointed out that the grouping of the sects will logically allow for considerable economy in the number of pastors, missionaries, and administrators. The inevitable tendency, which in the economic field leads to industrial concentration, is thus brought to bear upon religious organization. The Federal Council of the Churches of Christ in North America, now known as the National Council of the Churches of Christ in the U. S. A., which was founded in 1908, today groups together more than twenty-five Protestant denominations and five Eastern Orthodox bodies throughout the country. In forty years there have been fourteen important church unions, brought about through mutual sinking of small differences in order to reap the benefit of all that they hold in common. The movement toward union has not, it is true, reached the minor sects, but its scope can be measured by the American contribution to the foundation of a worldwide Protestant church, initiated by the United States, which has remained its most convinced and most efficient partisan. I do not know whether the enthusiasm shown for union represents a strengthening of faith, or whether it is not rather a desire for administrative efficiency. If the minor sects be considered as religious youth, then this liberalism, with its penchant for organization, would appear to be the sign of a kind of maturity.

Puritanism, on the other hand, which after World War I had led a new offensive, now appears to be diminishing in importance, the turning point being the end of prohibition in 1933. After a long period of repression, certain tendencies in human nature succeeded in making themselves felt in spite of an oppressive moral armor, but this liberation was carried out in a spirit characterized by Protestant individualism. It is in virtue of this religious conception, which is essentially Protestant, that formulas, such as "living one's own life" and "making one's own destiny," applied to the field of sentiment or even to sexual life, have undergone an unexpected renaissance in the United States; it represents a religious penetration into matters where it can scarcely be imagined by the European. There is in the Kinsey Report a sort of legacy of the tradition of Rousseau. The current of American religious thought has turned so definitely from transcendence to immanence, from heaven to this world, from the theocentric to the anthropocentric, from duality to monism, that it cannot be stemmed; but the original religious impulse is evident, under whatever form it may appear.

IV

To sum up, even where there is no authentic religious doctrine, America remains essentially Protestant and her problems continue to be considered from the moral and moralizing Protestant attitude. Even the Catholics share this outlook; while unbelief, closely kept in check by rather zealous conformity, does not exist in aggressive forms, but rather takes the form of a respectful agnosticism. The Protestant churches have used the increased number of people declaring church affiliation to claim a progress in their faith, or at least in attachment to church attendance. The European is struck by the large number of Americans who are faithful church members, thus bearing the imprint of a Protestant conscience. In this way the country is maintaining its Christian and specifically Protestant tradition and, though it insists on the separation of church and state, it is by no means of the opinion that religion should be a thing apart from the life of the nation. The country retains, also, its missionary vocation and is genuinely anxious to improve the moral destiny of mankind through a raising of the standard of living. If the outlook is often materialistic the inspiration is nonetheless idealistic, and its idealism is religious in inspiration. Europe, through its sufferings, sees religion and life as fundamentally opposed and is on its guard against philosophies that claim to sanctify success. America, which has not known suffering, retains the optimistic conviction that the two ideas are not incompatible.

CHAPTER 12

The Jewish Minority

★

In order to understand the Jewish problem in the United States, as, indeed, in any other country, both racial and religious factors must be considered, and this is why the discussion of it has been deferred to this stage. The delay may even be considered as a matter for criticism, so closely does the problem touch the very core of American life. In 1950 there were 5,000,000 Jews in the United States, and 2,100,000 of them lived in New York—an enormous percentage for an urban agglomeration of not quite 8,000,000 inhabitants. These figures, however, are far from indicative of the place that the Jews hold in a community where at first sight their assimilation appears astonishingly rapid, but where, after all, they remain a group apart.

I

The composition of this compact community is very diverse, ranging from the aristocracy of the banking world of London or Frankfurt to the wretched pauper escaped from the ghettos of Poland or the Ukraine, and including genial intellectuals who come from almost any environment. All classes of society are represented among the American Jews, and these are designated in American parlance by a great variety of names. All this is readily comprehensible in the light of the history of Jewish immigration into the United States.

This immigration was accomplished in four main phases. Those who came before the Declaration of Independence were mainly Dutch; they were not numerous and were chiefly of high social standing, and they played an important part in the early relations between Europe and America. The first half of the nineteenth century was marked by the arrival of German Jews, who came to seek in the New World a position in life which the Old World, at least that of central Europe, had denied to them; they were not poverty-stricken and their liberal outlook contributed to the formation of the American nation, in which, moreover, they found a number of their fellow countrymen. They naturally settled in predominantly German communities, especially in the Middle West, setting up small-scale businesses which were to develop into the large-scale Jewish department stores to be found in all the main cities. The standing of the Jews until then had been fairly high, but it deteriorated with the wave of Latin and Slav immigrants at the end of the century; these were from eastern Europe, Russia, Austria-Hungary, and Romania, where they had been persecuted and were often the victims of pogroms, and they came to the United States in search of refuge. They were humble people, pitiably poor and often starving, men marked by centuries of persecution; they brought with them the exotic atmosphere of the eastern ghettos and settled in the great ports of the East and the large cities of the Middle West; they were small-scale traders, artisans, and tailors; from the last-named group originate the important manufacturers of ready-made clothing in Chicago and New York. Then came World War I and the end of large-scale immigration, but persecution under the Hitler regime, with World War II and the spread of the Soviet system to the line known as the Iron Curtain, led to a new wave of immigration, which included a significant Jewish element, America having once more, at least temporarily, become a country of refuge and welcome for displaced persons. It is not possible to say whether the introduction of this new component will be harmful or beneficial. It has brought a new foreign element to the American community, but, just as England or Germany did after the revocation of the Edict of Nantes, the United States has gained an important group of intellectuals, even men of genius, such as Einstein. It is, however, true that crypto-Communists and spies also appear to have crept in, and that the Jewish problem, which had never been solved, has become more acute.

II

The essential personality of a nation depends above all on its reactions to religious questions, whether it has an optimistic or a
pessimistic attitude toward everyday life. In what category can
the Jew be placed, and more particularly the American Jew? Like
the Puritan, who indeed derives this belief from Jewish sources,
the Jew is assuredly an optimist. In his view the Kingdom of God
must come upon the earth by and for the chosen people; there,
addressed to a selected race, is a strictly terrestrial promise. The
persistence and the extraordinary vitality of this hope are expressed in the belief in the Messianic prophecy; it continues even
when the idea of the Messiah has ceased to be that of a person,
when awaiting the Messiah becomes synonymous with a kind of
aspiration toward social progress—or any other form of human development. "For us," a Jew once said to me, not entirely without
his tongue in his cheek, "the Messiah is not necessarily a man; it
may be social progress, or a rise in oil prices!" This optimism
about social achievement is fundamentatlly the most authentic
Jewish belief. From history we have learned of the faith of the
rabbis in which the hope of their race was concentrated, and
experience shows that, as with the Puritans, this zeal may be di-
verted toward the accumulation of wealth. But there is no mistake
about the fact that Jewish hope has a spiritual basis; the Jew is
never solely either a businessman or a dilettante, he has a desire
to fulfill the will of God. From Zangwill comes the heart-rending
cry: "Take from me the hope that I can change the future, and
you will send me mad." * There is a strange resemblance between
the Jew and the Puritan, neither has priests but there are pastors
or prophets, leaders, who on either side attract their flock by the
sanctification of success, so that belief in a life hereafter tends to
fade more and more into the background. And yet, who would
dare deny that the Jew is pessimistic? The metaphysical sadness
of the Bible is sufficient evidence. Who can fail to recall the verse
taken from the Psalms which is used in the burial service of the
Protestant church: "As soon as thou scatterest them they are even

* Israel Zangwill, *The Melting Pot*, London, William Heinemann, 1930,
Act II.

as a sleep: and fade away suddenly like the grass. In the morning it is green, and groweth up: but in the evening it is cut down, dried up and withered." Nowhere else are such utterances to be found. How can this nation with so much tradition, a race that forgets nothing, how can it ever forget the ever-renewed persecutions that it has suffered, the endless wandering that destiny has imposed upon it? This philosophical melancholy, one of the most poignant characteristics of Jewish thought, is also one of the most moving inspirations of Israelite poetry.

The combination, the tangle, the contradiction of these two tendencies form the backbone of Jewish personality. The Jew is certainly an optimist from the personal point of view, for his race, for the achievement of social progress; but he is a pessimist as far as life in general is concerned and particularly for the destiny of the society in which he has been forced to live through dispersal. He can judge it, even when he has become a member of it, with a kind of intellectual detachment, with the cold lucidity of a foreigner, even showing in his dissection of it a kind of indefinable sadism. Barrès wrote: "They handle ideas in the same way that a banker handles money, like counters sorted out on a cold marble slab." * A Westerner in his ease of manner as he moves through the mechanism of modern life, the Jew is an oriental in the depth of his religious feelings. Herzl, the founder of Zionism, was neither orthodox nor a believer, but one must not for one moment imagine that he was not religious. In the Jewish soul there is a feeling for God that cannot be uprooted. "He desired God," wrote Zangwill of one of his characters, "his soul was athirst for God, the God of his fathers. He could not reject the faith of a thousand years." But the Jew seems to find his religion in the form of suffering, in his conversion seeking a burden to bear rather than a source of happiness. In contrast with the insipid social optimism of the pragmatists, this pessimism, this eternal sense of tragedy, takes on an added grandeur.

III

These are the particular conditions under which the problem of the assimilation of the Jews must be studied. Superficially, Jews

* Barrès, *L'ennemi des lois*, Paris, E. Paul, 1910, p. 170.

are Americanized very rapidly, with almost lightning speed. As in law school training where one can compress a three-year course into three months, the bearded Jew from some eastern European ghetto seems to become American, so to speak, at the end of an extremely short course. From the second generation onward, sometimes from the first, there is nothing foreign in his appearance and he often changes his name. It is, indeed, a way of "passing," but the passage is easier than for the Negro, even with the whitest skin. The adaptability of the Jew doubtless facilitates his assimilation, but his essential qualities also make their contribution, especially as far as American Protestant circles are concerned; he has a hereditary sense of duty, he respects family virtue and puts it into practice, and more than most immigrants he possesses a civic sense; above all he is an outstanding leader of social reform. Immediately at his ease on the stock exchange or in a university, he frequents the societies of ethical culture, where he finds liberal-minded Protestants who also are fired with the spirit of social reform.

And yet, even after three generations, the assimilation is not complete. There is clearly something that keeps the Jew aloof. This age-old being has existed, felt, suffered, long before becoming part of the nation that is now his, and by this past tradition he remains to a certain extent a man apart. His soul is like the palimpsest of which we have spoken, bearing the traces of the impact of countless nations. To the morning hymn, pictured by Barrès, his memory "secretly mingles the songs learned yesterday in a foreign land." Reactions of Jews are not the same as those of other Americans; they have a greater wealth of feeling which extends beyond the national boundary, moved by religious impulse and unexpected returns into the past. In fact the Jew does not belong to the American tradition and, when he has not "passed," he feels the need of remaining apart. Moreover, in the United States outward assimilation of the citizen is not enough, there is that desire to assimilate the souls, to use them, to direct them toward the mill of production, toward all that is the aim of Americanization. But the soul of the Jew cannot be tamed, it remains at the bottom of the melting pot as a residue incapable of fusion. In this respect the Bible does not offer good counsel.

Jehovah, who knew how to pardon, did not forgive the Jews for sparing their prisoners, for He feared the intrusion of foreign souls among His chosen people.

It is, therefore, easy to see how the Jewish problem of the United States has arisen. It is less virulent than in Germany but more acute than in the other countries of western Europe. The points of comparison and similarity between Americans and Jews are, however, numerous. The optimistic outlook of the Calvinists in social matters, the desire for success of the Puritans of the New World, and even the extraordinary wanderlust found among Europeans who have crossed the Atlantic, all these factors ought to combine to unite and almost merge the sons of Abraham with the sons of Calvin; are not the last-named also sons of Abraham? But the points of difference between them appear to be more fundamental than the points of similarity. There is first the intellectual level of the Jews, too rapid in rhythm for the mental simplicity of this young race, the Americans. There is a tendency to forget that the Jew, an oriental, is more precocious than a Westerner of the same age, and in school and university he outclasses his American fellow students without difficulty. To raise the standard of the examinations would only have the effect of excluding those for whom protection is desired, and thus the Jew at times finds himself inadmissible under a virtual *numerus clausus*. Equally disturbing is the bitter, pessimistic criticism of Jewish thinkers in a country where national optimism is the first duty of the citizen. Finally, a grudge is borne against the Jew because he remains in his separate racial group in a society that is too given to assimilation, and this appears as provocation.

It must be admitted that the Jew is not always wholeheartedly sincere in his desire for integration. If he penetrates anywhere, a group of his own people will follow him, in a racial group whose solidarity is contrary to the spirit of assimilation. His advent, therefore, appears as an intrusion, which in its turn provokes defense measures. Welcome one Jew and there will immediately be ten. Should a Jew become a customer at a hotel, it will soon be exclusively his. If he settles in a district, the Christians will desert it. In reaction against this, by a sort of unwritten law, especially in New York, Jews are excluded from whole sections of social life

as the result of an anti-Semitism unknown in either England or
France. Numerous hotels refuse to have them as customers, land-
lords do not want them as tenants, even though refusal is contrary
to the Constitution. Many New York clubs do not admit them,
whatever their individual merit or their position in the country.
One certainly meets Jews at social gatherings, but what is known
as "society" has set up against them a barrier more effective than
any known in the most closed circles in Europe.

The same discrimination applies to certain fortresses of national
interest. It is often believed that Jewish bankers dominate Wall
Street. They are certainly powerful, but less so than the great
Protestant bankers. The famous names in the history of American
industry are Protestant: Rockefeller, Carnegie, Ford. Even in politics Jews are powerful in the municipal field and provide members for the Senate and House of Representatives, but it is rarer
for them to be governors of states; in New York, however, no
party ticket has any chance of being adopted unless it has a
Jewish name beside an Irish and an Italian one. Brandeis, Car-
dozo, and Frankfurter are, or have been, among the members of
the Supreme Court. Roosevelt grouped around himself a Brain
Trust, several of whom were Jews, but in this he has been followed neither by Truman nor by Eisenhower. If the Jewish outlook has become important, especially in foreign affairs, it is because a minority of five million, possessing such great financial
resources and so adept at making the best use of them, cannot be
neglected by governments which are always at the mercy of the
voters. The American attitude toward Hitler's Germany, the Israeli
state, and Arab questions in general would certainly have been
different, or at least less emphatic, if it had not been influenced
by the Jewish minority. It would, however, be incorrect to believe, as the Nazis did, that America is dominated by the Jews; it
is essentially a Protestant country.

IV

It is thus clear why America has not absorbed or assimilated this
foreign element, which elsewhere in the world has shown an
extraordinary capacity for assimilation. The Jewish community remains a group apart in the United States probably more than

anywhere else. Part of the explanation would appear to lie in the fact that immigration was carried out in large contingents. Also, contrary to what has happened in western Europe—not central Europe—Jews from the Middle East are particularly numerous. These immigrants from the Middle East, in whom the ancient Jewish traditions survive in a more marked manner, give from time to time a new impetus to the religious fervor of those of their race already established in America, and it often happens that Jews who had betrayed their faith turn back to it again. Did not Péguy say that the Scriptures which the Catholic has been reading for fifty years and the Protestant for four hundred have been known to the Jew for two thousand years? This mystical tension has a rhythm and depth which prevent adaptation. Assimilation is easy when it is a question of business, mode of dress, language, or even attitude to civic affairs, but in order that it may be complete something other than language, customs, or even outlook must be thrown into the melting pot; unless the soul also is cast in, there can be no assimilation.

Thus in the United States the Jews act as a sort of leaven, in the sense in which Bismarck said that they provided "a certain sparkle which is not to be disdained." The American appreciates the value of this but considers that the proportions of the mixture must be measured carefully if the dose is not to become dangerous. When the old-established, traditional elements of the nation come into contact with this Biblical flame, with this bitter, insatiable intelligence, ever restless and dissatisfied, so unlike the Anglo-Saxon in its sharp outbursts, they take fright, stiffen and withdraw into themselves, and it is from them that the deepest American anti-Semitic feeling springs.

CHAPTER 13

A General Survey of the American Nation

★

We have considered the various human elements that have gone to form the American nation as it exists today, and the problem that must now be considered is whether these elements have been mingled in such a way as to form a psychological individuality. The striking feature in this development has been the transformation that has occurred between the nineteenth and twentieth centuries and which has affected the physical composition of the nation, its psychology, and the conditions under which it lives.

I

In one sense, and rather paradoxically, the American civilization was more stable at the end of the nineteenth century than it is today. Before the Slavo-Latin immigration wave the introduction of the Irish, German, and Jewish elements, superimposed on the old-established English colonial background, had brought into being a community that remained Anglo-Saxon but with certain features that made it deviate from the classical British tradition. This society had its legendary types, which people of my age have had the privilege of meeting: Uncle Sam, Buffalo Bill, the captain of industry, the New England aristocracy, the four hundred, the beautiful American woman with the bearing of a goddess, bedecked, exacting, like an actress. One has only to reread *Les Transatlantiques* by Abel Hermant to get a picture of America at that time, a country still looking westward, creative, eccentric and anxious to set up records. The different areas had their own types of civilization, which had evolved according to their particular environment and traditions: that of New England with its Puritan-

ism; Philadelphia with its Quakers and its memories of Franklin;
Baltimore, already Southern in outlook; New Orleans with its
French heritage; the Middle West with its Germanic background;
California, Latin rather than Anglo-Saxon. There were the distinct
schools of cookery, that of Baltimore, the most typically American
of all, with its Virginia ham, turtle and mulligatawny soup; Louisiana with its Creole recipes; San Francisco, where the culinary tradition was a mixture of French and Italian. Although deeply influenced by the English Protestant tradition, the writers of the period
were nevertheless essentially American: Mark Twain, Walt Whit-
man, Ralph Waldo Emerson, Henry James, Henry Adams, Henry
David Thoreau, Louisa M. Alcott. But perhaps, like Lincoln with
his classical and Biblical education, the Americans of that time
were nearer to us Europeans and easier for us to understand than
the Americans of today, whose links with the Old World seem to
have been completely severed.

Why has this America ceased to exist? In the first instance a
a change was brought about by the mingling of the Slav and Latin
element with the essentially Anglo-Saxon background. This was
further increased by the moving west of the center of population;
the authentic force of the Protestant tradition passed to the Middle West, and the Atlantic coast, once a Puritan fortress, became
unrecognizable by reason of the flood of immigrants, while the
Pacific states came to count more and more in the general picture
of the country. Even the physique of the race has changed. It is
difficult now to find the types that were so familiar in 1900; it is as
though people of an entirely different race filled the streets of New
York and Chicago. The same is true in the universities, where there
is a striking number of professors whose accent betrays their German or Jewish origin. There has certainly been a markedly foreign
influx; and in the Middle West and now spreading toward the
South a new type of solid, serious businessman has appeared, indefinably German in his bearing and with not a twinkle to be seen
behind his spectacles. Zangwill wished to see an America that
was American without necessarily being Anglo-Saxon. Perhaps his
wish is now nearing fulfillment.

I nevertheless consider that the factor which has contributed
most to this transformation is the new standard of living. Twen-

tieth-century technical equipment, with its high degree of mechanization and its mass production, has indeed given life a new aspect. The inevitable and ever-ruthless effects are applied to the machinery and methods of production, to all the adjuncts of daily life, to the complete range of social relations, whether those of the press, of literature, of education, of religion, or of politics. The age of the pioneer is past; the conception of a life of personal effort and hard work and the acceptance of asceticism has given place to the organization of a collective community with mass discipline and large-scale teamwork. American society now appears as a first-class piece of organization; it is a whole nation of workers each with his own job. This nation enjoys a high standard of living, not Germanic in atmosphere, for it contains a greater degree of humanity and a certain measure of unconstraint, but it is nevertheless a society where phantasy and liberty do not reign as they did formerly.

Under these conditions, is it really possible to speak of an American nation? There is certainly not an American race, for in a cross section of the American people all the European types are represented from Celt to Slav, from Scandinavians to the inhabitants of the shores of the Black Sea, not to mention Turanians and Arabs. The official list of nationalities represented among the immigrants in the period 1900-1910 is fantastic: African, Armenian, Bohemian and Moravian, Bulgarian, Serbian, Montenegrin, Chinese, Croatian and Slovene, Cuban, Dalmatian, Bosnian and Herzegovinian, Dutch, Flemish, Indian, English, Finnish, French, Greek, Hebraic, North and South Italian, Japanese, Korean, Lithuanian, Magyar, Mexican, inhabitants of the Pacific islands, Polish, Portuguese, Romanian, Russian, Ruthenian, Scandinavian, Scottish, Slovakian, Spanish, Syrian, Turkish, West Indian, and the scrupulous statiticians considered themselves bound to add, "other peoples." Apart from the South, remote country districts, and high society, it would be incorrect to say that the Anglo-Saxon type is now dominant. I have often been entertained by considering from this point of view groups of American students visiting Europe; they are racially just as typical of the Mediterranean lands or of eastern Europe as of England or Scandinavia.

At the same time it must be recognized that this kaleidoscope of races has produced a nation in the full sense of the term. All Americans, whatever their racial origin, have a similarity in bearing, they all dress alike, have similar ways of standing, walking, listening, replying, telephoning, even of waiting. They all have the same spontaneous reactions, a similar slowness of thought and movement which contrasts sharply with the vivacity of the Latin races, but the deliberation is accompanied by a restlessness that contrasts strongly with the habitual calm of the Englishman. It is the paradox of a sluggish temperament swirled along in a hectic, relentless rhythm; this doubtless accounts for the prevalence of nervous breakdowns in the United States.

This degree of conformity in manner is probably a result of the material uniformity of the American way of life, in a society which is so well-equipped solely because of its high degree of standardization. The same type of train, the same hotels, restaurants, cooking, the same newspapers are to be found everywhere; and it is important to realize that this monotony is not only accepted but even highly esteemed. The American, who formerly appreciated eccentricity, has now become conformist in his habits, he prefers to be exactly like all his other fellow countrymen rather than individually distinctive in his appearance or his mode of life; it is the means by which the immigrant can show that he is truly assimilated. While it must be admitted that this assimilation was necessary if the country was to preserve its initial unity, it is also true that it has had somewhat the effect of a steam roller. It is doubtless the price which the American has had to pay for his prosperity.

II

The American nation can thus be considered as a single entity, but the question remains as to whether American psychology can be considered in the singular. This is a question that can have both an affirmative and a negative answer, for within certain limitations it is possible to state that the American is still seeking the fulfillment of his personality. The Frenchman or the Englishman may be likened to the man who has finished building his house; this cannot be said of the German and less still of the American, who, having remained a nomad, is still undergoing a process of evolution, not imprisoned, like we are, behind the stone walls of an edifice built to withstand the centuries. It is perhaps advisable to consider where the psychological center of the United States is to be found, and to what the typical American really corresponds. It is tempting to describe him as the Middle Westerner, his strong Puritan tradition paralleled with the most autonomous form of economic progress. But New York is equally representative of the nation's civilization. It was in New York that I saw a play written by a Jew, produced by an Armenian with Negro music, and the critics spoke of it as a triumph of American art. They were, indeed, quite justified in their opinion. If each state has its own personality, as is illustrated in John Gunther's *Inside U.S.A.* or Cartier's *Les 48 Amériques*, these forty-eight states have a common denominator which is the American way of life, of which they are so proud and which they even go so far as to consider the finest justification of their patriotism.

There is thus diversity of origin combined with unification in the application of modern production methods to create a common way of life. The two currents which flow together in this great American stream remain, nevertheless, distinct. It is possible to distinguish between the leading elements of society, which correspond to the original stock with its old-established traditions, and the mass of the people who still remain largely foreign, who have not taken part in the founding of the nation and who are to a certain extent passive. It is a distinction of caste rather than of class, for ethnical origin is still important, and it is also a question of social structure, of the distinction between management and the workers. On this Jacob's ladder, which stretches from the least of the manual workers to the President of the republic or to the multimillionaire, there is every scope for free movement, economically and socially speaking, if not racially. It is a condition indispensable to the well-being of the country, without which it would be a prey to the insoluble social problems of the older-established European civilization.

The leading element is characterized by the activity springing from its Puritan ancestry. Its individual members are efficient, have an innate sense of responsibility, and are conscientious and systematic in their efforts. An even more important characteristic is their sense of social service, of their duty toward the commu-

nity, also their missionary spirit, which is expressed in their instinctive need to pass on their convictions and zealously to improve their fellow men and their material conditions. It would be
difficult to exaggerate the part played by these men in the formation of the nation, men whose efforts between the eighteenth and
twentieth centuries made of the United States the leading nation
in the world.

But it must be acknowledged that this psychology is restricted
to an elite among the nation. The millions of immigrants from the
European continent, whose children and grandchildren today form
the mass of the American people, are of a completely different
moral stock. They have been integrated into a social structure in
whose formation they have not participated. This structure, which
has at its base the initiative, effort, and responsibility of the individual, has, owing to modern conditions of production, been
changed into a highly organized society. The idea of the West,
the "frontier" of the pioneers, no longer exists; it has given place
to an industrial society where collective discipline goes hand in
hand with large-scale enterprise. No longer are the qualities of
the pioneer adventurer required; all that is necessary is to be a
steady worker and a good member of a team. It is important to
emphasize the fact that social advancement is still possible, but
it is now carried out within the framework of a hierarchy where
everyone, from the latest recruit to the President, is a paid employee. From the middle of the nineteenth century onward the
new immigrants displayed a psychological attitude very different
from that of the early settlers. As individuals they were more fully
developed artistically or as artisans, they had distinctive natural
gifts and a type of resourcefulness unfamiliar to the Anglo-Saxon.
They came hoping to profit from the higher standard of living
prevalent in the United States, and they possessed nothing of the
civic sense of the old-established Americans; following the example of the Irish, past masters in this connection, they had every
intention, not of serving the state, but of drawing the maximum
benefits from it in the form of jobs. As industry became more
and more concentrated, and formed of larger and larger groups
of workers, so the preoccupation with finding a job came to be
of greater significance.

Thus the mass of the American people has a very distinctive attitude toward life. The American accepts the prevailing system without discussion, compares it advantageously with the systems existing in Europe, and, even under the influence of an orator gifted in swaying the mob, he never becomes a revolutionary. In spite of its undisciplined outward appearance, an American crowd is one of the most docile and patient that can be found anywhere in the world; if such a thing were possible, it would be more than 100% nationalist, and, proud of being American, it is supremely disdainful of anything European. This social discipline, which is on the increase, is not without its disadvantages, since it is applied to ideas as well as to action. The average American has a supreme belief in education; more mature nations have realized that there are things that cannot be learned. The American has not had to be convinced, for it pleases him to consider that industrial methods can be applied to the dissemination of thought, he appreciates canned science, science presented in the form of pills, simple ideas, prepared by the experts in an easily digestible form. This has given rise to a certain measure of intellectual laziness, further encouraged by motion pictures, radio, and television. The expert has thus become dangerously authoritative; critical faculties have diminished and are less and less easily exercised in a community where organization on all sides swamps the individual.

The American public may thus be likened to a sort of social dough, easily molded by mass-production methods, reacting admirably to publicity and propaganda. These are characteristics of extreme youth. How old was the immigrant who, fifty years ago, disembarked on the docks of New York, bent beneath the burden of centuries of tradition and of suffering! He has found his youth again, but has become rather less than adult in the process. He has lost all resemblance to his European ancestors and he is equally far removed in outlook from the original American colonists, founders of his new nation. But if he has not acquired their civic sense, he participates in the optimism characteristic of their continent, he accepts the American game with all its hazards and, passionately devoted to the United States, he is convinced that he can and must succeed.

PART III

AMERICAN ECONOMY

CHAPTER 14

The Heroic Period and the Beginning of Industrial Organization

★

Four main phases may be distinguished in the economic development of the United States in the period stretching from the beginning of the nineteenth century until the end of World War II.

The first phase covers the nineteenth century up to the Civil
War (1860-1865) and even from some points of view up to about
1890. It is characterized by the colonization of the West and the
development of the whole continent, up to the time when the
idea of a Western "frontier" ceased to exist and the whole country
became orientated toward a new conception and organization of
production. Then came the period of the growth of large-scale industry, set in motion by the Civil War; it was the heroic period
of trusts, characterized after 1870 by a program of rationalization, which was to reach its point of culmination immediately
after World War I. The third phase is that of the great economic
depression, which lasted from 1929 until 1941. It acted as a very
strongly applied brake and gave rise to fundamental readjustment and to the introduction of a social policy into the field of
American politics. The fourth phase, which coincides with World
War II and the period immediately following it, is one of renewed
prosperity and an astounding effort in technical progress, characterized by methods which, if not specifically new, at least appear
to be so because of their incomparable dynamic qualities. The
whole country is astonished by this prosperity and is continuously
wondering how long it will last.

I

Industry existed in the United States from the time of the Napoleonic Wars, but it was only after the Civil War that the lines on which it would develop could clearly be seen. At that period industrial development received encouragement on all sides. The war itself brought ruin to the South but prosperity to the North, and other factors influencing this development included the rapid expansion of agriculture and mining in the West, the carrying out of which required vast equipment. The period was characterized by an atmosphere of creation and adventure, filled with a colonizing spirit and its consequent exaggeration, disorder, and romance. Unfettered, integral capitalism was mingled with a credit policy splendid in its confidence and its acceptance of risks; the stage was set in a new country, as yet unpolished, where there seemed to be no limit to possibilities and where optimism overflowed because every kind of hope appeared legitimate. The initial capitalism was financial rather than, properly speaking, industrial; the bankers were the prime movers and the directing force. Initiative flourished in a society free from restraint and tradition, in which each member hastened toward action, achievement, and success, in which the strength of the individual made its bid against relentless competition, to which the integral liberalism of the background imposed no limitations. Strictly speaking, this America was not liberal in the sense of the word as understood by Cobden or Gladstone inasmuch as it became, in a continental sense, protectionist, the English doctrine of free trade not having crossed the Atlantic. It nevertheless vaunted itself on its liberal philosophy, in the sense that everything was carried out by individual enterprise without any element of state control. Respect for competition became almost a religion, and thus came about the liberty to do anything one wished, and this can be explained by the very youth of the community which reacted in favor of meteoric advancement. In this connection the saying of La Bruyère would appear relevant: "The youth of the prince is at the root of vast fortunes." It was, moreover, a period of corruption, characterized by collusion between business and politics, a period of triumph for bosses and political machines. Is it not natural that so powerful a current should carry dross along with it?

The pioneers of this great achievement were the captains of industry. Their aim was to create industries rather than to organize them. It was the period when the controlling interests in enterprises could be bought on the stock exchanges, when industries could be amalgamated and acquire some of the initial characteristics of large-scale organization; there were sensational corners and extensive strangulation of short sellers, as happened with the Panama Railroad and the Northern Pacific. Politicians were involved in these transactions, where their help was required. Certain financiers bought whole legislative bodies. "I needed," declared Jay Gould in giving evidence, "the good will of the legislators of four states. I 'formed' the legislative bodies with my own money. I found that it was cheaper that way." And Henry O. Havemeyer, president of the sugar trust, stated: "We always contribute to the funds of the political parties for their election campaigns in the states. Where the issue is too uncertain, the trust subscribes to the funds of both parties, in order to have some influence on the winning side, whichever it may be."

Abel Hermant, in his *Transatlantiques,* has furnished excellent portraits of the great magnates of the period; the famous Jay Gould of the Erie Railroad figures under the guise of Jerry Shaw. But there were also industrial personalities of even greater stature, such as John D. Rockefeller, the founder of the oil industry, Cornelius Vanderbilt, of the New York Central, Andrew Carnegie, the iron and steel king, J. Pierpont Morgan, the banker. The fantastic wealth of these men seems to us today all the more phenomenal, since there was no income tax to limit it and public opinion went beyond the bounds of tolerant acquiescence, approving the eccentricities of these millionaires, with their sumptuous town houses on Fifth Avenue, their summer residences at Newport, and their parties worthy of ancient Rome. It was a romantic period, and every American could say to himself, "Perhaps it will be my turn tomorrow!"

The motivating center of the whole system was Wall Street. Everything, in the West as well as in the East, was financed from New York or New England; it was there that all capital resources would be concentrated if a break occurred in the supply of funds coming from western Europe. In this passionate and dynamic development it was less important to possess capital than to be able to borrow, and it was a question of creditors and debtors rather than owners and nonowners. This age, characterized by dominant personalities and for so long taken as the standard picture of the United States, drew to its close in about 1900, though it survived by the force of its own momentum for some time after. Carnegie and Ford belong to two distinct periods. Toward the end of the century came the formation of trusts, precursors of the new age; they marked a first attempt at rationalization of production, though this was jeopardized by a desire for monopoly, dependent on a spirit of adventure and not destined to be approved in the future.

II

Toward the end of the century the trusts concentrated on industrial organization because the colonization of the whole continent had been completed. In the Far West the age of the pioneer continued, but geographically speaking the dream of a West filled with unlimited prospects had ended. This dream which knew no limitations had given place to the ambitions of a reality which, although magnificent in scope, nevertheless implied certain conditions of fulfillment. At the same time, economic enterprises had tended to become so vast that organization and consolidation were necessary. The inconsequential romanticism of the creative epoch gave place to a period of administration. The pioneering spirit had certainly not disappeared, but it had been transposed, and the organizers were no less creative than had been their pioneering predecessors. The movement was generalized: in 1890 there were only 24 trusts, in 1900 this number had risen to 183, and by 1904 trusts controlled 40% of all industrial capital. Twenty-six of those trusts controlled 80% of the total output of their special product, and eight of them as much as 90%. Although after 1920 a second movement toward concentration occurred, and subsequently this tendency has been maintained as being in keeping with the age of the triumph of machinery, there was something particularly distinctive about the formation of the first trusts.

The early trusts were formed because of the necessity of decreasing the cost of production by means of mechanization and greater concentration, the latter becoming more and more necessary in view of the enormous capital outlay which the increased mechanical equipment necessitated. There was a tendency toward vertical amalgamation on the part of enterprises that desired to safeguard their own raw material supplies and their means of transport. These enterprises, therefore, considered logical the acquisition of their suppliers and transport companies as well as of their small competitors. It was from that time that the first signs of a grave problem became apparent: Should the stimulus of competition be sacrificed to the greater technical efficiency of monopoly? Charles Beard, who was a shrewd observer, remarked upon it in the following terms: "The new barons of industry were organizers of men and of materials, masters in the art of administration, with penetrating eyes which saw the wastage and the imperfections of the competitive system." Technocrats before their time, they were the ancestors of the advocates of state control. Their conception was on the whole a sound one, in keeping with the technical demands of large-scale modern production, but the trusts interpreted it in a fashion which failed to take into account the economic and social problems involved. As soon as their monopoly allowed them to impose what prices they wished upon the consumer, disposing of surplus goods by dumping to allow for the conditions inherent to mass output, they were tempted either to put a strangle hold upon the customer, who was at their mercy, or to suppress by force competitors who appeared troublesome, since the prices were no longer determined by normal market values but by the will of a small number of powerful manufacturers. These manufacturers came to participate in politics through sheer logical necessity, since, without strictly applied customs tariffs, foreign competition would operate in bringing down a price system maintained artificially at too high a level. They doubtless would eventually encounter, particularly as far as the Republicans were concerned, an acquiescent state, but they were running counter to basic American opinion, which was deeply and instinctively hostile to anything which savored of monopoly. It was the political feelings of a democracy that was jealous not of wealth itself but of the way in which certain people tended to abuse its power.

This attitude gave rise to the antitrust measures which, more than half a century later, remain fundamental in American politics. In 1887 came the formation of the Interstate Commerce Commission; this was followed in 1890 by the Sherman Antitrust Act, which Chief Justice Hughes described as having the characteristics and the scope of an article of the Constitution: "Every contract, combination or conspiracy in restraint of trade or commerce among the several states . . . is illegal. . . ." The principle of this legislation, today just as much as when it was formulated, is in keeping with the will of the people, and no political party dare run counter to it. There is always the question of its mode of application, particularly the interpretation given to it by the Supreme Court. The Republican party is always anxious to spare the trusts, and the pettifogging offensive of Theodore Roosevelt was certainly not in keeping with its policy. The Democrats are more sincere in their hostility, since they retain in the lowering of the customs tariff a weapon which they have never used. On May 15, 1911, the Supreme Court, in a decision which has acquired historical significance, dissolved the Standard Oil trust under the application of the Sherman Act and authorized it to be reformed under conditions which would restrict competition in a reasonable manner, considering that any legislative measure which forbade reasonable restriction would be unconstitutional and in opposition to the principle of liberty of contract. The trusts thus became consolidated in point of fact, though they had lost any opportunity of forming themselves into monopolies. In spite of numerous legal ups and downs, the trusts have never regained their initial importance; if in our times gigantic corporations still exist, they are watched over carefully by the Supreme Court, and they respect the fundamental principle of competition, a matter on which legal opinion has never wavered.

Nevertheless, the period of the trusts left a decisive imprint on industrial development. It represented the first attempt to organize mass production in a rational manner, and from this point of view the foresight of these early planners was logical. But they appeared unaware of the fact that mass production of necessity implies mass consumption, and that the latter is incompatible with a monopolistic policy, with restrictions or overhigh prices. Theirs was error of judgment rather than crime, and it was an error of

judgment into which Ford, another forerunner of modern industry, did not fall. The magnates who followed the cul-de-sac of
the monopolistic system thus remained, in spite of their genius
for rationalization, adventurers who must be grouped with the
pioneers of the romantic period. At the same time they mark an
age of transition, that of the way leading to twentieth-century
large-scale economic enterprise, dominated by a technical equipment which holds it prisoner, a collective entity of superhuman
size, no longer human. This neocapitalism no more obeys the dictates of individual liberalism; it tends to become overrigid and
leads to technocracy. We are at one of the great crossroads of
modern industrial evolution—at one of the great crossroads of industrial development of any age. Marx overturned the social aspect of the whole world when he raised the question of the nationalization of the means of production, but the fact that large
scale enterprise is no longer within the scope of a single man is
one that marks a stage in human—or inhuman—development, one
whose consequences are perhaps even greater.

I I I

There is a philosophy that has been evolved from the youthful period of American capitalism. Although it is not in keeping
with twentieth-century conditions, it marked American society so
deeply that it still survives, not only in the propaganda of large-
scale industry, but also in popular tradition, where, paradoxically,
it has remained particularly flourishing. It is a moral outlook, basically conservative, which endeavors to prove that energy, hard
work, and intelligence engender material success and that such
success is possible within the existing economic framework. This
doctrine has been so insistently stated that some may be beginning to doubt it. But at the end of the nineteenth century when
the slogan "Go West, young man, go West" still held a practical
appeal, the idea of success, believed in in its entirety, encouraged
this. Each held the conviction—expressed in the saying attributed
to Napoleon—that he had a field marshal's baton in his pack.

Once Carnegie, himself a symbol of the most fabulous success,
had arrived at the top, he constituted himself the apostle of a
moral philosophy which took as its basis the conscience and the

initiative of subordinates destined to become leaders. "Do your job," he would say to them, "but don't be contented with just doing your job; distinguish yourself as you do it by demonstrating through your personality and character that you are worthy of promotion." It is a precept as old as the world itself; the difference is that today we do not believe in it sufficiently, while the background of the United States during the last century encouraged all kinds of beliefs in the possibility of achievement. Carnegie was not unjustified when he stated, "There is always room at the top," concluding, "Be king in your dreams." The subsequent comment of this Scot who had come to settle in the New World was so typically American that even today it has not lost its value: he said that no man suffered more than the employer when he could not find a man suitable for a vacant post. There was no concern in Pittsburgh that was not on the look-out for men with commercial capacities, for all employers would say that there was no rarer commodity on the market. "There is always a boom in brains." This gift should be cultivated, for men who possess it have always a marketable commodity, and need never fear overproduction. The more intelligence one has to sell, the better the price to be gained for it. An outlook of such complacent optimism as this pleases me, because it is so truly in harmony with the New World. How strong is the American's sense of moral security, which enables him to define success as the reward of virtue!

In this connection everything breathes an air charged with the oxygen of a heroic age, of which one should speak in epic style. But Carnegie's philosophy survives in the propaganda, official or camouflaged, of large-scale production, and even today we can find an authentic trace of it in the systematic optimism of the *Reader's Digest*. Thus the initial impetus continues, in spite of a social structure in which the adventure of conquest has had to give place to the needs of rational output.

CHAPTER 15

The Formation, Composition, and Character of the American Labor Force

★

From 1918 onward, in spite of subsequent important transformations, it is justifiable to speak of American industry in the present tense for, whether it is the Coolidge period, the Roosevelt period, or the Truman period to which reference is being made, it will be seen that both outlook and methods have their root in the same inspiration, through periods of prosperity or crisis, of peace or war.

The first problem to be encountered is that of the labor force, and the question under consideration is that of the population problems discussed above, viewed from the angle of production.

I

During the nineteenth century, in order to fulfill the needs of an ever-increasing consumer demand and a never-satisfied development of equipment, the recruitment of labor for industry outstripped the pace of the natural growth of the population, so that immigration became a decisive factor in this recruitment. The new immigrants indeed furnished a valuable supply of labor, ready to serve as an additional force in times of boom, and more flexible by reason of their docility than the long-established Americans or the already assimilated immigrants; moreover, the new immigrants were young, consisting of 60% males, 80% of whom were between the ages of fourteen and forty-four. The number of foreign-born workers in the labor force was therefore considerable. In 1870 they accounted for 65% of the total in Idaho,

58% in Utah, 54% in California, in the West, generally speaking, they totaled 42%, in the Northeast 28%, and in the Middle West 26%, but prevalence of Negroes in the South restricted their proportion there to 3%. In 1930, after the call of the "frontier" had disappeared and the wave of Slavo-Latin immigrants had flooded the Atlantic coast, the percentage of foreign-born workers was reduced to 16% in the West and 17% in the Middle West, while it remained as high as 24% in the Northeast, but was no more than 3% in the South.*

Especially after 1880 the immigrants sprang mainly from the lower-grade agricultural laborers of eastern Europe and the shores of the Mediterranean, or from an old-fashioned type of artisan class. They were generally offered jobs as unskilled laborers in heavy industry. They could frequently have become skilled workers had not the language handicap and the disdain in which they were held deprived them of access to the higher positions, which were virtually reserved for Americans or for earlier immigrants who had adapted themselves to American ways. A division not dissimilar to that of the caste system reigned in the field of labor, and from this point of view American industry in its early stages was not unlike a colonial system, where an elite of white people supervised the mass of colored workers. Assimilation, later followed by the suppression of immigration, has now led to an increasing measure of integration of these diverse elements, but the original differences can still be detected.

Assimilation allowed the immigrant to rise in social position, while the place at the bottom of the ladder which he had deserted was filled by new arrivals. When he landed he was forced to accept the lowest-paid jobs, either as an unskilled heavy worker or as a craftsman in a small way. His son, who had adapted himself to American ways, was able to fill a better position, which brought with it an increase in his standard of living and a tacit admission into the American social background; his improved position usually brought about also a change in his living accommodation, his original poor, downtown dwelling passing on to some new arrival, who would again begin the cycle. Thus the

* A. J. Jaffe and Charles D. Stewart, *Manpower Resources and Utilization; Principles of Working Force Analysis*, New York, John Wiley, 1951.

same lodging in the same house might succesively shelter the most astonishing succession of Irishmen, Italians, Russians, and Negroes. The movement appears to continue, for according to a recent survey, it is recorded that, in the space of five years, in a certain district of New York 78% of the inhabitants changed their address. The textile industry of New England up to 1870 employed Englishmen, Scotsmen, and Irishmen; these were later replaced by a wave of French Canadians, but from 1890 onward the new recruits were Russians, Italians, and various workers of Slav or Latin origin. It is interesting to follow the change in status of the original workers. The Englishman or Scotsman became a foreman, shopkeeper, or factory owner, the Irishman a politician or a building contractor; as they achieved success, all of them, though the Irish more slowly than the others, became assimilated into the background of American life.

Thus the distribution of the different types of jobs has followed the racial groups of the workers. By reason of his natural gifts the American, followed closely by the assimilated immigrant, prefers intelligent and speedy teamwork, dependent on machinery but not requiring any physical effort, work necessitating a high degree of mechanical technique and a good sense of organization. Craftsmanship is not his line; he is happier to specialize in technical or organizing jobs which require competence and team spirit rather than individual ingenuity or resourcefulness. The immigrant, and more particularly the first-generation immigrant, will be used for heavy labor, the fatigue of working automatic machinery, or for small repair jobs, tasks that he alone in the United States is willing to undertake; and, as far as any peasant labor is required in American agriculture, he will supply it, with a patience and a sense of the laws of nature that place him above those who despise him as a traditional serf whose back is always bent over the soil.

As the immigrants become assimilated and the flow of fresh arrivals is stopped, these distinctions fade, and it is now possible to imagine a time when they will have ceased to have any meaning. They were still very pronounced in the decade 1920-1930. People of American descent then formed more than half the labor force in the liberal professions and among office workers of all categories; they accounted also for the majority of the skilled workers in large-scale industry and of farmers working on their own account. On the other hand, workers of foreign extraction were predominant among the unskilled laborers, semiskilled workers in the textile and footwear industries, and in those industries with a high proportion of machine tools; they were also numerous among workers in the food-processing industries, as well as in certain trades that had retained their artisan tradition—bakers, tailors, masons, painters in the building industry; domestic servants and market gardeners were also mainly of foreign extraction. In the iron and steel industry foreigners accounted for 53% of the total number of workers; in the copper mines 52%; in the ready-made clothing industry 77%; in furniture production 50%; in the bakeries 49%; in domestic service 60%, of whom 39% were Negroes. Moreover station porters (redcaps) and Pullman porters were and still are 100% Negroes. In 1925 I noted with some care the predominant occupations of the different nationalities to be found in California; Mexicans and Negroes were mainly concerned in the cultivation of cotton; Portuguese in growing artichokes; Italians, Frenchmen, and Armenians in the vineyards; Germans, Swiss, and Italians in dairying; Southern Slavs in apple growing; Japanese in cultivating melons; Japanese and Hindus in rice growing; Portuguese, Greeks, Finns, and Japanese in fishing; Mexicans in heavy work and road repairs; Frenchmen, Italians, Greeks, and Dalmatians in the restaurants. A similar survey carried out in 1950 yielded the following results: Frenchmen and Italians figured as small-scale farmers; Italians and Frenchmen were employed in the vineyards; Mexicans in tomato growing; Spaniards in the cultivation of walnuts; Americans in scientific market gardening; Mexicans as day laborers in agriculture, though until recently these workers had been mainly Japanese or Filipinos ("A little yellow devil is worth three Mexicans!"); Basques, Frenchmen, and Chinese as laundry workers; while Frenchmen were in great demand as shop assistants—one large store showed itself particularly keen to recruit salesmen who either had a French accent or who could imitate one.

By reason of this hierarchy, ethnical rather than social, and implying caste rather than class distinction, American society would appear to be somewhat less egalitarian than is popularly believed, and it remains democratic only because these divisions are not fixed but slide as if impelled from the bottom upward by an ever-flowing current. There is a whole series of types of employment that the American will not undertake, either because he considers them too hard or too poorly paid, or because he despises them: such tasks include milking cows, working as a domestic servant, or undertaking repair work. Indeed, the United States until recently has been provided with a servile class, for whom one had to put oneself to no inconvenience and whose useful contribution was very similar to that of the natives in an exploited colony. In their severe criticism of colonial systems, the Americans too often forget that they have shown, not only to Negroes, but to lower-class immigrants, the mental outlook of the colonist toward the native.

II

The new regime introduced after World War I, which had the final effect of virtually suppressing immigration, deprived employers of a source of labor on which they had always relied. The crisis was all the more serious since it coincided, in about 1924, with an almost sensational recovery of industrial output and a new prosperity. The effort of adaptation made by industry in that period had far-reaching consequences, particularly from the point of view of the resultant large-scale increase in mechanization. Industrialists had recourse to all types of workers to replace the immigrants: Negroes transferred from the Deep South; Mexicans, who were used in the Southwest for heavy labor; Filipinos, who had much the same qualities as the Chinese; poor whites from the South, who were not difficult in the matter of wage scales; women and girls as an additional labor force. These were mainly unskilled or semiskilled workers, who were poorly paid and not organized in trade unions; they were capable of handling straightforward machinery, which the ingenuity of the technical staffs endeavored to make simpler to handle. This tendency had the effect of orientating output toward the sole aim of maximum mechanization and mass production.

Since immigration has never returned to its former importance,

labor conditions have maintained similar tendencies, as is testified
by the persistent migration of Negroes and Mexicans toward the
North and West. But World War II caused decisive action to be
taken in the matter of the composition and distribution of the
labor force and has left it considerably changed. When the army
removed millions of men from civilian life and at the same time
it became necessary for industrial production to be increased beyond measure, enormous manpower needs were felt. The Government had taken over the general control of production and, though
this was carried out without either conscription of workers or
suppression of private enterprise, it certainly gave the Government
power over the recruitment and even the geographical distribution
of the workers, according to the needs not only of efficiency and
social equilibrium but also of security. Even more than in 1924
an attempt had to be made to recruit all possible workers; an
appeal was made to women, particularly to those who normally
would not have considered taking paid employment, to elderly
people who had already retired and who otherwise would not
have taken up work again, and to all people who did not need
to earn their own living. The total labor force thus increased
from 55 million in 1939 to 65 million in 1944, 54 million of whom
were in civilian employment and 11 million in the service of the
armed forces. The gap caused by the latter had been filled by
recourse to exceptional strata of the population.

The circumstances were indeed exceptional but they had lasting
consequences, the main one being the large-scale geographical redistribution of the labor force. It is estimated that between 1940
and 1945 fifteen million Americans changed their domicile, and
in the immediate postwar period there was a further migration
movement involving several million workers. The economic, social,
and political repercussions of these enormous population transfers
are extensive, though they cannot yet be assessed in detail. A general exodus from the country toward the towns has been observed;
more than five million people have left the countryside to settle in
the cities, or rather in their suburbs, swelling their population out
of reasonable proportion, often to the detriment of old-established
urban centers, where anxiety is shown over the tendency of large
stores and blocks of offices to be transferred toward the outskirts.

Statistics show, under the heading of "rural, not farm," whole urban populations settled in the country but in no way participating in its life. Farmers are attempting to overcome the dearth of farm laborers by the overmechanization of agriculture. It has already been pointed out that many of the new industries established during and after the war have been set up in California and Texas and more recently in the South, which has at last recovered from its long period of lethargy.

These remarkable population transfers have had the effect, not only of unifying a labor force which until recently was still characterized by the diversity of its racial origins, but also of swelling permanently its total effectives. Many women and elderly people, whom the war had encouraged to work as an exceptional measure, are now accustomed to drawing their salary and wish to continue to do so, and are quite ready to declare themselves as unemployed if the demand for labor slackens; and shortly what may be only a return to normal may be termed an unemployment crisis.

Thus once again, as in the days of the pioneers, the West has sent forth its appeal. An increase of nomadism is again apparent among this essentially nomadic nation; its time for stability has not yet arrived, its dwelling house has not yet been built.

III

According to the census of 1950, the civilian labor force of the United States totaled 60 million, or about 39% of the population as compared with 42% in 1940. Three men out of four are gainfully employed, but only one woman out of three. The female labor force is composed mainly of girls under the age of twenty and women over thirty-five, most women between twenty and thirty-five years of age being engaged in household duties and the care of their children. Generally speaking, the working age in the United States is from fifteen to sixty-five years of age, but 41.5% of men over sixty-five and 7.8% of women are still gainfully employed.

Since the last century there has been a considerable decline in the rural population, which fell from 71.5% of the total in 1870 to 36% in 1950. People are no longer willing to live in the country, and moreover the need for a large rural labor force is no longer felt, since most of the important processing is now carried on in the towns. Recriminations on the subject of demoralization resulting from the rural exodus have no longer any sense in a modern industrial society, in which it is normal that for every man working in the fields there should be six or seven men engaged in urban activities.

Since the nineteenth century there have been vast changes in the numbers employed in the different groups of activity. Agriculture, which in 1870 accounted for 6,849,000 workers, employed in 1950 a number not, comparatively, very much different— 6,837,652. Numbers employed in mining and manufacturing have increased from 2,930,000 to 15,856,000; and those in the distributive services (using the term in its broadest sense, that of tertiary activity) from 2,889,000 to 23,149,000. These figures are more significant if considered as percentages; agricultural workers have declined from 53% to 11.6% of the total labor force; the number of those employed in mining and manufacturing has increased from 23% to 31.5%; while the distributive services have risen spectacularly from 24% to 49.7%. Thus, in comparison with 1870, agriculture has lost 41.4%, industry has gained 8% only, while distribution has increased by 26%. This is the effect of a basic tendency which in industrial production places greater emphasis on the needs of the administrative side, that is to say, organization. It is, therefore, not surprising that the number and percentage of employees in offices, in transport, banking, commerce, the professions, and domestic service (hotels, restaurants, etc.) show a progressive increase. A recent survey has shown that the posts which would be most likely to offer the greatest number of openings in the next few years would be those in offices, transport, commerce, the professions, scientific research, primary education, the police force, the fire brigades, telephone and electric companies, domestic service, and building. In this movement toward the greater importance of the distributive services, which is being felt throughout the whole of Western civilization, the United States has once more filled the role of the pioneer.

This transformation is the result of the change first from an agricultural to an industrial community, and subsequently from a highly mechanized to a highly administrative industrial organization. The changes in the social equilibrium which have resulted from this arise from the fact that increased mechanization has released one-quarter of the, strictly speaking, productive workers, and they have been transferred to the distributive services, so that there are now relatively fewer agricultural and industrial workers and more office staff. This swing-over, which has changed the United States from a country of manufacturers to one of distributors, has been brought about without any spectacular clashes. Apart from periods of crisis, it has been carried out in an expanding and supple economy, which has been able to absorb without difficulty the ever-increasing excess of workers. It is a new form of economic civilization, founded on industrial methods which are specifically American, and which it is now important to study.

CHAPTER 16

The Spirit and Methods of Production: Basic Principles

★

The Industrial Revolution which ushered in the machine age was born in Europe, but it is the United States in the twentieth century which has carried its development farthest, giving in its turn a demonstration of creative ability.

The originality of the American experiment resides essentially in its development of organization, which is independent of any technique or particular source of power. This organization may be applied to any type of production, for it comprises a method which transforms the whole of human life. There is a universal temptation to make use of this, for it has a corrosive action which may operate on any type of civilization and any type of culture, more particularly if the general standard of living is low. The U.S.S.R. is a disciple, technically speaking, of the United States, and it is on the American plan that the world of today will find its renaissance.

This outstanding success may be explained by three particular circumstances which have influenced the industrial development of the United States: an amazing abundance of natural resources, a highly paid labor force, and an enormous home market guaranteed by a policy of protectionism—a market continental rather than national in its proportions.

The United States is a country well-endowed by nature. It represents 6.4% of the total land surface of the globe and houses 6.3% of the total world population; yet in the period following World War II it produced 47% of the free world supply of coal,

67% of the crude petroleum, 49% of the iron ore, 55% of the pig iron, 61% of the steel, 54% of the aluminum, 52% of the phosphates, 30% of the lead ore, 50% of the meat, 60% of the corn, and 20% of the wheat. These resources are available within the country itself, being, generally speaking, easy of access and often present in almost unlimited quantities. Any signs of exhaustion, as of iron ore, are very recent, and in general the economic history of the country is one of great abundance. On the other hand, labor demands have almost invariably outstripped the progress of the natural increase in the population. The employer seeks the worker, so that wages have risen to a level unprecedented in any other country in the world. But the unique advantage with which the United States is favored is the possession, inside a customs barrier comparable to the Great Wall of China, of a national market which is continental in its scope, dominated by a policy of free trade and all that this implies. The regime is one which is admirably suited to mass production and mass consumption.

These conditions have given rise to a particular form of psychology. If it is possible to waste materials without serious consequences—and this is done constantly—man's efforts must be spared as far as possible, since the competition for labor is too costly. In Europe materials are guarded jealously while manpower is wasted, but in America, where there is great wastage of materials, it has become of prime importance to spare the manpower, and this is the basis of the whole of the American industrial philosophy. It seems obvious to point out that the New World is new, while the Old World is not, and that not everything should be imitated. Our admiration is checked when we consider the barbarian fashion in which, during the nineteenth century, America squandered her natural resources and reduced some of the richest tracts of countryside to the point of erosion. The European peasant, close to nature, has shown a finer understanding of how to preserve his soil.

American production methods, often described in Europe as rationalization, consist of four distinct but co-ordinated operations: a systematic recourse to mechanization, mass production, scientific organization of labor, and concentration of industrial administration. It is not a system of five-year plans like the Russian, nor a controlled economy, but it is the work of a whole nation, at the same time collective and individual. It is assuredly one of the great achievements in the history of mankind.

I

The high level of wages would soon become prohibitive if no effort were made to reduce the number of workers needed for each unit manufactured. Indeed, industries where mechanization cannot be applied to the maximum will never succeed in the United States. The recourse to a high degree of mechanization is doubtless a result of the spirit of progress, but it also corresponds to a vital necessity which in the long run is imposed upon the workman himself. Fifty years ago there were textile workers in New England ready to break up new machinery, but there is now greater understanding on the part of the trade unions. The very opposite is happening to what occurs in countries where labor is cheap; high salaries in the United States bring about progress.

American industrial equipment is not technically superior to the European, but the American factory owner enjoys far greater facilities for procuring loans to install more powerful equipment, for acquiring at any given moment any spare parts required, and, finally, for obtaining machinery of a higher quality. He can also, if he wishes to increase his mechanical installations, dismiss without any scruple as many workers as he considers necessary, knowing that they will experience no difficulty in finding other jobs either in their specialized work or in some other employment, on the spot or in some other locality, and that these dismissals will not be considered by the workers in general as a cause of grievance. This is the privilege of an expanding economy, in which experience has proved, contrary to what has been felt in Europe, that technical progress always pays.

Nowhere has the automatic force of machinery made its effects felt so relentlessly, progressively replacing the muscular exertion of the workers, their initiative, their intelligence, and this has given rise to a decrease in the significance of the individual as compared with the total output. It is a large-scale operation of the elimination of man by man, from the moment when, deprived of the necessity to use physical force, he found himself also relieved of the task of using any effort of intelligence; he will thus in the long run be doomed to disappear from workshops where, night and day, self-operated machines continue their work alone, capable even of complicated operations which would appear to require reasoning. It is true that intelligence is still necessary and even more indispensable than ever, but it is no longer required of the ordinary worker; it is limited to the upper level of production where the machinery is conceived, manufactured, put into operation, and repaired. The gamut of industrial operations has come to require a new hierarchy in which the supervision of the beginning of the work and the control of the finished product occupy the essential roles, the carrying out of production having become something automatic once the machinery has been put into motion, something which now has no more than secondary significance.

Under these conditions production depends on power derived from natural sources, which has been substituted systematically for the power of man's arms, and man is thus freed to fulfill other tasks. The United States has abundant supplies of these sources of power, easily accessible, transportable, flexible, and increased still further by well-developed technical equipment. Motive force penetrates everywhere in a multiplicity of forms, hand in hand with machinery of various kinds, invading every domain. The American makes no attempt to resist this invasion, on the contrary he encourages it, associates himself with it, having no regrets about the passing of an artisan tradition which he has never known. Aeschylus made Prometheus say: "It is I who first brought animals under the yoke, made them henceforth the slaves of man, and the mortal body was thus relieved of the burden of the hardest toil." The United States could, by transposition, apply those proud words to itself, assured of speeding along the line that runs from the Caucasus to Detroit and Chicago, along the great highroad of human technical progress.

II

Europe understood mass production but America has understood more fully the immense power that can be derived from a highly mechanized industrial regime. Machinery can be used to its full significance only when output is confined to a strictly limited range of models, and when raw materials are specifically prepared with that end in view. The raw material, in order to be suitable for regular but, so to speak, blindfold transformation, must be rendered homogeneous, since tools are unable to adapt themselves to irregularities of quality as the hands of the artist can. If this primary condition is fulfilled, then the machine works more efficiently than man, with no errors or weakness, with relentless regularity, making any finishing process or milling unnecessary. Frederick W. Taylor wrote: "Even better results are obtained with materials of mediocre quality than with high-class instruments or materials of different qualities, some good, the remainder average. It is uniformity which is the essential factor."

This uniformity allows for a multiplicity of operations with a restricted number of machine tools, and this results in a remarkable economy of raw materials and equipment, together with easy replacement of spare parts. It is a matter of logical necessity to apply the process in an almost infinite manner, reducing to the absolute minimum the number of models manufactured. For example, a particular textile mill which specializes in the manufacture of one single fabric will be able to market it at a price that will allow for no competitors; in the same way standardization will be brought about in the production of spare parts, screws, typewriter keyboards, the formulas of commercial correspondence, and anything else that one cares to name. But this conception goes beyond purely technical considerations and impinges on social problems, for there is more to the question than pure standardization; collective competition is necessary, either on the part of other manufacturers or on the part of the consumers, since, in the long run, the collaboration of the latter will be necessary. The United States Government has again played the role of an initiator in the education of the industrialists and the consumers on these lines. When he was Secretary of Commerce in Coolidge's Administration, Herbert Hoover achieved the reduction of the number of different types of bottle from 210 to 20, of wheels from 174 to 4, of bricks from 66 to 7, and of baskets for containing grapes from 71 to 11. This simplification is advantageous when it is a question of machine tools, spare parts or standards of measurement, but it is certainly more contestable for consumer goods, particularly if it leads to the relentless standardization of any product, be it a vanilla sachet, the color of wallpaper, or a program of music.

Moreover, regimented by publicity, public opinion has allowed itself to be educated along these lines with the utmost ease. It has realized that mass production is a *sine qua non* of an abundant and cheap supply of consumer goods and thus of a constantly rising standard of living; and since American industry has never descended to the production of goods that are cheap and poor, the public has never associated the idea of mass production with poor quality. Moreover, the American does not hanker after the "made to measure," since he does not conceive any necessity for being different from his neighbor, on the contrary preferring on all occasions to fall into line with his fellow citizens. Elegance is in no way exclusive, it indubitably exists and can with the greatest of ease stand up to any competition, but it is mass elegance. These circumstances, which are really providential as far as industry is concerned, have enabled publicity to have full rein, it has become an instrument indispensable to the American industrial system, which, with its high degree of mechanization and its mass production, offers the public an ever-increasing abundance of goods. Skillful publicity has educated the public into a restricted series of tastes and preferences in keeping with the needs of a standardization, and without which the system as a whole would be unable to operate.

In order to produce cheaply, output must be in large quantities, that is to say, nothing short of mass production can be conceived as a paying system. There is no other way. If machinery is regulated permanently to perform the same operation in automatic rhythm by means of a continuous uninterrupted stream, then the fullest advantages can be gained from the system. W. Butterworth, one of the presidents of the United States Chamber of Commerce in the period between the two wars, cites as examples of industries that followed this mass-production system: motor vehicles, tires, bathroom equipment, bottles, nuts and bolts, confectionery, preserves, electric refrigerators, internal combustion engines, calculating machines, chewing gum, combs, pharmaceutical products, electric motors, pins, Portland cement, radio equipment, glassware, handkerchiefs, agricultural machinery, gas pipes, paper, mineral oil, shirts, footwear, tractors, typewriters, valves, vacuum cleaners. The industries to which mass-production methods are applied are decidedly those for which the United States cannot be surpassed.

III

In all this America had done little more than develop and perfect on a large scale principles that Europe had already discovered and to a certain extent put into practice. But the scientific organization of work represents something truly creative on the part of the United States.

The problem involved is that of obtaining the maximum output from costly equipment and a very highly paid labor force. Only well-developed organization can achieve efficient results in this field. The problem is social as well as technical for, in order to rationalize the effort of each individual worker, that worker must be integrated into a whole system in which everyone occupies his own particular place and where he can be of maximum efficiency. To a certain extent this problem has existed since the beginning of civilization and has been attacked quite simply by the application of common sense; peoples such as the ancient Egyptians, the Chinese, the Dutch shipbuilders of the eighteenth century, or even Vauban, are in a way precursors of the present-day Americans. If the Americans have made outstanding achievements in this field, it is because they have been the first to envisage the problem in all its amplitude. The environment was propitious, there was no old-established routine among industrialists who were creating new industries, there was no artisan class to regret the artistic value of craftsmanship, the management found no tactical problems in handling a labor force that was often foreign in origin and needed no particular consideration; they had, moreover, the intelligence to pay the workers well. There was complete liberty of outlook, and in this environment Taylor's theories could effectively be applied.

These theories represent only one aspect of scientific management, but from them are derived all other systems that aim at rationalizing production. Taylor's methods have been greatly improved by modern psychotechnology, but it was he who was the initiating genius in this field. He reorganized the Bethlehem Steel Company and the Dodge works. He was, moreover, the author of a number of standard works, among them *Shop Management* (1911) and *Principles of Scientific Management* (1911), and it is he who by his work and his writing proved decisively that without interfering with wage scales it was possible, by rational organization, to reduce the cost of output by considerable percentages.

Taylor's formula, "High wages and low labor costs," contains nothing really paradoxical if the output of each worker is increased to the maximum by the intelligent direction of his activities. The real originality of this doctrine lies in its rational character, which might be described as almost aggressively rational. It has been the practice to consider that the workman should know how to carry out his own job, the tradition of which has been handed down the centuries. Taylor, on the contrary, considered that each act carried out by the worker should be closely studied and directed and that the management should superintend in detail the work of every single workman, however apparently insignificant his job might be. The aim of this control is to find the best methods of procedure, that one best way which can be achieved only by rational study and which can subsequently be controlled and confirmed by chronometers which analyze each movement carried out and which are now used universally. The whole outlook of this method is completely revolutionary, for it replaces artisan tradition by the science of the study of operations, substituting for the responsibility of the individual workman the responsibility of the management, making the research office a center more important than the workshop, substituting collective organization for individual initiative.

Man's intelligence had discovered tools and their use, but so far reasoning had not had to intervene to regulate and co-ordinate the mass movements of large numbers of workers operating machinery and conforming to the laws of the rational division of work. Each action of each worker must be preceded, accompanied, and followed by other actions performed by other workers according to a pre-established harmony of the whole process. It is not sufficient to determine what process shall be carried out by which worker, the movement of the whole must be co-ordinated like that of a clock, the handling of both materials and workers being regulated so as to exclude all useless operations. The relative positions of the various pieces of machinery must be studied, so that each worker has at hand, at the precise moment of need, the materials and tools required. Time lags must be considered as enemy number one, for workers have to be paid for periods of idleness just as much as if they were in active production. The assembly line is one of the most spectacular aspects of this method. The slaughter-houses of Chicago were the initiators of this in the period immediately after the Civil War, and Ford subsequently became the standard example, but the real creative genius in this field was Taylor. He organized the division of industrial operations into three stages—preparation, execution, and verification.

Under this system the real creative producer is not the workman but the management. Manual dexterity yields pride of place to organization; the workers as a group require less technical skill but the managing staff need much more specialized knowledge. The labor force thus changes in scope. The heavy manual worker has disappeared, since machinery now replaces anything savoring of great physical effort. In certain supermechanical factories there is a tendency to eliminate semiskilled workers, since the control of the machinery has become so automatic that skilled intervention on the part of its operator is no longer necessary. On the other hand, technical workers of the highest degree of skill are necessary for the manufacture, maintenance, and repair of the machinery. A new category, that of the organizer, has been introduced, taking its place between the main body of workers and the owners. It is a highly educated group of planners, whose task is to reason, to construct, and to solve problems. It consists of extremely complex personnel and includes advisers, co-ordinators, foremen, speed bosses, route clerks, disciplinarians, psychologists, regulators and repairers of machinery, inspectors, and all types of draftsmen. From the technical standpoint, have the working classes passed the peak of their importance, although they have now achieved their maximum of social influence? The new leading class is that of the managers who, strong in their power as experts, are moving toward a technocracy that recalls the enlightened despotism of the "century of light."

Modern industry has thus become a complex organism which must move in all its separate parts in a predetermined rhythm. In assembly-line production any variation in the speed in any one of the various links would bring about a blockage, if not a complete stoppage of work. Zealous work and aiming at greater speed than that of one's neighbor are of no account; what is necessary is to follow the collective rhythm. The worker who is unwilling to adapt himself to this runs the risk of disrupting the whole system; this was illustrated by Charlie Chaplin in his witty satire, "Modern Times." It is not surprising that the dignity of the worker should rebel against these methods imposed by the management. Taylor respected the policy of high wages, but showed that he did not understand the human aspect of it when he replied to a worker: "You don't have to think; there are people paid for doing that." Psychotechnology is now studying the introduction of a more human element into the mass-production system, but it is something that can be applied only by means of a new ethical outlook, since the worker must be prepared to accept integration into a system that by-passes consideration of the individual.

IV

As production has become a series of collective operations which are strictly co-ordinated, it is natural that it should tend toward concentration, otherwise neither mechanization, nor mass production, nor the scientific organization of work are possible. This concentration can take different forms; it can be carried out in the field of technical operations in huge factories; it can be geographical, with the output of certain specialized products restricted to certain localities; it can be managerial when there is unification of control, particularly in financial matters, even when production is decentralized; it can also be political, when the state intervenes in the direction of production, as it did during World War II. The important aspect is that industrial problems can be envisaged from above and therefore they can be considered and solved on a much broader basis.

The advantage which this gives is very striking. It is thus possible, in any given industry, to suppress the less efficient factories and make each unit specialize in the output of one particular product; raw materials may be purchased in a more rational manner, and distribution can be organized on a large scale, with country-wide publicity and a general public relations policy; duplication can be avoided, and powerful, well-equipped research centers and offices can be instituted. Such a program can be fully developed only where markets are sufficiently large-scale. When it was envisaged by American industry half a century ago, the United States already had 100 million inhabitants, and the 160 million potential customers of today are not too many to keep this huge vessel afloat. The system can be applied only on a continental scale, and it would have been rendered impossible after the Civil War had not Lincoln maintained the Union in spite of all opposition.

While the basic tendency favors concentration, it is certainly not geographical concentration that is implied. Geographically there is an increase in decentralization, the reasons for which have become much more obvious since the last war: the new sources of power that have been developed throughout the country; the anxiety to escape the burden of heavy transport charges by locating the processing centers near the sources of raw materials; the attraction of industry toward supplies of labor that can be obtained for lower wages and that are not organized into powerful trade unions; the advantage of carrying out assembly work in centers convenient for the distribution to consumers in the locality; the desire for independence on the part of the regions on the periphery which are no longer willing, so to speak, to be colonies of Wall Street or the East; a movement toward the areas of better climate and the coastal zones, particularly since the Panama Canal has formed an easy link between the Pacific and the Atlantic. Although the East and the Middle West remain the chief financial centers, they no longer have a monopoly, and there is now not one single state that is without its group of factories.

This geographical decentralization runs parallel with a policy of financial concentration which leads to the unification, often on a nationwide scale, of whole branches of production. The period of the trusts has been succeeded by an age of large corporations increasingly independent of the bankers, with the power of a state within a state. The grouping of enterprises, which never really stopped, has been carried out with even greater intensity since World War II. Half of the total production capacity is in the hands of less than four hundred enterprises. There is, however, no question of monopoly. A jealous public opinion is opposed to this and is upheld by the precedents of the Supreme Court, remaining faithful to the basic principle of competition as being a vital necessity to the economic prosperity of the country. Beside these industrial giants, medium- and small-scale enterprises continue to flourish and are capable, in their more restricted field, of dynamic activity and rationalization. Solidly entrenched in their chambers of commerce, Rotary Clubs, and numerous commercial associations, they are able to exert on Congress an influence sufficient to operate in their defense, and thus, in a country that is moving toward industrial integration, they stand out as bulwarks of individualism and economic independence.

The spirit behind the system is, nevertheless, one of integration, under the aegis of the technical orientation that is common to the whole of Western civilization. After a negligible phase of crafts- manship and a triumphal period of mechanization, American industry has now arrived at the administrative era. Industry has become so complicated that pure technicians alone are not competent to direct it; administrators, or what James Burnham termed managers, are required. Among the presidents of the leading industrial enterprises, organizers, lawyers, and men trained in administration figure predominantly. Raymond Cartier speaks of this evolution from the artisan to the administrator via the technician in the following terms:

The first generation was one of mechanics and the second of trained engineers. Walter P. Chrysler began as an engine-cleaner at five cents an hour. The first of the Fords achieved wealth and fame because of his passion for experimenting which gave birth to the famous model "T," and then the equally famous "A," and which made the car a necessity for the poor rather than a luxury for the rich. As far as General Motors are concerned, after an initial period of oily-faced mechanics, William S. Knudsen, an amazing technician, took over the reins and ushered in the second phase. Today, the great names of the automobile industry are nearly all administrators. Lester L. Colbert, the President of Chrysler, studied only law, and was "stolen" from the bar by the automobile industry. Wilson, the ex-president of General Motors, is a trained engineer, but on the electrical side. . . .

This is necessitated by an age of organization following a period of adventure.

CHAPTER 17

The Spirit and Methods of Production: The New Industrial Society

★

World War II added nothing specifically new to the basic principles analyzed in the last chapter. It could scarcely have been different had it been written in 1939. In spite of astonishing technical progress, methods have remained constant, and a man such as Henry J. Kaiser in his mass production of ships only adapted them, giving greater scope to already familiar processes. It is above all the scope and rhythm of production which, stimulated by the state, have increased in so astonishing a manner; research now occupies a decisive position which it would appear certain to maintain henceforth. In its social aspects, however, postwar industry has evolved rapidly; enterprises have made an astounding effort to integrate themselves into the community, a far greater effort than they made in former times, and this is illustrated by the greatly increased emphasis placed on human and public relations. It is now possible to speak of a new society and a new capitalism.

I

Human relations in American industry have undergone three phases during the last century. First of all there were the combatant industrialists who followed the pattern of the Pittsburgh captains of industry of the time of Frick and Carnegie, men who possessed their private police forces and who could easily break up strikes by wholesale importation of "yellow" labor. They were at the same time paternal and in the long run they did good; they were passively accepted by their workers, and a trace of this attitude still survives in that curious lack of sensitiveness about the intervention of the industrialist, with an indiscretion which would appall the European, into the private life of the worker. The second phase, which is contemporary with Taylor and Ford, was a period of 100% efficiency, with little preoccupation beyond the maintenance of a policy of high wages, which was supposed to suffice all needs; it was a rudimentary form of psychology which was soon to be shown up in all its insufficiencies by psychotechnology, but it nevertheless allowed the scientific organization of work to be developed with practically no obstacles in a period of astonishing economic expansion. Finally, in the third phase, the industrial enterprise has come to be considered as a complex system where the human element must enter into the production as one of the essential factors of the cost of output. The spirit of this policy may in theory be entirely utilitarian, but it nevertheless leads in practice to the introduction of humanitarian considerations.

This conception of modern American industry means that the management and the workers have similar interests in the development and success of the enterprise. Every effort is made to maintain a belief in this solidarity on the part of the employees, so that they participate in any progress achieved in the field of technique, organization, and production. It is not solely a question of propaganda, for the management has every intention of making this solidarity a reality. In this rising tide of economic advance where every element of progress pays, such a program can all the more easily be realized, and the paternal tradition of the management has certainly assisted in the education of the workers. In this evolved capitalistic system the industrialist himself has changed his outlook, he discusses matters with his employees on terms of equality and there is no class consciousness to create a hierarchy or a barrier to the cordiality of personal relationships.

It must be admitted that contradictory impressions arise from these human relationships. There exists a cordiality which is deliberately social rather than truly personal and is marked by a certain element of standardization. I am tempted to believe that the French industrialist has more personal consideration for his workers, has greater regard for them as individual personalities, and would be more loath to sever contact with them. The policy of "human relations" adopted in the United States has not prevented discipline from being absolutely heartless; the management will unhesitatingly dismiss workers for whom they have no further use, and there is a certain harshness about relations in general. The worker has nevertheless been won over, particularly because he no longer feels that he is dealing with an employer possessed of divine rights; the employer has entered into the game in all good faith and has decided—from a utilitarian standpoint perhaps, but what does it matter?—to give his workers a place in the enterprise and to allow them to participate in its progress. This mixture of social duty and profit is in keeping with the utilitarian Anglo-Saxon tradition, and American outlook, far from taking exception to it, has on the contrary seized all its advantages.

II

Public relations in American industry are founded on the same inspiration. In a century when mass production necessitates mass consumption, the economic regime cannot but be democratic, since in the long run it is based on the opinion of the masses. In order to win over and to keep its customers, each enterprise must justify its existence to the people as a whole. When it grows beyond a certain size, an industrial enterprise appears justified in setting up ministerial departments just like a government; not only has it, so to speak, a department of the interior and a department of labor, but also a department of foreign affairs or a department of information, that is to say, a propaganda department. Democratic governments live by votes, industries live by the consensus of opinion of the consumers; in either case the problem raised is one of contacts, publicity, and persuasion. Public relations may thus be defined in this way: everything that an enterprise or organization of any sort does or says to make itself better known and appreciated among its personnel, its clientele, and the public in general.

Public relations thus considered may appear somewhat like the prose of Molière's Monsieur Jourdain. They correspond, nevertheless, to a broad conception of industrial democracy, and it is not surprising that it is the Americans who first developed the technique, with their specialized personnel and those innumerable public relations consultants who are to be found today throughout the United States. The idea arises from this optimistic philosophy inspired by Bentham, in which service and interest go hand in hand: the prosperity of any enterprise can be maintained in the long run only if it conforms to the general interests of the community, but the public as a whole must be enlightened and persuaded on this point. To whom should the public relations officers appeal? To the personnel in the first place, for they should explain to them the aims of the enterprise, how it implements them, how it is managed, and how the profits may be justified. To carry out this program fully it is essential that there should be nothing to hide. There certainly must exist in the United States funds not publicly accounted for, but a policy of secrecy is becoming more and more difficult, as long as the field of atomic research does not introduce this element by another door. Then overtures must be made to the customers, in a manner not dissimilar to that of publicity, but at the same time differing considerably in tone. Finally, an effort must be made to reach the public in general, to find favor with it, even though it may have no direct concern in the enterprise. Once any industry has expanded beyond certain proportions it cannot afford to do without the good will of the public.

There is possibly nothing specifically new in this. The element of originality consists in the fact that in the United States this propaganda is accepted as a matter of course, and that it carries with it a whole technique, including a simplified yet significant psychology, proved methods, all the tricks of the trade expressed in succinct slogans, whose ingenuity would appear to border on cynicism if they were not in reality ingenuous in a country where publicity knows no limits. That is why the American public relations system must be substantially adapted for European consumption.

III

It is evident that a kind of neocapitalism is now coming into being in the United States. It is a phenomenon adapted to twentieth-century conditions and already completely different from traditional capitalism. It takes into consideration the revolution that has occurred in modern times, which consists of the extension of the whole conception of life to mechanized output and mass production. Its processes have relentlessly invaded all fields of human activity, from agriculture and office work to surgery and the organization of the armed forces. They are operations which go far beyond the domain of machinery, to include an entirely new system of the administration of human effort. Modern industry had its birth in this revolution and its constitution marks a major social transformation, more powerful than that of the legal or political systems under which it operates. The conditions of efficient production are on the whole the same in the United States as in Russia, in a society based on free enterprise as under a Communist regime. Perhaps the truly revolutionary innovation consists in the proportions of modern industrial units, which no longer come within the scope of a single human being. It is not surprising that in the age of the light-year and the micron the question of human relationships in industrial production requires revision.

With this scale of dimensions, industrial enterprises belong less and less to individuals, even when the latter are the legal owners. They show a tendency to be the property of the community as a whole, unless they end by owning themselves. Ford had already observed this tendency when he wrote: "The remuneration of the head, of the owner, of the personnel must be incorporated into the running expenses of the enterprise, but the profits properly speaking belong to the enterprise itself, and the enterprise alone can safeguard them and permit them to expand. Everything else must be considered as part of the production costs." According to this concept an industrial enterprise is in itself both a means and an end. It must ensure social service, but the remuneration of those who serve it must be in proportion to the services rendered. Americans have realized more than Europeans that it is scandalous, and under modern conditions impossible, for an employee to collaborate in the enterprise and increase productivity if he himself has not reasonable and direct interests in its success. In this sense modern industry cannot restrict itself to using the proletariat, and there is no longer a question of serving the interests of individuals to the detriment of society in general.

American industry is becoming more and more orientated toward such conceptions. It doubtless confuses, with some measure of deliberation, the interests of the individual with general interests. Certain indiscreet propaganda has the effect of wearying us almost *ad nauseam*. The Anglo-Saxon outlook is particularly receptive to this facile and reassuring optimism. It must, however, be realized that this philosophy is characteristic of an evolved capitalism, extremely different from the unchecked capitalism of a century ago, and that, as far as it has been applied in the United States, it has served the interests and the status of the workers. I sometimes wonder whether America has not achieved an optimum difficult to maintain, and whether, still living in the momentum of the initial impulse of free enterprise, it is not already benefiting from all the possibilities of organization.

IV

In what does American industrial efficiency, reputed to be three or four times greater than the European, consist? One must immediately dismiss from one's mind the idea of the intrinsic superiority of either American workers or American industrialists, and it is far from certain that on the whole the industry of the United States is technically superior to that of Europe. But the equipment is of better quality, because the industrialist is generally in a better financial position, or can obtain credit more easily, so that he can acquire the most perfected type of machinery. Moreover, he is in an excellent position for obtaining spare parts easily and, though the machinery is not better, it is usually installed on a far larger scale and is more easily adaptable to mass production. The same observations are true as far as raw materials are concerned, for they are readily available in the United States and are, moreover, of the highest quality. This is an essential advantage for which no dexterity or ingenuity on the part of the workers can compensate. Power is also easily obtainable in the maximum quantities required and at the lowest costs, whether it be coal, oil, electricity, or natural gas. Finally, better results are obtained from the personnel because of the spirit of co-operation existing between management and workers; although there may be violent discussion, there is no element of class warfare. It is, indeed, an economic background admirably suited to the needs of mass production. It would be impossible to lay too much emphasis on the geographical simplicity of the wide expanses which seem created especially for the development of the use of agricultural machinery and the creation of great industrial enterprises from nothing. Emphasis must also be laid on the simplicity of their huge home market, free from tariff barriers, which has been rendered homogeneous by assimilation. Yet another important factor is the simplification of a social system which is the result of an environment where the idea of class scarcely exists, where people appear to be more willing to follow the dictates of publicity, and where the steam-roller action of Americanization is fulfilling the prophetic vision of De Tocqueville a hundred years ago of a community of 160 million inhabitants, grouped together in conditions of equality, with the same religion, language, habits, and manners, forming their opinions from the same propaganda—people who remain unhampered by traditions and prejudices, who look to the future rather than to the past, who are conservative only when they feel that they have something worth preserving.

I believe that, in order to understand thoroughly American industrial productivity, one should realize that it is not so much the result of certain determined and separate factors as of a general atmosphere which is conducive to high productivity, an atmosphere closely linked with the economic youth of the New World and the state of maturity of a nation composed of elements old in tradition but rejuvenated in their new environment. And it must be added that production enjoys a continuity that has never been compromised by revolution, foreign occupation, or even war. Loans bearing low interest rates can easily be procured, and there is no need for the holding of large stocks of raw materials or spare parts when they can be obtained swiftly merely by making a telephone call. These conditions may at times be temporarily upset by crises, but they form the fundamental basis of the economy of the New World, and will last while that New World remains.

These general economic conditions which are normal in America are by no means so on this side of the Atlantic, where in certain respects one may say that they have disappeared. The European industrialist, lacking capital and credit, cannot acquire such highly perfected equipment, and must at times economize on the quality of his raw materials, always provided that he has sufficient supplies of foreign currency to obtain them at all. Sometimes through his own fault he does not enjoy to the same extent the co-operation of his staff, and conditions are such that he must hesitate to dismiss workers no longer required after absolutely essential mechanization has been carried out. His market is more restricted, and at the same time composed of a clientele whose requirements are more diversified, with the result that mass production is frequently impossible.

Some of these circumstances are due to the aftermath of the wars which have weighed more heavily on the European continent, since they have been fought over its own soil, but the real disadvantages by which Europe is hampered are deeper than this. Europe and America are, from the social, political, and geographical points of view, two completely different continents belonging to entirely different ages. American simplification, which is an almost *sine qua non* of modern industrial production, is impossible in contemporary Europe. Europe consists of too many sovereign states, with their customs barriers, their currencies, their national traditions and languages, and their different ways of life, which create a great variety in the requirements of consumer goods.

It is an ancient and old-fashioned structure, as complicated as an age-old forest encumbered with liana, parasites, and impenetrable brushwood. The American background, on the other hand, makes one think of the clear, geometrical design of an immense California orchard, all in one block. Raymond Cartier gives the following picture of what California would be like were it situated in Europe:

Imprisoned by the customs barriers of the old world it would be, in spite of its oil resources, no more than an incomplete economic entity, condemned to languish. Even its agriculture would be deprived of the vast market formed by 150 million hungry consumers, nor would it have the colossal technical equipment which enables it constantly to improve the soil. A European California would be a poor Mediterranean nation. It owes its existence as an area of astounding wealth and its abundance of human happiness to the great nation in which it has been integrated, in spite of the natural frontiers of mountains, deserts and great distances which are still the unhealthy dream of European nations. It is the eternal and outstanding lesson of America which Europe, enclosed by its customs barriers and its walls of hatred, cannot manage to assimilate.

We have been urged to abolish these old-fashioned barriers and constitute a single European market west of the Iron Curtain, which would unite more than 300 million consumers. The advice is good, and the immediate benefits would be extensive, but abolishing the Franco-German or the Belgo-Dutch frontiers is a very different proposition from ignoring the frontier between the states of North and South Dakota. It would be a struggle, not only against established positions, but against customs inherited from a long-established past, where routine and egoism are not easily distinguished from the nobler aspects of tradition. And this is something which the American in his simplicity fails to understand when he tells us: "Follow our example!"

The truth is that a large-scale clearance must be carried out in Europe if it wishes to hold its place in the twentieth-century international market, or even if it wishes to survive. But the modernization of an ancient monument is a much more complicated matter than the construction of a new edifice, particularly when the monument in question is a Tower of Babel. The United States is unaware of the degree to which it has been favored by nature and destiny, and the extent to which things are made easy when one is borne along on a rising tide.

v

In the first phase of the Industrial Revolution Europe showed itself sufficiently well-equipped to stand as leader of world industry, but when mass production was fully developed, this little western peninsula of the Asiatic land mass proved inadequate. Germany in the post-Bismarck period had enough vision to create an ultramodern conception of industry based on mass production, but in attempting to carry out its theories it proved to have mounted an inadequate steed. Twentieth-century industry requires the support of vast continents, rather than the highly jointed skeleton of the European peninsula: it is the age of the United States and the U.S.S.R.

The origin of this new system is nevertheless European, and the industrial methods of the United States are based on the philosophic and technical traditions of Europe. The Americans are, paradoxically perhaps but nonetheless effectively, Cartesian in their systematic and even aggressive recourse to reason. This is how Oliver Sheldon sees it:

A standard is the outcome, first, of analysis, then of synthesis. The expert, set upon the standardization of some process, will first analyse the process into its component parts; he will then subdivide each part into its elementary constituent parts. He will examine each part and devise the most effective way of operating it. He will then begin to rebuild, adding part to part, adjusting where necessary to fit the parts together, till he has fashioned the process into a synthetic whole. Similarly, he will analyse the material used in the production of any article, and the tools, machines, and speeds employed in the process. Finally, he will record what he has found to be the best way of performing the process, the best materials and equipment to use, taking into account the variables of working conditions, of varying outputs, and of the human agent. Adherence to these written instructions then becomes the duty of the management and workers.*

Is not this deliberate method of reasoning, applied to thought and action, in direct line with Descartes' *Discours de la Méthode?*

By his Anglo-Saxon tradition the American is inclined to experiment, so that it would be unjust and almost ridiculous to try to make of him a sort of French polytechnician. When he has reasoned and come to conclusions, he then verifies by experiment, always allowing for a wide margin of error, just like an Englishman, mistrusting logic and conclusions based on theory. I sometimes wonder whether it is not France with her metric system who was the real pioneer in the matter of standardization. The American would well be capable at some period of standardizing measurements not based on the metric system.

* Oliver Sheldon, *The Philosophy of Management,* London, Pitman, 1923, p. 213.

Finally, there appears to me to be a certain link with Machiavellian philosophy, to the extent to which Machiavelli was a realist rather than purely Machiavellian. The American, like the German, is capable of pure objectivism in the pursuit of his goal, carrying out the processes necessary to achieve it without being hampered by doctrine, prejudice, or routine. He sets himself before the problem he has to solve as before a clean sheet of paper, in a completely unprejudiced state of mind. Certain market studies, carried out to determine the capacity of demand and the saturation point of the markets of the goods in question, are real masterpieces. Dale Carnegie even considered the application of this method to personal relationships in his famous book *How to Win Friends and Influence People.*

I am the first to recognize that from the American point of view such a comment is completely superfluous on my part. I shall be told that the Americans had never considered this at all, and that Taylor was probably completely unfamiliar with the works of Descartes. I can imagine myself, like Professor Nimbus, asking Henry Ford in an interview whether he was a Cartesian, and he, like the elder Cato chasing the Greek sophist from Rome, taking me for a madman and hounding me out of Detroit. I am, nevertheless, of the opinion that this analysis of the American point of view is justifiable.

American methods have today carried off the victory in the industrial battle, not so much with their technique as with their sense of organization, the outstanding characteristic of this new era of humanity, which may legitimately be called the American age.

CHAPTER 18

The Lesson of Ford

★

At the time of his death in 1947 at the age of eighty-five, Henry Ford was already a figure of the past. In the lightning speed of his career he belonged to the age of the adventurers. By many of his ideas in the social field he joined the ranks of the great captains of industry, and, as a pioneer in a new mode of transport, he has become a legendary figure. Nevertheless, it is impossible to exclude him from a study of modern American industry, for on the question of the administration of an enterprise and its role in the life of the community, there is still a lesson to be learned from him. Whenever American industry has spurned his precepts it has experienced difficulties, and it is doubtless due to the increased measure in which it has followed them that it has achieved the success that has astonished the whole world.

I

The whole of Henry Ford's philosophy is contained in his simple but productive attitude toward modern industry. Mechanization has made possible—and desirable—mass production of consumer goods at a low cost to meet the needs of the bulk of the population who, by means of these methods of output, have become potential purchasers. The conception is thus a method of production linked with economic democracy. It is in this that Ford was original, for, even though he inherited from them, his methods are not to be confused with the capitalism of the trusts, which were, before him, pioneers in the matter of rationalization.

Ford recognized as a basic principle the fact that production has a social function—that of serving the consumer. Since an enterprise exists only through the support of the consumer, it must work for him, thus fulfilling the typically American aim of social service. But the problem arose of how to keep one's customers in an age of overproduction, which assumed threatening proportions in view of the never-ending possibilities of mechanization. Henry Ford's reply was to fix the sale price extremely low and to concentrate on making it progressively lower. This, according to him, was the only means of preserving, stimulating, and even of creating purchasing power among the masses. Since profit is essential, the price must be determined by the cost of production and the margin of profit necessary to the producer. He therefore began by fixing the sales prices and then saying to the manufacturing departments: "Work this one out!" He was like Cortez burning his boats, or, to choose a more recent example, Foch refusing to give his generals a line of retreat, since he refused even to envisage the possibility of retreating. Ford himself said that there were always men ready to buy, provided that the manufacturers supplied their requirements at a suitable price. People may say that the market is overcrowded with products that do not sell, but they would sell if only the manufacturer asked a more reasonable price for them. Ford's own principle was to lower prices, to extend operations, and to perfect his cars, but the reduction of prices was the most important aspect. He did not consider the cost of output as something fixed. He therefore began by reducing the sales price in order to sell more, and then set about linking this reduced sales price to a new cost of output. He considered standardization a bad thing if not associated with a constant and systematic reduction in the sales price, and such a reduction should not be associated with discontent on the part of the public, for it should be made possible by progress in manufacturing methods.

This policy is possible only in conjunction with a high degree of technical perfection, which itself is possible in this machine age only by means of increased standardization. Since low prices can be obtained only through mass production, the public is forced to collaborate in this progression, being willing to accept the limitations which it implies and once and for all abandoning the phantasy of goods made to measure. Ford's formula on this subject is legendary: "The customer may choose whatever color he likes for his car, provided that he chooses black!" This represents a new phase of orientation in human evolution. It has led to an optimistic conclusion, as we shall realize when we study the question of the essential nature of American prosperity: if technical progress permits of sufficient lowering of output prices, then there can be no such thing as overproduction.

Ford considered that this technical progress was as limitless as the possibilities of mechanization. He stated that it was always possible to conceive a machine capable of executing any piece of work better and with greater precision than could man's hands. This concept was in the interests of production, and also of man, who should be spared effort. Specialists are too precious to be wasted on work which the machinery they set up can carry out better than they can.

It is often considered that handmade goods have a greater degree of finish and perfection, but this idea should be revised, for mass-produced goods are infinitely more even in quality. The automatic nature of the manufacture has eliminated the imperfections. Then comes the question of assembly, and here Ford described possibly the most original aspect of his method, in the character of the organization, or the collective administration. He stated that he considered industry above all as a question of organization but that for him administration and management were one. When management becomes arduous, then output is unsatisfactory. Each square foot counts in the overhead; therefore the consumer has to pay for a higher percentage of the overhead and transport charges if the machines are placed even as much as six inches too far apart.

These are doubtless well-known truths based on common sense, but in order to understand their full scope they must be considered in the light of mass production, where the slightest simplification may make a startling difference to the cost of output. A small factory manufacturing one single product and using cheap power is more economical than a large factory producing a considerable number of products, even though its power is equally cheap and it is divided into several sections. No factory is large enough to make several different sorts of product.

Then the question of the worker requires consideration, and in this field Ford also showed himself to be an initiator, even though, from certain points of view, some of his social ideas belong to the old regime. He pushed mechanization to its maximum extent, even almost aggressively, but he admitted that he needed the co-operation of the worker. His policy toward the wage earner was utilitarian, generous, and relentless. He expressed as a basic principle that costs must not be reduced through a policy of wage reductions, and here he was in complete harmony with American tradition. Publicly, with a fanfare of trumpets, he declared himself to be in favor of a systematic policy of high wages. And why? He considered in the first place that this would increase the output of the worker, and, in the second place, that the worker's purchasing power would be augmented. He should possibly have added a third reason, that the publication of this policy served as an advertisement for his firm. It is, however, essential that any increase in wages should be related to a corresponding increase in productivity. This basic point is too often forgotten, for without it the cost of output rises, thus automatically preventing any decrease in the sales price, and the whole balance of the system is imperiled. To increase wages and to decrease production is to hover on the edge of the abyss of industrial depression. It is the product, not the industrialist, that should pay the wages, and the task of the management of a factory should be to orientate production in such a way that this is so. The most prosperous industrial enterprise is the one that increases wages at the same time that it decreases prices. If it cannot do this it is practicing self-destruction, inasmuch as it is limiting the numbers of its potential customers. Ford himself set an example in sensational fashion. In 1914 the average daily wage at Detroit was two dollars; he raised it to five, and by 1920 to six, for eight instead of for nine hours' work. His competitors considered that he was quite mad, but it was to be seen that he was in the right.

The industrialist, then, is ready to pay the worker a high wage, but what does he ask in exchange? It is not great physical effort, for this has been rendered less and less necessary by the perfection of machinery, but rather the maintenance of a level of output below which he must not fall. It is a question of regularity in work rather than technical competence or even conscience. He must show attention, agility, constancy, and endurance under a supervision that is almost excessive in its control. When one visits the River Rouge factory one is inclined to think that this type of monotonous, boring work would disgust the workers. Do they not feel nostalgia for the varied efforts of the artisan, which call for use of the intelligence? Henry Ford, disillusioned, did not think in this way, and if he himself was an admirer of his own system it was with this sort of disillusionment: that he himself, a former artisan, realized that his employees appreciated it only too well. "For most minds," he wrote, "this kind of work has no terror, and on the contrary it is thought which is feared by many types of mind. Our difficulty does not consist in finding men worthy of promotion, but men who are willing to accept it."

The assembly line, first developed on a large scale at Detroit, had as its psychological basis this attitude of semipassivity. "The thing is to keep everything in motion and take the work to the man and not the man to the work. That is the real principle of our production, and conveyors are only one of the many means to an end." * Real specialists are thus no longer necessary and their place is taken by men described as semiskilled workers.

The rank and file of men come to us unskilled; they learn their jobs within a few hours or a few days. If they do not learn within that time they will never be of any use to us. . . . They do not have to be able-bodied men. They have jobs that require great physical strength— although they are rapidly lessening; we have other jobs that require no strength whatsoever—jobs which, as far as strength is concerned, might be attended to by a child of three.†

Henry Ford showed a remarkable reaction to the mechanization that he had set in motion. On the one hand he showed himself justifiably gratified by the indubitable progress achieved. Why should one insist on men continuing to make an effort that machines, once regulated, can perform unaided, faultlessly and with-

* From: *Today and Tomorrow*, by Henry Ford and Samuel Crowther. Copyright 1926 by Doubleday & Company, Inc., p. 100.

† From: *My Life and Work*, by Henry Ford and Samuel Crowther. Copyright 1922 by Doubleday & Company, Inc., p. 79.

out fatigue? An infinite vista of a country governed by machinery is opened up like that of a country ripe for unlimited conquest. All mechanical progress is from this point of view human progress, and to oppose it would be ridiculous, even wicked. But at the same time Henry Ford experienced a sort of melancholy at the thought that so many workers were contented with this type of task which he himself had imposed upon them. He would have preferred them to seek for promotion, clamor for greater initiative in their work, more technical skill, greater scope for their intelligence in their daily life. It is easy to guess that he felt the nostalgia of the artisan in the depth of his heart. The word "guess" is perhaps inappropriate. There is indeed sufficient proof of this nostalgia in the amazing museum which Ford, the pioneer of rationalization, set up beside his factory. The museum is deliberately archaic; one reaches it in ancient horse-drawn landaus, and in it are displayed examples of all the technical progress achieved throughout the course of the centuries by artisan labor. It is the supreme act of homage of high-powered machinery to the hand tool, of the age of mass production to the age of ingenuity.

It was also in Detroit that I was privileged to meet William Knudsen, then head of General Motors, and he also expressed to me his admiration for the French workman with his long artisan tradition, proud of his craft, a student of all the multiple problems of his work, which he attempts to master. The automatic nature of the machine threatens to dry up many sources of imagination and individual creation. It is significant to note that the great industrial leaders have made every effort to maintain the flow of this spring and to preserve in the heart of a century of mass production the seeds of individuality.

II

But this is far from being a complete picture of the powerful personality of Henry Ford.

In the first place he made a penetrating analysis of the conditions essential to the success of an enterprise, and in this matter his example is one of a pioneer. In the capitalist background in which he worked, he considered that the proof of the health of an enterprise consisted in its profit. A business that loses money or works without showing a profit is not worthwhile. But he did not stop there, for he had started with the point of view that the main object of an industry is to serve the consumer. "But when any one attempts to run a business solely for profit and thinks not at all of the service to the community, then also the business must die, for it no longer has a reason for existence." * Profit, therefore, must be considered as a proof of a well-balanced conduct of the enterprise, a sign of its vitality and its activity. An enterprise must certainly fulfill its social functions, but the incitement to production which the consideration of profits stimulates is of another degree, following the laws of nature, and there is to be found the deep-seated instinct which brings about creative action.

Thus the workman is not one of the essential parts of the machinery but, according to Ford, he has his place among the overhead expenses; he must be offered a generous share in the profits, though they do not belong to him but to the organization. This term is generalized and includes the capital, the shareholders, the owner, the administrative staff. Whose, then, is in reality the profit? According to Henry Ford it should not be the capital, or the owner, or even the shareholders, except to a limited extent. Once their demands have been satisfied, the profit belongs to the enterprise itself, and it should spend these funds on machinery, which can always be perfected, on increasing the wages of the workers, or on lowering the price of the goods offered to the consumer. As is so often true in life, the means becomes the end. Originally one might have thought that the end in view was the making of a profit, but in the long run the enterprise becomes an end in itself, which the industrialist follows with a passion that amounts almost to a faith. He becomes the servant of his creation, and makes a distinction between his own salary, which he includes in the overhead charges, and the profits in the strict sense of the term, which he allocates to the business with the aim of assuring its survival and its future development.

* Henry Ford and Samuel Crowther, *Today and Tomorrow*, p. 28.

III

Henry Ford's company, now headed by his grandson, Henry Ford II, is today, together with Chrysler, no more than a "good second" to the gigantic General Motors Corporation, and the old Ford is now legendary. Its descendants are, at present, three in number, the Lincoln, the Mercury, and the modern Ford. On looking back, it is evident that the work of the great Henry Ford contained no element of technical invention. His contribution was of a deeper and more generalized significance, and in one sense it went beyond the limits of the automobile industry. It is not incorrect to say that his influence extended to the whole conception of American industrial production, and the effects of it are still felt.

It was essentially a question of methods of production, at first applied only to the automobile industry, but now extended to include all types of large-scale production. I am even inclined to believe that the main lesson to be learned from Ford is the method of considering not solely the organization of an enterprise but the place that it occupies in the community. By his example and his success Henry Ford taught the common-sense lesson that the only way of increasing the purchasing capacity of the consumer is by reducing the price of the articles offered for sale. It required, perhaps, a genius to formulate this doctrine, which had not been understood by the trusts of the earlier period, and which was not considered in a later period by Roosevelt in his New Deal, and the full significance of which is certainly not grasped by French industry. On the other hand it appears that an increasing number of American industrialists are now returning to Ford's point of view, realizing that it is more profitable to make a smaller percentage of profit on a greater number of articles than a large percentage of profit on a restricted production. They, moreover, consider that the ever-present danger of overproduction can be eliminated only to the extent to which increased productivity allows for a reduction in prices. This policy may be compared with a sheet of water which as it recedes discovers fresh surfaces, formerly unoccupied, over which it may spread. The United States has found the equivalent of a new western "frontier" in the application of democracy to purchasing power. That American industrialists will associate themselves with this policy is a sign of their understanding of contemporary conditions. The fact that they convincedly pursue a policy of social service is possibly inherent in their Protestant traditions.

I find disappointment and even humiliation in the fact that this economic wisdom, which is becoming widespread in the United States, is not yet to be found in Europe, which from this point of view still belongs to the old regime. America has not arrived at this stage without a certain amount of hesitation and even backward steps, and it is, moreover, by no means certain that under conditions of economic crisis the country would not revert to former methods.

CHAPTER 19

The Limitations of the System:
Mass Production and Quality

★

The American system of production has arrived at a sort of perfection, through a technique the rules of which are infallible and the logic of which necessitates integral application. But in the long run it comes up against limitations, for it is a technique of quantity, which is not always compatible with quality, and even in the field of quantity it can operate to its full advantage only if the increase in consumption is parallel and complementary to the increase in production.

The system encountered a crisis, from the point of view of the quantitative balance of production, at the time of the Great Depression. In the subsequent period the war prevented the problem from arising, and, since the war, industrialists have shown an intelligent practical approach to the question, so that, following the example of the doctrine of Ford, they appear to be able to postpone almost indefinitely the threat of overproduction. If mass production is not wholly compatible with the interests of quality, experience has proved that it can make great strides toward attaining it, if it cannot actually reach its goal. This is not really a point of paramount importance in the United States, where a new civilization based on mass production has succeeded the ancient civilization founded on the importance of quality. The problem must, nevertheless, be considered, even though American opinion would tend to consider it unnecessary and old-fashioned.

I

It is important to distinguish between certain terms which might appear synonymous: quality, high quality, and luxury; or technical progress, progress in mechanization, and human progress. Production founded on any one acceptance of these ideas will carry with it essentially different conditions, either on the part of the producer from the point of view of technique and methods, or on the part of the consumer in his education and his critical sense as a purchaser, or in the general atmosphere of the community, whose level of culture will be different according to whether it aims at artistic perfection or an increase in the standard of living.

Even in the United States there are certain operations that cannot be carried out by machinery because of their very nature; this necessitates the physical intervention of man and the application of his brain. It is true that the limitations on the possibilities of mechanical equipment are receding farther and farther. Perhaps nobody will ever invent a machine for picking strawberries, but a cotton-picking machine is already widely used in the southern states. On the other hand, a more serious limitation exists when it is a question of producing quality goods, since then the standards of mass production are no longer applicable. One encounters the opposition of two different epochs, that of the artisan with his hand tools and that of the engineer with his powerful machinery. It is also a clash between two civilizations, since quality remains a European preoccupation.

Quality production necessitates the application of art and individuality. There is a fundamental opposition between art, which is, in a way, manual, and industry, which is collective and anonymous, based on automatism and repetition. It is a contrast between personality and uniformity, between an article made to requirements by an operation that is different on each occasion and one that is successful only when mass produced; between the subtle approach and the geometric, for if the artist or artisan must apply the personal touch, anything savoring of personality must rigorously be excluded from the action of the worker in charge of a piece of machinery. It is a difference not of degree but of essential nature, and it is impossible to pass from one regime to another, or to practice both at the same time, just as one cannot pass without a break from the straight line to the curve.

The repercussions on the psychology of the worker of these two methods are significant. The era of the artisan, which extends from the time of neolithic man to the Industrial Revolution, saw the building up through the ages of a technique of production with all its aesthetic and moral values, in which man learned from his tools. "I have been making clogs for fifty years," an artisan once said, "and they still have plenty to teach me." In the machine age, which is now in the process of conquering the world, the situation is quite different, progress comes from the equipment itself, not from the man who uses it. Thus a new industrial civilization is coming into being, with entirely different technical, aesthetic, and moral standards.

The distinction must be made here between quality and high quality, terming "high quality" goods those which are well-finished, solid, practical, elegant, and pleasing from the aesthetic point of view. None of these characteristics is impossible in mass-produced goods. Moreover, if machinery is fed with raw materials of uniform quality, it will produce, by reason of its automatic nature, goods of a higher standard than man's hands can accomplish. Thus in large-scale enterprise mass production logically leads to high-quality products, the quality becoming to a certain extent a by-product of standardization. As far as the United States is concerned, nothing is more false than the description "cheap and poor," which was applied to the first mass-produced articles at the time of the 1878 Paris Exposition.

If the material that is to be processed is one that has remained distinctive, then the use of machinery is no longer suitable. The scissors of the tailor-artist will draw something from a piece of material which a machine cutting blindly through fifty thicknesses at a time will only massacre, leaving the clothing manufacturer to make the best of it. The tools of the sculptor can follow the veins of a block of wood or stone, while the machine is bound by its very nature to ignore them. The same differences are evident in matters of setting and adjusting, where the brain or the hand of an artist is required. Quality production is thus characterized by a certain finish which gives the article a personality denied to it by mechanical work, which by its nature leads to impersonalization. The machine improves the standard of production, giving it high quality but not quality in the artistic sense. It raises the minimum standard and generally improves the average, but it has definite upper limitations.

In this sense there is fundamental opposition between the products of industry and artistic quality. A work of art is unique, and a true artist cannot paint the same picture twice. If he yields to the temptation of seeking to obtain quick returns, then he is no more than a commercial artist, in the worst sense of the term. Nevertheless, industrial art and artistic industrial production do exist, where individuality is given to machine-made goods. In the lost wax process each model is individualized; in art editions only a limited number of copies is printed; *haute couture* would be completely ruined were the models repeated. There is thus a whole range of activity which cannot admit of standardization: we appreciate an individual diagnosis from our doctor, a personal talk from a lecturer, or a well-designed garden.

But can one not, by means of mass production, reproduce in large quantities individual creations so that they cease to be the privilege of the few and come within the range of all? Modern processes of reproduction and transmission have reached such a stage of perfection that one can believe oneself to be in the presence of the masterpiece itself, that one can believe oneself to be actually listening to the orator whom one sees on the television screen. The social benefits of this are enormous, but again we are faced with the difference between a product of a high quality and a product of artistic value, for there is something that cannot be transmitted. At the time of the 1952 presidential election, the candidates realized that contact by radio and television was not sufficient and that the voters wished to see the candidates in the flesh.

What conclusion should we draw from this? It seems to me that there are two distinct fields of activity—that of art and that of industrial production. It is dangerous to industrialize art, since artistic value is threatened by multiplicity, and this may serve to demoralize the artist himself. On the other hand, prototypes of high aesthetic quality may be reproduced indefinitely, but this leaves the scope of the humanities and comes within the field of industrial production. It would be disastrous to conclude that in the future the only original things to exist will be the prototypes for production in series, or that the reproduction of something good has the same value as a creation both original and unique. John Steinbeck in *East of Eden* wrote:

> Our species is the only creative species, and it has only one creative instrument, the individual mind and spirit of a man. Nothing was ever created by two men. There are no good collaborations, whether in music, in art, in poetry, in mathematics, in philosophy. Once the miracle of creation has taken place, the group can build and extend it, but the group never invents anything. The preciousness lies in the lonely mind of a man.*

II

There exists, then, industrial production to which the term quality, in its absolute sense, can be applied, but it is based on particular technical and economic conditions. The raw materials used are of little importance as compared with the ingenuity of the manufacturer, and the principal aim of production is the artistic value of the finished article, without consideration of its price, since the potential purchasers are, by the nature of the industry, limited in number. Industrialist and workers alike must have a whole artisan or artistic tradition, and they must serve a discriminating and critical clientele. The manufacturer should have a background in which a high degree of culture and technical tradition are combined; his industry is thus not easily transplanted, since it depends on environment as well as on persons. Typical examples of such industries are the *haute couture* of Paris, the hand looms of the Cambrai district, or the silk industry of Lyons.

The question now arises of how far the United States can succeed in this quality production and also to what extent they wish to attempt to compete in it. It is a fact that American industry appears to have little interest in products that can be manufactured in small numbers only. By a kind of tacit agreement, the output of goods made to specified requirements has

---

* John Steinbeck, *East of Eden*, New York, Viking, 1952, p. 132.

been left to Europe, including the high-precision machinery that is the speciality of Winterthur, Baden, or Mulhouse. In the United States progress is measured quantitatively. Goods of a very high quality are produced, the standards being so high that they are often confused with "quality" goods, as in the production of luxury cars. But with rare exceptions there is an upper limit to this high-quality production, that of the article which can be manufactured in large numbers. American industry is handicapped in the production of quality goods by lack of desire rather than lack of capability. Its genius is for organization rather than for creation, and does not naturally orientate itself toward quality. Its inventiveness operates mainly in the conception of labor-saving devices, and once its equipment is installed it calls for a restricted range of products rather than for the fantasies of the individualistic imagination. Its whole outlook is weighed down by a preoccupation of serving a large market.

Thus, by virtue of its inward logic, American industry succeeds in the mass production of silk stockings, but the fine silk tissues that are characteristic of Lyons or of China do not come within its scope. America may produce the most elegant women in the world, but *haute couture* models will not be designed in New York. I have often noticed that in the large department stores the mass-produced articles are American, but quality goods and fancy goods are foreign. The American appears to lack the critical sense that can distinguish between high quality and intrinsic quality. It takes an experienced observer to distinguish the subtle difference in quality between a Cadillac and a Rolls-Royce; and if the Agen prune is an individually better article, the California prune has easily an advantage over it in the guaranteed standard of its quality. There is, therefore, a tendency to prefer to manufacture articles in series with highly mechanized equipment and to reduce the ranges of current consumer goods. Hoover's advice has been followed, and the public no longer looks for quality goods since it is ignorant of their existence.

This regime has produced remarkable results. The American lives better than any other man on this earth from the point of view of his home, his clothes, his transport, and his food. He has the greatest number of goods available, and of a quality the average of which is of a higher level than can be found anywhere else. He profits from a general democratization of comfort and even mass-produced luxury, which is the socialized form of modern luxury.

Does this amount to incontestable social progress or quite simply a general progress in civilization? Is it not now rather unnecessary to speak of distinctive intrinsic quality as distinct from quantity, quality that cannot be measured by the standards of mass production? The reply to these questions depends on the extent to which the answerer has become assimilated to the general outlook of the United States on these matters. Raymond Cartier, from his American background, wrote:

Approximately one out of every ten chickens eaten in America comes from Iowa, and the number of eggs laid annually in this single state reaches the phenomenal figure of 4,398,000,000, compared with 58,000,000,000 for the United States as a whole. Consequently each American eats on an average one egg a day and chicken is a working man's dish. When faced with this magnificent abundance of food, and all that it represents in strength, health and democracy, the question of whether a chicken from Iowa is slightly less succulent than one from the French province of Bresse seems completely futile.

According to the same author, the presumptuous French couturiers, faced by the powerful clothing manufacturers of New York, will be reduced to supplying models for the garment center to copy. On the other hand, Rodier once told me that a few years ago, when talking to an American couturier, he had told him that his ateliers in the Rue des Moulins made five hundred models a year. "You are mad!" exclaimed the American. "You should reduce your models to twenty-five or thirty at the most." But Rodier had replied, "I understand; next year I shall make six hundred." Which of the two is right? It is a conversation between representatives of two civilizations, and I fear that the European is fighting a rear-guard action.

CHAPTER 20

The Limitations of the System: The Threat of Overproduction

★

As far as American industry is concerned, the criticism that goods of intrinsic quality are not produced is, indeed, of no significance. There is, however, a source of danger that appears to arise from the very nature of the industrial organization: as it has freed itself from the control of the will of the individual, it is logically driven toward a conception of unlimited development of output, which can be achieved with a progressively small number of workers. Overproduction, as we have seen, can be avoided if new groups of customers can be put in a position to purchase the increased supplies, and there need be no unemployment if workers who become unnecessary by reason of new equipment can be given other jobs, either in the industry itself or in distribution. But the rhythm of this threat, which is essentially a technical matter, has shown itself capable of outstripping the speed at which it can be checked; this is a social matter, and the whole problem hangs constantly like a sword of Damocles over American optimism.

In considering this race between production and consumption, the last fifty years of American economic history may be divided into three periods, each of which merits separate study. There is the period of Republican prosperity between 1896 and 1929; that of the Great Depression from 1929 to 1941; and the post-Pearl Harbor period of neoprosperity, which received its initial impetus from the war, but which, nevertheless, has persisted in the immediate postwar years. These three periods correspond to

176

three distinct psychological outlooks. In the first period prosperity was considered as a sort of American divine right, received without any conditions and for which the crisis could be considered as a chastisement. In the second period the American nation underwent a pathological reaction, becoming pessimistic and having no longer any faith in its destiny. In the third period the nation once again recovered its faith, though at the same time it had learned its lesson from the period of depression; the new prosperity is doubtless based on firm foundations, but it has reached an abnormally high level through the influence of World War II and subsequently the cold war. The optimism known in the past has reappeared, but it is tinged with a spirit of misgiving about a future which is, after all, uncertain.

I

Prosperity was continuous between 1896 and 1929, being scarcely interrupted in 1907 by the speculation crisis and in 1921 by the crisis that was the aftermath of World War I. From 1924 onward it progressed triumphantly, and this success has been attributed to the new industrial methods which deeply impressed Europe, and which America itself has adopted almost as a doctrine. The extreme end of the nineteenth century and the beginning of the twentieth seemed to contemporary opinion a period of certain, guaranteed progress, which was permanent in its nature. It originated first of all from the youth of a continent filled with immense sources of wealth, as yet undeveloped, with a constantly increasing population, where the need for equipment became the source of substantial profits, while the country, although already industrialized, was at the same time an important exporter of raw materials, cotton, oil, meat, and cereals. The words of a poet spring to mind: *"Quand on est jeune on a des matins triomphants."* * This rapid growth, the memory of which has long since been lost to the European mind, was associated with the prolonged period of supremacy of the Republican party, politically conservative, well disposed toward industry and allowing free rein to its initiative.

* Victor Hugo, *Boöz endormi.*

This prosperity increased immediately after World War I from a mixture of causes, some of which were permanent by nature and thus healthy, and others incidental to the cessation of hostilities and therefore unhealthy. Rationalization, which led to an increase in both productivity and wage levels, and eventually to the increased purchasing power of the masses, belongs to the first category. This is also true of the social equilibrium resulting from a low population density, which allowed for a place for all in the system and a reasonable hope of success. There was also the spirit of progress manifested by a people which had made its way in times of peace and had emerged from the war the leading nation in the world. In the second category, emphasis should be placed on the abnormally favorable position of a country which had become a creditor through the war and which, nevertheless, continued to maintain a favorable balance of trade. To this must be added a chain of circumstances where success borders on imprudence; under artificial stimulation consumption reached giddy heights by methods other than that of the lowering of retail prices recommended by Ford, and turnover became more and more dependent on speculation overencouraged by a credit policy, which led to the habit of spending beyond one's means; it was a policy of excessive investment.

In this expanding American economy, which inherited from the nineteenth century an outlook typical of a boom period, business was carried on the crest of an ever-mounting tide. The market was insatiable, and production had only to follow an upward curve, with no anxiety as to sales, which were quasi-automatic. Thus an unlimited confidence in the possibilities of an economy which appeared in truth exceptional came into being, and its optimism was reflected by stereotyped slogans, such as: "Unlimited Possibilities," "Unbounded Potentialities," "America Unlimited," "God's Own Country," "The Country of Opportunities." These are more than mere words, for everyone believes in the idea behind them, convinced that daring pays, that technical progress is of necessity profitable, that one should not hesitate to install expensive equipment, that speculation on a rising market is a source of wealth, and that if crises occur they can easily be overcome and leave no aftermath. The period of postwar prosperity was in full swing in about 1926 or 1927, and it was at that time that the New Era doctrine came into being, with its theory that prosperity would continue uninterrupted. The classic theory of ten-year economic cycles was abandoned in favor of a belief in minor readjustments every three and a half years in an economy which maintained every new high level reached. In a country such as the United States the old laws of political economy were out of date. It was an outlook tinged with satisfaction, ingenuous rather than aggressive, recalling that of the Pharisees. It is confirmed on an official level in President Coolidge's message of December 4, 1928:

> In the domestic field there is tranquillity and contentment, harmonious relations between management and wage earner, freedom from industrial strife, and the highest record of years of prosperity. . . . The main source of these unexampled blessings lies in the integrity and character of the American people. . . . We must extend to other countries the largest measure of generosity, moderation, and patience. In addition to dealing justly, we can well afford to walk humbly.

II

There was, nevertheless, something unhealthy about this excessive well-being. As early as January, 1928, I remember having written an article entitled, "Is a Crisis in Preparation in the United States?" The Americans did not hold this opinion, as we have just seen, but certain symptoms which were making their appearance should have given rise to anxiety.

Sales difficulties were making themselves felt for the first time. Production strode ahead of consumption, whose steps showed signs of flagging. A feeling of superabundance was experienced. A contributor to the *Atlantic Monthly* expressed these sentiments, in the issue of September, 1928:

> In my town, which I know better than any other town, there are too many merchants, too many hardware dealers, too many banks, druggists, newspapers, coal dealers, plumbers, painters, carpenters, florists, restaurants, lawyers, garages, filling stations, contractors, blacksmiths, doctors, and far too many unemployed.*

* Walter Henderson Grimes, "The Curse of Leisure," *Atlantic Monthly*, Sept., 1928, p. 355.

It thus became important to pursue the tedious task of tempting the purchaser, with the result that the expense saved by rationalization of production was squandered in outlays on sales and publicity, and the costs of production again became excessive.

Thus, the distributing services had to be enlarged. For example, in order to maintain its output, a certain brush factory was obliged to maintain more than 2,000 salesmen under the aegis of 100 branch offices, and a silk hosiery company more than 10,000 salesmen and 250 branch offices. Within any one enterprise there was friction between the production department, desirous of increasing standardization, and the sales department, demanding a greater range of models to stimulate the slackening market. This change from the old equilibrium, which operated in favor of the so-called tertiary services, may be considered as normal in a period when the emphasis of production is changing from mechanization to administration, always provided that the administration in its turn be rationalized. The effort would be made in the future, but on the eve of the Great Depression the lesson propounded by Ford had not yet been universally learned. In order to stimulate a flagging clientele, manufacturers had recourse to expedients that were not only inadequate but in the long run harmful.

When normal demands are insufficient to maintain the flow of business, manufacturers endeavor to create new needs by "educating" the consumer—an education indeed suspect! The consumer must be canvassed in such a way that it will require more effort for him to abstain from buying than to make purchases. Everything must tempt him, not only publicity, ease of delivery, and installment terms, but he must also be brought to a state of mind which will make buying appear a duty. It is in the interests of propaganda to teach him that the good citizen is not he who saves but he who spends. General Motors even invented the "Two Car Consciousness."

It was at this time that the installment-buying system entered into the American economy. The customer takes delivery of his purchase on payment of the first installment and settles the remainder by monthly payments, having to relinquish the goods if he falls behind with even a single payment. There is nothing inherently unhealthy in the system, but if it becomes widespread it has essentially the effect of making the customer spend his money before he intended doing so, thus accelerating the sales rhythm by pledging the future. The purchaser may enjoy the goods before he has paid for them but, having become a debtor, he is obliged to earn money in order to pay his debts. The old practice of saving first goes by the board, but this does not appear to be a cause for anxiety to the American temperament, as it would be to the French. The economists who preached prosperity by means of this system, true descendants of the jurists of Philippe le Bel, maintained that they were creating purchasing power. Much was written to prove this point, but experience has shown that installment buying had rather the tendency of engendering a sort of unreal purchasing power, which allowed people to live about a year ahead of their means. A period of hiatus is bound to come when the market is blocked, even more so because the monthly payments will generally continue to be made. Efforts were made to accelerate continuously the rhythm of the system, since catastrophe would occur should it stop, its balance being maintained solely by its momentum.

At the same time it was necessary to develop publicity, particularly where optional expenditure was concerned, and where the customer could easily be persuaded to change from one product to another. Products affected in this way included motorcars, soap, perfume, tobacco, specialized food products, toilet necessities, lingerie, kitchen equipment, travel tours, and insurance. This in itself is only normal, but it becomes unhealthy if a fictitious purchasing power is borrowed from the future, or if, because total purchasing power cannot be increased, industries strive among themselves, each enticing customers away from its rivals. In this feverish predepression period there was great rivalry in publicity, not only between different manufacturers of the same product, but between whole industrial groups: iron tried to outbid cement, oil pitted itself against coal, rayon against pure silk, ice against electric refrigeration, cigarettes against confectionery, town against town, California against Florida. Some of the slogans have remained famous, such as: "Reach for a Lucky instead of a sweet," or "Change to Shell."

As even this stimulus seemed insufficient, it appeared essential to offer credit, not only for the purchase of consumer goods but also so that speculation on the stock exchange might offer potential customers the means to buy an increasing volume of goods. Speculation became widespread in this period of abnormal stimulation, where the market was constantly rising. Not only professionals bought and sold on the stock exchange; there were also those who had no connection with business of any sort, office workers, messengers, commissionaires from hotels or clubs, and many enterprises used any funds available for similar purposes. Thus, in spite of effective prosperity with a perfectly sound basis, the country's standard of living was raised to an artificially high level, maintained by the necessarily exceptional profits of speculation on a rising market, any check to which could not avoid being catastrophic.

CHAPTER 21

The Great Depression

★

The boom of the postwar period came into being at the time of the election of the Republican Calvin Coolidge against Democrat John W. Davis and Progressive Robert M. La Follette, and it was confirmed when in 1928 the Republican Herbert Hoover became President, defeating the Democrat Al Smith. Following the doctrine of the New Era, the economist Irving Fischer envisaged prosperity as a permanently high plateau, and the new President considered himself justified in saying, "Soon, with the help of God, the time will come when the nation will be rid of poverty." The soaring of the markets on the stock exchange bore out this optimism; United States Steel rose from a low of 132¾ in 1928 to a maximum of 261¾ in 1929. At the same time, while the salary index had risen from 108.4 to 109.1 between 1923 and 1928, the index of profits on the stock exchange rose from 100 to 410. It was an environment which favored the middleman; there were 70,950 stockbrokers in 1930 compared with 29,609 in 1920. Thus the rise in the market was insufficient and it became necessary to maintain a constantly accelerating pace. Europe had begun by mistrusting this atmosphere, which seemed to be the calm that precedes a storm, but then, seeing that nothing occurred, had followed America in its illusion. I was in the United States during the summer of 1929 and not one person said to me, "It can't last this way."

It is well known that the crisis burst suddenly that October, like a thunderstorm in a calm sky. At the beginning of the month there had been some wavering on the stock exchange, but it had not seemed likely to produce serious repercussions. By October 29, it had become impossible to shut one's eyes to the truth: a crisis had occurred, or, rather, to employ an old-fashioned term the meaning of which reappeared with full force, there was a crash. In a few weeks U. S. Steel had fallen to 151 and General Motors to 36, but they were to fall still further and to remain at 30 and 11 respectively in April, 1932. It nevertheless seems, and this is also my personal recollection, that people failed to understand the gravity of the situation. It was termed a stock exchange crisis. But as American prosperity, generally speaking, was to a large extent founded on the profits made through rising markets on the stock exchange, the economic depression could not remain confined to Wall Street. The whole economic structure of the country was put to the test, and there was the risk of a general crisis within three months.

It is interesting to study the reactions of public opinion to this state of affairs, which was a new experience for a whole generation. People refused to believe in the possibility of crisis, and anyone who dared mention the word was termed a disloyal citizen and a defeatist. A great deal of propaganda was put forward, magnates and presidents affirming that the economic structure was perfectly healthy, that instead of selling in panic one should profit from falling prices and buy, for "Prosperity is just around the corner," and it is only good American common sense that "Wall Street sells but Main Street buys." Then, as the uneasiness persisted, reassurance was sought in the belief that a general outlook favorable to recovery could be achieved through the power of suggestion. "Ninety per cent of the slump comes from fear," stated President Hoover. In June, 1930, an editorial in the Middletown *Journal* entitled "Loosen Up!" affirmed that the whole story of the crisis was a mental problem. "If tomorrow morning everybody should wake up with a resolve to unwind the red yarn that is wound about his old leather purse, and then would carry his resolve into effect, by August first, at the latest, the whole country could join in singing, '*Happy Days Are Here Again.*'" * It was the period of the autosuggestion clubs so reminiscent of the Coué system, of the Buy More clubs, the Confidence Will Committees, and the Pep Committees. Extraordinary slogans sprang

---

* Robert S. Lynd and Helen Merrell Lynd, *Middletown in Transition,* New York, Harcourt, Brace, 1937, p. 17.

up: "Buy now whether you need it or not!" "Start your factory going whether you have orders or not!" "Spend five dollars a week more!" "Ride in taxis instead of walking!" "Keep money in circulation!" "Eat a steak instead of eggs for breakfast!" Babbitt adopted the habit of wearing a Booster Club button, with an attitude akin to that of the disciple of Coué or the Christian Scientist.

By reason of these influences, and also of intervention on the part of the banks, the market rose a little at the beginning of 1930; U. S. Steel rose to 180 and General Motors to 45. Confidence had been shaken but not completely destroyed, and even Europe refused to abandon hope. But soon, as had been foreseen, the crisis spread from the stock exchange to the economy of the country as a whole, and brought about a general stagnation. Unemployment appeared and spread until there were more than thirteen million without work; investments became almost completely worthless; bankruptcy was frequent; and there was a landslide fall in purchasing power, all the more spectacular because of the system by which earnings were pledged ahead through installment buying. In 1933 at "Middletown," a city in the Midwest of about 50,000 inhabitants, the value of industrial output had dropped by 44% since 1929, the number of workers employed by 42% and the total wages paid by 53%.

From a psychological angle the fall was heavy, since it started from a great height. The postwar period had naturally created the illusion that everything was easy—jobs, profits, and speculation—that success was attainable without special effort, and that America, God's own country, had particular privileges denied to Europe. The American had to pass the test of a kind of *nuit de Jouffroy*—according to the legend the philosopher came to realize, after a night of meditation, that his faith in God had deserted him, and in the morning his hair had become white. The American, who had considered himself invulnerable from a commercial standpoint, realized that crisis could hit him too, just as much as other men—white streaks began to appear among the locks of his economy. His faith was beginning to waver. Public opinion slumped into deep depression, and it was no longer possible to recognize the old, familiar American. After a belief in permanent prosperity he had come to the point of wondering whether the Depression could ever end. Men were attracted toward the West by hereditary instinct, but the only response to be found there merely underlined their misery: "Go West, young man . . . and drown yourself in the Pacific!"

It was, indeed, a terrible testing time, and we find it difficult to understand exactly how catastrophic it appeared to contemporary opinion. Millions of men were ruined, the unemployed sought vainly for work. Workers, and even managers, who had lost their jobs were unable to find others. The crisis made an even stronger impression upon the people than World War II, and, indeed, the Great Depression is as important a milestone in the history of the United States as 1917 or 1941. It had far-reaching psychological, economic, social, and political repercussions.

II

There had been crises before, sometimes serious ones, but it had always been understood that individuals concerned should work out their own solutions. The slogan "Go West, young man" was an example of this. If assistance were required, it would be given through private charitable organizations; it was in no way considered to be a matter of concern for the state. President Harding considered matters in this light in 1921, as did President Hoover in 1929, though the latter felt compelled to change his outlook in instituting the Reconstruction Finance Corporation. Public opinion clamored for action, though without knowing what sort of action it wanted. There was no sort of Communist or Marxist reaction, in spite of the cosmopolitan population and the large Jewish minority, but rather a spirit of genuine confusion. Protests by farmers about the payment of mortgages led to actual riots. There were tragic, wandering exoduses of the unemployed, often in old cars. But there was no revolutionary spirit, using the expression with the European significance. There was a vague anticapitalist tendency, and a reaction against former propaganda, expressed in publications hostile to financial or industrial magnates: *The Tragedy of Henry Ford, Mellon's Millions, America's 60 Families.* An unfamiliar philosophy arose which denied the glory of success, the value of happiness dependent on wealth, as illustrated by the film "You Can't Take It with You."

This idea spread all the more rapidly in view of the fact that the crisis was not one marking the end of an economic cycle but something more fundamental, which attacked the very roots of the capitalist system. "Before the Crisis" and "After the Crisis," B.C. and A.C., became common parlance like B.C. and A.D. Three new doctrines, all pessimistic and all attacking those of the New Era, concluded that production was condemned for the rest of time to exceed consumption, that mechanization of industry engendered unemployment, and that the American monetary and banking system made a healthy distribution of purchasing power impossible. The old jealousy in the West of the Wall Street monopoly of credit reappeared. Thus, in reaction against the laissez-faire doctrine, there was a movement toward a government assumption of power, which was the novel aspect of Roosevelt's administration. The Democratic party made capital of these tendencies, which were interpreted by able politicians; but, independent of politics properly speaking, an extraordinary number of panaceas, now forgotten but not without their effect, came into being.

According to technocracy (a pessimistic doctrine of controls), capitalism for private profit necessarily causes overproduction and unemployment. A technocratic economy, managed by experts, could solve the problem of rewarding work with "power" certificates, which would be the equivalent of liquid assets. Walter Lippmann referred to it as the pretentious ignorance of cranks, but it nevertheless reflects this "managerial" age.

Father Coughlin, the radio priest, whose Irish eloquence stirred millions of listeners every Sunday, preached the doctrine that credit is the only source of wealth, that it belongs to the People (with a capital P), and that this powerful instrument must not be abandoned to the arbitrary will of the bankers. It must, therefore, be nationalized, together with the currency in general, in order to reconstitute the now-deficient purchasing power of the people. With countless subscriptions which he received, he founded at Royal Oak, near Detroit, the Church of the Virgin of the Little Flower, dedicated to Saint Thérèse of Lisieux. He thus acquired immense popularity, for he touched a responsive chord by defending debtors and protesting against the monopoly of the powerful. The church, concerned about this use of ecclesiastical authority, forbade him to broadcast any more and, as a disciplined priest, he relapsed into silence.

Social credit, according to the doctrine of an English engineering expert, Major Douglas, who was very popular in certain circles in the United States, affirmed that society attributes too much money to production and not enough to consumption; and that, in order to re-establish the equilibrium hitherto continually threatened, a "social dividend" should be distributed to each consumer. If each citizen were to receive a monthly dividend, say of twenty-five dollars, having free purchasing power but constituting an asset which had to be liquidated by the end of the month, the volume of business would automatically be increased, and this would permit a decrease in the cost of output since it would allow for the resumption of a mass production while maintaining the balance with consumption. The profits made, however, would belong to the community, which would recoup them by fixing a just sales price. There is here again the same preoccupation with the creation of purchasing power. This plan was destined to be tried out, not in the United States but in the Canadian province of Alberta by the pastor-politician William Aberhart, but it has yielded no decisive results, in spite of the fact that in 1953 its partisans were still in power there.

The Townsend Plan, conceived on a similar basis by Dr. Francis E. Townsend, was exceedingly simple. Everyone over the age of sixty should receive a monthly pension of two hundred dollars, on the condition that these two hundred dollars should be spent before the end of the month, by which time they would lose all their value. But how should this pension be paid? When the question was put to him by a congressional committee, Dr. Townsend appears to have shown a certain amount of impatience. It was not his business to work out such affairs, it was a question for the legislators! He admitted, however, that a 2% tax on all commercial transactions would easily furnish a means of financing his proposal. And it consisted of no more than that. Its advantage was that elderly people, instead of continuing to compete with the young in the labor market, would become solely consumers, all the more reliable in that they could not accumulate their money, and thus business would be stimulated and consumption increased.

Dr. Townsend was an ordinary medical practitioner from Long Beach, California, until then wholly undistinguished in his profession. He was an elderly man, the typical respectable Anglo-Saxon in appearance, whose spectacles and pointed evangelical beard gave him a somewhat professional air. He had an appearance of conviction which was not in the slightest degree tinged with irony. There was nothing of the fanatic about him though he was possessed of that indefinably disquieting quality that one encounters at times among inventors. He had seen large numbers of elderly people retire to live on their small incomes in the pleasant climate of southern California, only to be completely ruined a short time afterward. Having seen their suffering the doctor wanted to help them, and, at the same time, to restore prosperity to his country. Townsend Clubs sprang up everywhere in order to claim from Congress the two hundred dollars for the over-sixties.

All these movements, whether doctrinaire, opportunist, demagogic, or merely naïve, sprang from the same depth of public opinion and had their source in the same problem of how to restore purchasing power in order to counterbalance the limitless power of production. They had all the same doubting and pessimistic attitude toward the possibility of realizing this aim by the simple means which, in its optimism, American tradition had hitherto envisaged. In the period of rapid expansion which preceded the 1914 war the country had found it quite natural that production should be countered by insatiable consumption. Then, after the cessation of immigration Ford had realized that rationalization, combined with a policy of lowering prices, would open up to industry a never-ending vista of markets. The result of the crisis was that this policy was no longer accepted, that America doubted her own powers, for the course which was being urged was entirely foreign to her. This basically inflationary demagogy, the work of social planners of limited outlook, demanded an intervention on the part of the authorities; if purchasing power no longer existed, then it must be created; if latent, it must be mobilized; if diffuse, it must be concentrated on those exact points where its power would be felt to the maximum.

The Roosevelt administration was born in this atmosphere. It introduced into the American economy an entirely new outlook, which would appear to be permanent in its effect.

CHAPTER 22

Roosevelt, the New Deal, and the Welfare State

★

Since the Civil War the Republicans had governed the country almost without interruption, and their rule ensured prosperity. In 1932 the crisis gave back the power to those storm birds, the Democrats. They governed for twenty years, at the end of which the old America had become completely unrecognizable, the Democratic regime having imprinted upon it an indelible mark. This change was not, as one might be tempted to think, a result of World War II, but rather of Roosevelt's policy of the New Deal and the welfare state, which now has doubtless come to stay in the United States, whichever party may hold the reins of government.

When Franklin D. Roosevelt was installed in the White House in 1933, the crisis had fully developed and the country was hovering on the edge of an abyss. The debts on mortgages amounted to thirty-six billion dollars, industrial and banking debt to fifty-eight billion, the public debt to nineteen billion, and the general short-term debt to about one hundred billion. These figures, which would not astonish us today, seemed astronomical at the time, and signified catastrophe. Stagnation had become chronic, and economic life was threatened with complete stoppage. Prices were at 80% of their 1913 level, and the national income had dropped by 50% since 1929. Wheat had fallen to 38 cents, its lowest quotation for a century, industry was working to only a very small percentage of capacity, there were thirteen million unemployed, and five million families were receiving assistance. By the day the new President took up his functions, almost every bank in all the states had either declared bankruptcy or been closed by state

action. The United States was sinking toward virtual anarchy. In
the West, ranchers abandoned their herds; riots by farmers prevented sales for bankruptcy; in several large cities officials were
no longer receiving their salaries and the public had no money
left for daily transactions. Because of the enormous fall in prices,
debts contracted when they stood at a higher level became impossible to honor, so that, by whatever name one might choose
to call it, some form of bankruptcy became inevitable.

This was the problem set before Franklin Roosevelt when he
became President on March 4, 1933. Looking back on this today,
we realize that that date marked a turning point of immense significance in the history of the United States.

I

The personality of F.D.R. played a decisive role in this great ven-
ture. He belonged to a New York family of Dutch stock, which
had already provided one President. It was a wealthy, aristocratic
family, of enviable social standing, and Franklin Roosevelt was
not under the pecuniary necessity of following a profession. He
belonged to the highest ranks of American society, and when he
first entered politics he was considered rather a snob. "Speaks
through his nose!", "Arrogant fellow, that Roosevelt!", people said
of him. Nevertheless, his tactical gifts raised him to the position
of senator in New York State, of which he became governor in
1928. It was a stepping stone to the presidency, which he was
to obtain in 1932 by his victory over Hoover.

His career can be understood to the full only when one considers the attack of poliomyelitis from which he suffered in 1921
and which made him a cripple for the rest of his life, never able
to stand without support. His extraordinary energy enabled him
to overcome this disablement, and his personal suffering made him
more ready to understand the suffering of others; that is perhaps
the secret of the astonishing contact which he was able to establish with the people. This sensitivity, coupled with exceptional
gifts in the political field and an unmatched knowledge of political machinery, made him one of the most powerful leaders of
the whole of American history. One must have seen him, have
heard his golden voice (he was irresistible when he began his

radio speeches with, "My friends"), have seen his look, so full of humanity, his winning smile, have felt personally the extent to which his instinct led him to gauge and welcome his questioners, in order to understand the incredible power that he had over all those with whom he came in contact. This influence was partly due to charm and ease of manner in his relations with both great and humble, but above all to his spontaneous humanity which pierced through the finesse of the politician. One had the impression that he loved people, the whole of humanity, that he understood them and sympathized with their troubles. His stereotyped smile, which I had seen a hundred times at the cinema, had at first struck me as a mass-produced article, but when I met him and he smiled at me, I immediately succumbed, and when he said to me, "I am glad to see you," I must confess that I believed him, naïvely enough. Millions of voters must have been impressed in the same way that I was.

It is improbable that he had a doctrine. He was, in fact, a pure opportunist, and probably an essentially lighthearted man. Some have wanted to find in him a revolutionary, or a sort of fascist. In point of fact, he was more like an intelligent Whig who saved what there was to be saved in a tradition. It was not that he favored the interests of capital or the business world; he did not like businessmen, never having belonged to their ranks because of his inherited wealth, and he was perhaps, for that reason, jealous of the power of the multimillionaires. His policy resembled a perpetual see-saw. He was neither obstinate nor self-deceived; he was like a man steering a rowboat—if he turned the tiller to the right, the vessel veered toward the left and vice versa. It is possible, indeed, that he was a lighthearted man who did not worry. He never allowed himself to be the prisoner of his counselors and changed them frequently. Not one of them exerted a lasting influence on him, not even Cordell Hull, the only one whom he retained during his whole lengthy term of office. He liked to group around himself his famous Brain Trust of intellectuals, professors, lawyers, and economists, who were often men of the left, in principle hostile to capitalism. The atmosphere around him, particularly at first, was one of quest for new solutions. The New Deal is in line with the New Era, though contrary to it.

It is necessary to employ caution in the use of the European terms left, right, Marxist, fascist, the corporate system when applying them to the United States, since there are often differences, in spite of superficial similarity. The truth of the matter is that Roosevelt, faced with a crisis of unprecedented magnitude, had no plan. His policy consisted of a series of independent tentatives, linked only by the personality of the leader, who remained at the helm when his collaborators and the program itself were changed. Roosevelt took an oath of allegiance to the people: "I pledge you, I pledge myself to a New Deal for the American people." He said this when, on the day of his inauguration, he spoke standing—a tremendous effort for a man with his physical handicap—in the open air, on a March day, without a hat, in a firm voice and with an almost defiant chin. And the following is the tone which he adopted toward the financial leaders: "The money changers have fled from their high seats in the temple of our civilization. We may now restore that temple to the ancient truths. The measure of the restoration lies in the extent to which we apply social values more noble than mere monetary profit." Finally, not as a revolutionary but as a demagogue, he advocated a new state which should be considered as a beneficent friend, a planned economy in the place of the former rugged individualism, the regime of mass man replacing that of the anarchic individual; in short, a welfare state as compared with a liberal state which remained indifferent in the face of struggle for advantage. According to an enlightened observer, William Allen White, this was a new attitude in American outlook, the firm intention on the part of the people to use the Government as a sort of agent for the provision of human happiness.

Thus Roosevelt's methods resembled those of a dictator, but a dictator who received his legal mandate in the very spirit of the American Constitution. If he delegated presidential powers to men in whom he had confidence, apart from or over the heads of his Cabinet, he had a legal right to do so. Since he frequently changed the administrators, commissioners, and countless delegates whom he used within the framework of existing institutions, and transformed and reorganized commissions and agencies, the general impression given is one of improvisation, confusion, and disorder, but in this state of turmoil Roosevelt maintained his general trends, which drew their permanence from his temperament. Miss Frances Perkins, who was his Secretary of Labor, wrote in her book, *The Roosevelt I Knew:*

That phrase, "new deal," which gave courage to all sorts of people, was merely a statement of policy and emphasis. It expressed a new attitude, not a fixed program. When he got to Washington he had no fixed program.

The notion that the New Deal had a preconceived theoretical position is ridiculous. . . . There were no preliminary conferences of party leaders to work out details and arrive at agreements.

The general situation, however, was clear in Roosevelt's mind and in the minds of his supporters and party. He represented the humanitarian trend. The idea was that all the political and practical forces of the community should and could be directed to making life better for ordinary people.*

II

Implemented by necessity, the first measures taken under the new presidency depended on the most severe deflation. There was a general moratorium, renewed from week to week, and a closing of all banks, only the most solvent of which were subsequently authorized to reopen. An improvement in the budgetary position was obtained by a revision of pension scales, and federal salary scales were reduced up to 15%. This strictly orthodox policy contributed, by the abolition of deposits and by the suppression of certain unhealthy parts of the organism, to a measure of improvement but—and this fact proves the absence of any preconceived plan on the part of the President—it was completely opposed to the line that he was next to take. As is common experience, the deflationary policy quickly proved too unpalatable to be followed for long in a democracy. The politicians protested, particularly those from the West, where the inflationary tradition is strong, and then, and only then, the real policy of Roosevelt was put into operation.

There were two alternatives, deflation or inflation, and the President chose the latter. When faced with the choice between op-

* Frances Perkins, *The Roosevelt I Knew,* New York, Viking, 1946, pp. 166-67.

portunist remedies and structural reform, in order to stimulate economic recovery he chose structural reform; and in order to implement this, he chose a controlled rather than a liberal economy. These are the tendencies of Roosevelt's second phase of orientation, and they were to last until the end of the Democratic regime. But one must not be misled by his methods. Under a cloak of false dogmatism, partly due to the Brain Trust, he moved forward by a series of experiments and tactical plans, unrelated and often contradictory, often formulated according to the dictates of the moment. Roosevelt proceeded like a skipper who constantly trims his sails to allow for the slightest changes in the wind.

Nevertheless, to the extent to which Roosevelt's policy may be said to have had a guiding idea, there was always the desire to relieve the debtor who had pledged himself beyond his means; since he contracted his debt before the drop in prices, he can redeem it only if prices rise. An increase in the general level of prices will increase the purchasing power of the masses—by means of higher prices for farm products as far as the agriculturists are concerned, and by means of an increase in wages for the industrial workers. Thus equilibrium, then compromised, would be re-established between industrial prices and agricultural prices which, having fallen too low, were preventing the farmer from making purchases. Equilibrium had also to be re-established between the wealthy classes who saved and invested too much, a policy which leads to overproduction, and the mass of the people who did not spend enough because they lacked means to do so. Generally speaking, purchasing power had to be transferred from the rich to the poor.

It is easy to see that this policy reflected current ideas which had spread through public opinion because of the crisis: the struggle against overproduction, the reconstruction of the purchasing power of the weak, the defense of the debtor against his creditor. But something specifically new arose, inasmuch as a social factor, hitherto almost absent from American politics, was introduced. The President made himself the champion of the people. "I shall not abandon you in your trials," he said to the distressed man in the street. The popular response was immediate and almost unanimous. There was no revolutionary attitude. On the eve of his second election, in October, 1936, Roosevelt could justifiably say: "It was this Administration which saved the system of private profit and free enterprise after it had been dragged to the brink of ruin by these same leaders who now try to scare you." In the American environment demagogy does not lead to revolution, it rather acts as a vaccine.

III

It is not within the scope of this book to analyze in detail the measures which constitute the New Deal, but it appears pertinent to outline the main stages, for, if the majority of these measures have not survived, they have, nevertheless, left permanent traces in American politics.

In order to stem the ebbing tide of prices, America had recourse to her tradition of "silverism." The Government undertook through monetary manipulations to depreciate the dollar in relation to gold. The gold standard was abandoned on April 19, 1933, and on June 5 clauses requiring payment in gold were abrogated and existing stocks of gold had to be handed over to the Treasury. The President had himself granted the right to issue up to three billion dollars in notes and eventually to devaluate down to 50% of the former parity (January 15, 1934). The note issue was not floated to the maximum, but there was a continuous series of short-term loans, consequential upon a systematically unbalanced budget. The aim in view was to inject voluntarily into the organism a purchasing power artificially maintained at a high level, and this was attained by a policy of premiums, subsidies, public works, unemployment relief, and large-scale creation of new employment. It must be recognized that this policy, though not without its effects, remained largely inefficacious. In 1934 the dollar had been devalued by 40.4% compared with 1933, but wholesale prices rose by only 22%. Even by 1937 wholesale prices had risen by no more than 33% and retail prices by 17%. This slackness in prices was an indication that the economy was not recovering and that confidence was not being felt.

The President and his collaborators, however, endeavored to probe more deeply into the problem. The National Recovery Administration (NRA), which was founded on June 16, 1933, aimed at stimulating industrial recovery by pump priming. The problem was to put factories back into operation, either by restoring the purchasing power of the workers by an increase in wages, or by reorganizing the industrial machinery in general by subjecting the private interests of the owners to the urgency of general interests. This tentative was in the nature of a structural reform but it was badly conceived and ill-prepared to the point of improvisation, and its deeper aims were not sufficiently apparent. The procedure consisted in inspiring and, if needs be, imposing collective conventions drawn up in each industry or profession as codes, drafted by the interested parties, management and workers, and then given by the state the force of laws. The Government told the industrialists, "Do this, or we shall do it for you." Liberty was respected in principle, but, nevertheless, pressure was brought to bear and the state was ready to impose where it could not convince. It is in this way that the system was to a certain extent corporate.

But the system had unexpected repercussions, doubtless unforeseen by its authors, which go as far as repudiating a political orientation in existence for several generations. The state recognized the right of personnel to form organizations, and—here is the new aspect—did not conceal the fact that it favored the worker against the employer. With the basic idea of increasing purchasing power, minimium wage levels were fixed, and, so that the work available might the more evenly be distributed, hours of work were limited. On the other hand, by encouraging in each branch of work a collective organization of employers, the aim of maintaining prices through industrial agreements between producers was upheld; the establishment of minimum prices must counterbalance minimum wages. The NRA recognized the workers' right to a trade union (without saying what union), and the principle of minimum wage levels and genuine state protection. This meant that, during the whole of the Democratic regime right up to the election of President Eisenhower, the worker rather than the employer was privileged to be received at the White House. Without wishing to do so, moreover, the President admitted the legitimacy of agreements between producers, thus favoring large enterprises; this was something that antitrust legislation had always refused. At the same time the employers were extremely opposed to the intervention of the state in business and the favor with which it viewed the claims of the workers. The business world conceived a hatred for Roosevelt which even his death has not appeased.

In carrying out this policy the Democratic party renounced its tradition of defending the consumer and protesting against the monopolistic tendencies of the trusts. It disregarded Ford's wisdom in advocating a lowering of prices by means of an increase in productivity as being the only means of stimulating sales. Wage levels were raised, but no compensatory increase in output was demanded. Production without high productivity was contrary to all that had made for American prosperity. The Depression did not yield to such an effort. At the same time a real effort was indeed made, under the sign of the Blue Eagle and with an enthusiasm in which ideals of social service were curiously mingled with typically American publicity according to the classic principles of national ballyhoo: this system embraced 22 million workers, included 546 codes and 185 supplementary codes, 685 amendments, 139 general rules, 70 executive orders, 11,000 circulars, and literature which ran to 18 volumes and 18,000 pages.*

The National Recovery Administration was not, however, destined to last in this form. In May, 1935, the Supreme Court condemned it as unconstitutional, inasmuch as it impinged on the rights of the states, to whom belonged the power to formulate regulations for commerce and industry within their own boundaries. The Federal Government had no right to interfere in this. Roosevelt, faced by this judgment, allowed the institution to fall into abeyance and returned to the praise of good, honest competition. He had already replaced General Hugh Johnson, former head of the NRA, by a less convinced successor, Donald Richberg. After his second election in 1936 the President reinstituted an attenuated form of the NRA; this organization retained a large number of the codes which were already, from a practical point of view, accepted by the parties concerned. The original NRA with its ambitions and aggressive outlook had had its day, but it

* Louis Rosenstock Franck, *L'expérience Roosevelt et le milieu social américain*, Paris, F. Alcan, 1937, p. 53.

left a permanent influence, particularly in the recognition of the legitimacy of trade unionism, something quite new in the history of the United States. The crisis, however, outlived it.

Along with this great effort at industrial reorganization, the President undertook to establish a controlled agricultural economy. The Agricultural Adjustment Act (AAA), of May 12, 1933, sought an increase in prices by the reduction of agricultural output, in order to ease the weight of farmers' mortgage debts. At this period there was fear of superabundance, since its dangers had so recently been experienced. The farmer thus had to be persuaded to reduce the acreage planted. Compensation was paid to those who fell in with the scheme, but the others were submitted to pressure bordering on compulsion, since all the main basic products were controlled—wheat, corn, rice, tobacco, cotton, dairy produce, hemp, barley, sorghum, ground nuts, sugar, and livestock, including pigs. Nevertheless, on January 6, 1936, the Supreme Court condemned in its turn the AAA. The Government once again took up the basic ideas of the AAA in the Soil Conservation Act, which advocated reduction of areas under cultivation as part of the struggle against erosion. Helped by the period of drought that was experienced at this time, agricultural prices rose by 50%. There was to remain in the American economy an idea of agricultural planning that was to prove very expensive to the country, but from which neither of the political parties could break free if they were to retain the farmers' votes. Indeed, agriculture truly recovered only with the war.

Independently of these measures, which may be classed as structural reforms, there was a systematic policy of expenditure which included compensatory payments and subsidies of all kinds; this, I think, must be considered as the most typical aspect of Roosevelt's era. A planned budgetary deficit covered by loans permitted the taxpayer to receive more than he gave; public works, useful or the reverse, to be undertaken; wages and subsidies to be paid; public assistance given; not to mention the creation of new jobs, for which the President's credit appeared to be without limit. The sums of money which he had at his disposal were so extensive, even astronomical for the period, that he seemed to find some difficulty in utilizing them to the full. As one traversed the country, one gained the impression that it was doing all that it could to achieve success, but without reaching its goal. Every request for funds, whoever the asker and whatever the purpose for which they were needed, appeared to be granted a favorable reception, naturally all the more so if made by members of the political party in power. Work of the most unexpected nature or the least justifiable had a chance of being carried out.

This is all the more striking in view of the fact that in 1932 the platform of the Democratic party had included a balanced budget, restriction of expenditure, and typically Gladstonian retrenchment. Henceforth a veritable flood of economic stimulus was to characterize the policy of the party, and this was, moreover, the part of the presidential program that found most favor with the public. Though Republican businessmen took refuge in furious opposition and the liberalism of bitter protest, denouncing the "caprices of bureaucracy," the "tyranny of autocratic power," and pursuing their hatred of "that man, a traitor to his class," the masses thought otherwise and triumphantly re-elected Roosevelt in 1936. In May, 1937, according to a Gallup poll, four Americans out of five approved of his policy. It is, therefore, not astonishing that he continued this lavish expenditure. He reaped an obvious advantage in the fact that Capitol Hill and the White House replaced Manhattan and Wall Street as the brain and nerve center of the nation.

IV

It now remains to consider into what channels the funds disbursed by the state, with the aim of stimulating economic life, were directed; after a few years, experience showed that it was less into heavy industry which would produce equipment than into the industries working directly on the manufacture of consumer goods. The unemployed or the farmers who received compensation from official funds did not acquire machinery but, instead, purchased radio sets, household equipment, and even motorcars. The wiser spent some of these sums on the repayment of debts. The interesting lesson to be learned from this is that, while the state can put money into circulation, it cannot have effective control over the spending of its subsidies toward those ends which it would be most beneficial to attain. Doctors experience similar difficulties in the application of medicaments, which they can make the patient absorb but which do not reach the part of his organism that must be reached in order to effect a cure. It would have been necessary, in order to put a final end to the crisis, for industries manufacturing capital goods to resume full activity. The state can encourage the production of these capital goods by measures such as tax exemption, reinvested profits, and accelerated amortization, but it is necessary for industrialists to be willing to collaborate; and businessmen refused to have the same confidence in Roosevelt as had the people as a whole.

The New Deal thus succeeded as a measure of social reform, but failed to bring the crisis to an end, and, indeed, the Depression lasted until the war. But a new element was introduced into American politics, one that will doubtless stay, for the Democratic party relinquished its traditions and became the champion of federal control, the upholder of trade unionism, and above all the dispenser of social benefits. From this point of view, even when one considers the two World Wars, the Great Depression is probably the most important event in the history of the United States since the War of Independence.

CHAPTER 23

The Neoprosperity of the War and the Period That Followed

★

Coming to a country with a long tradition of optimism, the 1929 crisis had appeared in the guise of a warning, the writing on the wall. It had made America doubt its own powers. For the first time in its history it had known overproduction, and that fact changed the center of gravity of its problems. Formerly the slogan had been, "Constant production and yet more production," but it had been brought to a state of anxiety about sales, like the rest of the world. This meant that potential buyers, in spite of their capacity to pay, hesitated to buy for fear of future unemployment. It also brought about anxiety regarding security, an element new and alarming in a country characterized by enterprise and confidence. The question to be considered is whether this moral depression, which ran parallel to the economic depression, would permanently mark the American character. The answer to this is not simple, for if America, fortuitously or directly, refound her former basic prosperity during the war, the period of crisis has not been forgotten and the renascent optimism has not the former full, ingenuous assurance.

I

The war brought back an atmosphere of prosperity which contrasted strongly with the stagnation of the Depression, and with prosperity there returned the particular psychological outlook associated with it. When I returned to the United States in 1945, after an absence of four years, this is what struck me most, with

a simple and direct impression that could not be deceptive. I
found a familiar America, but it was the America of 1925, not that
of 1935 or 1939. It was impregnated with the genuine legendary
Coolidge atmosphere of a society swept along in the general well-
being of production and upheld on a sort of powerful tide. The
country had shaken off the burden of a long period of testing and
had become itself again, with the same characteristics with which
we were familiar in the past. It had prodigious activity, rapid momentum, and achievements that constantly surpassed themselves.
I wonder whether it is really possible to picture in mere words
this particular atmosphere. To understand it fully one must have
breathed this air of another world; in what a melancholy contrast
it sets the European scene!

In the spring of 1945 the war had not yet ended, but victory
was certain. It is interesting to note the characteristics of the
striking American recovery at that period. Between 1939 and 1944
the war had stimulated the economy in a remarkable manner, since
the United States was constrained by circumstances to intensify
production to an extent unforeseen by the most vivid imagination.
The volume of goods and services increased by 50% and the output of raw materials by 60%, while the production of manufactured goods trebled. Agricultural production was increased by
one-third, and the industrial potential by 40-45%. Military and
economic mobilization absorbed nine million unemployed without
difficulty. Forty per cent of this increased production went to armaments, 50% to civil consumption, and 10% to investments and
exports, for America became an efficient and indispensable source
of supply to her allies. In spite of the immense production effort,
consumer goods, although abundant, were rationed to civilian clientele, and this gave rise to an intensified demand when peace
came.

This activity, urged on to its maximum, was universally profitable. The full employment dreamed about nostalgically during the
period of unemployment had become a reality. Every worker drew
his wages and thus was supplied with a purchasing power which
he showered on the country like beneficent manna. At the same
time, since the system still maintained some degree of control, the
demands of the civilian population were restrained with admirable

firmness. Taxation inexorably absorbed the excess purchasing power which was constantly being created. The tax on an income of $10,000 was $2,875, $8,290 for $20,000, and $76,010 for $100,000. Thus resources were canalized to supply the needs of the struggle and, following the good nineteenth-century tradition, there was no need for anxiety about markets. But manpower was scarce because of large-scale mobilization, and since workers were sought on all sides anxiety about unemployment ceased to be felt. The "boom" atmosphere appeared again, large-scale mechanization was once more necessary in order to replace manpower deficiencies, and each worker had to be urged to work to his maximum output, according to the classic tradition of Taylor. The atmosphere was thus technical rather than commercial. The producer was unfettered, and the war appeared as a magnificent cause of progress, the whole difference with the European attitude being that the war was not waged on American soil. The public did not fail to realize this, and these exceptional years appeared to them as the achievement of conditions ideal for production freed from the fear of unemployment and from anxiety about markets, a period in which one could unreservedly abandon oneself to the intoxication of speed and movement. Americans, inasmuch as they were not in the front line, and considering that relatively few of their number were killed, not surprisingly associated the war with a return to prosperity. I realize that this suggestion will shock Americans, but it is nevertheless true.

The return of peace may appear as a threat, for it is dubious whether it is reasonable to suppose that these exceptional circumstances will continue. Public opinion, nevertheless, wishes it. The industrialist is clamoring for a return to liberty, but he wishes to maintain markets as wide as those which he enjoyed when the state gave orders, took the goods, and paid without discussing the price. If the home market, which he considers as his private preserve, were threatened with invasion, his old protectionism would reappear; moreover, the solutions that he instinctively looks for are by no means lazy ones, and one can look to him for a superb effort of adaptation.

The workers are above all desirous of maintaining full employment, since this economic doctrine has now passed into the realms of popular imagination. It goes without saying that this full employment must be associated with the maintenance of such wage levels that, whatever length the hours of work may be, the pay envelope remains the same as before. It is a new form of the old "right to work," which meant a maintenance of the standard of living. It is also assumed that the additional labor force, recruited to meet wartime exigencies, shall be kept in employment, and the term "unemployment" would be used in connection with the dismissal of these auxiliary workers who in normal times would have remained peacefully at home with no thought of gainful employment. More money is now required in order to live, either because prices have risen or because people are now accustomed to earning their living. There is, moreover, still a fear of unemployment, since the bitterness of recent experience has not been forgotten. There remains, as a legacy of the Depression, a need for security, for which the optimistic American of the past found no need. Jobs and security are words introduced frequently into the conversation of today, and they signify a change in both preoccupations and political attitude. There is no question of revolution, nationalization, or even state socialism, but the idea has been established that full employment must be maintained at all costs, and that, if private industry does not succeed in this, then the state must see to it. The experience of the war years has persuaded the public that the Government can achieve much in this matter and that it would be unpardonable to fail to attempt to keep up, during the years of peace, the rhythm of economic activity achieved during the war.

It is thus evident to what extent the memory of the Great Depression remains alive and influences the reactions of the public. All people over the age of twenty-five have suffered from it and fear within themselves a possible return to it. They also remember Roosevelt and his New Deal, with his promise not to abandon the unemployed, not to wash his hands like Pontius Pilate when the people were in trouble. A page has been turned in American policy and a governmental attitude of *laissez faire* is now unacceptable to the masses. President Truman's acknowledged attachment to free enterprise did not prevent him, in continuing Roosevelt's program, from feeling obliged to promise that, in the event of a crisis that would bring about unemployment, the Government would do all in its power to guarantee full employment.

In spite of the optimism that was restored by the war, America thus appears to believe in the possibility of another crisis. This was, moreover, the almost unanimous opinion of the experts, who did not consider that the reconversion or readaptation of the economy to an equilibrium suitable for peacetime needs could be carried out without a period of painful readjustment. The Americans for once were doubtful of the capabilities of their country, but on this occasion they were wrong.

II

The forecasts of the economists and the fears of the public have not materialized, and no crisis has appeared in the immediate postwar period. On the contrary, the return to peace seems to have brought with it a return of permanent prosperity, although some hesitation was felt from 1949 onward. In 1950, threats of war appeared on the horizon and the outbreak of the Korean War occurred. The prosperity continues from year to year, becoming firmer and stronger, to the astonishment of all observers who are seeking signs of a storm and marvel that they see no cloud on the horizon. Industrial output has recovered in all its branches, and yet the dreaded lack of equilibrium between production and demand has not materialized. Cassandras declare that the situation is unhealthy, that this atmosphere of well-being will exhaust itself with its own success, but continued prosperity gives the lie to their fears. Though the fine, lighthearted security of 1925 has not returned, one is bound to admit that days of prosperity equal to the best that the past could offer have returned again, and have returned to stay.

This return to prosperity is easily explained. During the war years, industry had worked to capacity, and thus those who were not mobilized into the armed forces drew high wages. But, because of restrictions, these wages could not be wholly spent on the artificially reduced amount of consumer goods available (though this reduction appears as plenty when compared with the European privations of the period), and therefore considerable bank balances accrued through saving, which, if not spontaneous, was nonetheless effective. It is natural that these savings, in addition to current earnings, should have contributed to swell the retail market of the immediate postwar period, the demand being all the greater because it had been so long restrained. Household and kitchen equipment, radio sets and motorcars were available almost without limitations, and the purchasing public appeared to have all the money necessary to acquire them. In 1949 a certain vacillation was apparent, the specter of a new crisis already seemed to be appearing on the horizon; but at that moment, returning to its most markedly national characteristic, American economy reintroduced fully the installment-buying system. This gave to business a new impetus which was soon to be accelerated by the rearmament program. Ten years had then passed since the dark days of the Depression, and though the memory of them had not disappeared, at least the obsession about them was dying down. A new generation was growing up who had heard of it only through the stories told by their parents. The idea of a continent privileged in spite of everything was again springing into being, a continent in which the ancient Asiatic or European conception of wages did not apply. America was returning to the fundamentally isolationist conception of a national market capable of absorbing an almost unlimited production, and perhaps it was not mistaken.

What would have happened if at this stage peace had been permanently established and the economy had been obliged to adapt its equilibrium to its conditions we shall never know in view of the events which followed. On the other hand, what we know for certain is that, in January, 1950, the revelation of the treason of Klaus Fuchs, who was employed on top-secret nuclear research, showed America that it probably no longer held a monopoly in the production of the atom bomb. Large-scale rearmament, I believe, started with this. In the month of June of the same year the Korean War came, in totally unexpected fashion, to produce all over again the conditions which, during the five years of World War II, had stimulated unprecedented industrial activity. Thus, in addition to the openings for expansion made by a peace which continued in spite of everything, there was the stimulus of the cold war, while at the same time the progress of technical developments allowed manufacturers to put at the disposal of the public an ever-increasing volume of products at prices within the reach of the consumer. Running parallel to this stimulus, the Marshall Plan served as a sort of export subsidy, and acted as a kind of guarantee against unemployment in disposing of possible surplus production by dumping. Finally, the purchasing power of the masses was upheld by President Truman's Fair Deal, a successor to President Roosevelt's New Deal, which also followed the line of the new attitude adopted by the Democratic party since the crisis: budgetary deficits as advocated by Keynes, and substantial subsidies to agriculture, ex-servicemen, and a wide range of other beneficiaries. The critics cited all these explanations in order to justify the maintenance, which was considered somewhat paradoxical, of an unfailing prosperity.

The end of the Korean War in 1953 raised once more the same problems as those of 1945, namely, how to maintain in peacetime a level of economic activity equal to that reached under the stimulus of wartime conditions. In spite of the well-being which it creates, it is doubtful whether "this feverish state which full health cannot imitate" * can be maintained within the framework of a normal life. The question is difficult to elude in view of the fact that the Americans have become so accustomed to the progressive rhythm of prosperity that they interpret the slightest slowing down as an indication of a crisis.

Indeed, postwar American economy, both before and after the Korean episode, has been influenced by two opposing tendencies which between them have had the effect of giving a kind of stability to the whole, even though it is an equilibrium established by means of movement. There is on the one hand a persistent inflationary movement, which is a result not only of rearmament but also of a social policy instituted by Roosevelt and from which no political party in power can now completely dissociate itself. The Republican party is in principle opposed to inflation and wishes to establish a balanced budget, seeing in that balance a factor that would engender confidence and stimulate private initiative to create employment. According to this doctrine, the state should intervene only when it considers that these

---

* Pascal, *"Cet état fiévreux que la santé ne peut imiter."*

ends are not being fulfilled, and such intervention should obviously be reluctantly applied. On the other hand, the Democrats regard a balanced budget as a secondary consideration, and their chief aim is the maintenance of full employment. One should not, however, underestimate the significance of the deflationary aspect of industrial progress, which, in reducing production costs, lowers the prices of goods offered to the consumer. Such an effort, inspired by the principles of Henry Ford, contains great potentialities for economic development, for both peacetime and wartime. If it does not necessarily bring about an all-round decrease in prices, it nevertheless acts as a brake to the increases which are constantly threatening because of latent inflation.

Thus the American standard of living ceases to appear unhealthy or even abnormal, and one can understand how public opinion expects progressive amelioration of it under all circumstances, be it during peacetime, rearmament, or even war. The following definition was given recently: (Jan. 18, 1954)

Who is the Average American! Statistically he is a man or woman—about 47 years old, with a spouse and two children. He lives in a house which he owns somewhere in the mid-West. He is a high-school graduate. His income is somewhere between $3,500 and $4,000. He has a television set, one and two-tenths cars, two and eight-tenths radios, a 1947 refrigerator. He has about $1,150 in the bank or in some kind of savings. He goes to the movies twice a week and takes a two-week vacation every year with his family. Either his mother or his father are still alive and one member of that generation, either his or his wife's parent, lives with them.

According to the *Kiplinger Letter* of December 21, 1951, 51% of the American population own their own homes, 94% of these homes are equipped with electricity and a radio set, and 21% of them are new, having been built during the last ten years. In 1952 there were 52 million cars in the United States, an average of one per family. And since 1929 the income of each American has increased by 50%.

The maintenance of this prosperity is linked with the maintenance of full employment, which itself depends on the absorption capacity of the internal market, on which industry essentially depends, just as it did in the period immediately following

World War I. European opinion, which is pessimistic and does not fully understand the amazing elasticity of the American economy, believes that overproduction is inevitable, and that is also the opinion, and indeed the hope, of the U.S.S.R. It is difficult to determine how far this idea is justified. Progressive decreases in production costs, with their repercussions on retail prices, may almost indefinitely prevent purchasing power from reaching saturation point. America has understood better than we have the maxim of Henry Ford: "Progress is an attitude or an atmosphere rather than a definite frontier which has to be crossed." These factors operate in favor of continued prosperity, but it must also be borne in mind that American opinion has a particular conception of prosperity or crisis which upsets ordinary reasoning. The Americans are used to the highest level of economic activity —no matter what unusual circumstances have combined to permit them to achieve it—with a progressive rhythm which is constantly breaking its own records. They therefore use the word crisis, or more modestly recession, to apply to anything lower than the maximum, even though this new level may be considered as perfectly satisfactory. Moreover, as soon as any evidence of recession is seen, there is an immediate psychological reaction, as after 1929, and this is extremely serious, since Uncle Sam has not the same nervous resistance as John Bull. He has doubtless analyzed the contingency, and he knows that the neoprosperity after 1940, after 1945, and even after 1950, is associated with conditions which can only be described as abnormal; the cold war, the Korean War, and rearmament, without being the sole or even the principal causes of it, have certainly added an element of continually renewed support to this prosperity, and, after all, the Great Depression was conclusively brought to an end only by the shattering blow of Pearl Harbor. It remains to be seen whether without these stimuli, or others which the Government may apply in times of crisis, the American economy can be maintained at this maximum level of activity to which exceptional events have led it, since its industrial equipment is tuned to maximum output.

The effort of adaptation to a less feverish regime of peace or semipeace may bring about a fall in the economic temperature.

There is nothing here to which the American organism cannot adapt itself, but the psychological tendency is no longer the same; moreover, viewed in its world setting, it appears somewhat like a high tide just beginning to ebb. It will be seen that it is possible for America to do without Europe from an economic point of view, but it is doubtful whether she can isolate herself from an economic outlook which has spread over the whole world.

PART IV

THE SOCIAL BACKGROUND AND THE FORMATION OF PUBLIC OPINION

CHAPTER 24

The Different Stages of Life

★

In the United States everyone is ready to give his opinion on any subject with the greatest assurance, but how is this opinion formed? We shall consider the role played in this by the churches, business, the press, and the radio, but the basic part is played by the social background, where the family, men and women, young and old, hold their respective places in accordance with a sort of hierarchy of influence, subject to change but possessing a certain number of traits characteristic of the whole collective psychology of the Americans.

I

The European is generally contented to have a certain number of ready-made ideas, mostly false, about American family life, and he generally fails to realize that the American is first and foremost a family man. But there exists in the United States a particular conception of married life which is entirely different from anything known in Europe. In Catholic countries marriage is considered as a sacrament, and from this arises the idea of the family as an institution, and this institution as more important than the individuals who form part of it. In the United States, on the other hand, owing to the Protestant tradition, there is no idea of a marriage sacrament, the only sacraments recognized by the Reformed church being baptism and Holy Communion. Marriage is therefore considered as a contract, carried out under the auspices of the church, between two human beings who pledge their faith, and thus the individuals are more important than the institution. This aspect of the question is fundamental since, except for Catholics, it takes away to a large extent the sacramental character of marriage.

In the continental background of the United States, the absence of traditions, the instability of the situation in general, the trend of industrialization, a certain degree of nomadism, and the very Protestant conception that every man should take responsibility for his own life, have led to the development of an idea of marriage in which there is an increasing belief in the rights of the individual, and particularly of woman, in the household. No individual should be bound by a contract, particularly one of the nature of marriage, if his heart is no longer in it. This has led to a decrease in the force and stability of marriage as an institution. It is still recognized as being fundamental, but society no longer has faith in it as an instrument of progress. This tendency is undergoing some correction as the result of the increase in number and influence of Catholics, who do not hesitate vehemently to proclaim their opinions, and also because the Protestant moral outlook upholds the family, and because the Americans, more than the English and about equally with the French, are fond of children—genuinely and in their daily contact with them, not merely from a sense of duty.

In New England in early times the Puritan family was large and was ruled by strong paternal authority, with a severe family moral code, which was Biblical in inspiration. This tradition was passed down to the pioneer, who in his economically isolated environment maintained ascetic virtues and energy, obedience to the *pater familias,* and devotion to a restricted community. These characteristics lasted until almost the end of the nineteenth century, when mass migrations within the country made instability a dominant trait. People were moving from town to town, from job to job, and very often did not even know who their grandfathers had been. This fluidity was greatly increased during the twentieth century, particularly during World War II. In 1947 only 44% of all American households lived in the same house as they had in 1940, 37% of them had moved to another house in the same county, and 20% of them had moved to another county. It is not surprising that, as families lose their territorial stability, psychological instability should become one of the predominant characteristics of the American, and that the dream that one might be born, live, and die in the same house should now be considered old-fashioned.

As inherited tradition has receded before a conception of the life of a single individual, there are no longer family fortunes to be inherited, which established a link between succeeding generations. Taxation on inherited wealth has destroyed much of its value and, since dowries have never figured in American customs, it is for each generation to make its own life. The family has thus escaped from the sordid temptations to which it is subjected in France, but at the same time it has not that amazing solidarity which makes for the greatness of the French family. The conception of the family is reduced to a few duties, progressively decreasing, of parents toward children; the wife, who has become increasingly independent, is often gainfully employed, so that the role of the husband has changed. He has become a partner, not always the senior partner and not necessarily the best paid, even though he may earn more money. In 1947 only 56% of all American families stated that the husband was the sole wage earner, while 25% of married women between the ages of 18 and 64 were gainfully employed. Under these conditions there is naturally a tendency for the family unit to become smaller; while in the nineteenth century five or six children in a family were frequent, in 1950 about two were considered normal. It should be added that in accordance with usual educational practices the children leave their family at an early age and thus escape parental influence very young. When they are away at school, or have left home for good, the family is reduced to a husband who is fully occupied all day with his business and a wife who either has a job or, being freed from other obligations, is ready to undertake social service or to busy herself with any other aspect of the social life of the community. This essential outlook explains very much in American life.

Relations between the sexes are founded on the acknowledgment of the rights of the individual, and there is, traditionally, great liberty of contact between young men and women, which contrasts with the continental and Catholic European outlook. It has for a long time been considered normal that young men and

women should go out unchaperoned, and coeducation is widespread. This attitude has now been accepted almost everywhere
in Europe, but it is not so long ago that it was considered as
American. With this background, marriage is a matter of free,
mutual inclination, something which concerns only the interested
parties and in which love should be the primary consideration;
marriage for financial advantage or marriages of convenience are
judged shocking and immoral. In such unions the intervention of
the family is reduced to nothing; a conception of complete equality between the two partners has been achieved, all ancient ideas
of hierarchy having disappeared, leaving rights and duties exactly
the same on the part of each partner. This is contrary to the tradition of the Mediterranean countries and to a certain extent of
France. The consequence of this conception is that divorce has
become normal and logical. If husband and wife no longer love
each other, honesty demands separation rather than the maintenance of a hypocritical façade, and the Protestant pastor will give
that advice from a moral standpoint. The Catholic church sees
the problem from the angle of respect for the sacrament, which
is the most important consideration; from the moment when God
enters into the matter, any rupture, for whatever excuse, is sac-
rilege, and the priest will rather tolerate some violation of the
marriage pact than allow the scandal of a divorce. A whole literature on the right of happiness, depending implicitly on the
Protestant respect for sincerity, concludes that the rights of the
individual must take first place, that true feeling is the source
and the justification of the union. In this gregarious and pub-
licity-ridden country, the maxim of La Rochefoucauld seems more
appropriate than anywhere else: "There are people who would
never have been in love had they never heard of love." *

From the heights of this dream one descends to the realities
of a household, the American household. There is nothing about
it which resembles European tradition, and particularly French
tradition. There is no idea of the general management of the
house with the husband as administrator in chief, and with detailed organization of the household by the wife, who superin-

* "Il y a des gens qui n'auraient jamais été amoureux s'ils n'avaient
entendu parler de l'amour."

tends the whole domestic side and attends to the constant and prolonged care which her children need. The American conception of the household is at the same time lighter and more wearisome. There are generally no servants, but merely a daily woman; husband and wife have to do all the household chores themselves —cooking, washing, cleaning the shoes, attending to the heating system. Moreover, with perfected household equipment, American homes are usually very well kept. It would seem that while the children are young the responsibility is wearing and amounts to real slavery for the wife; in spite of the practice of baby sitting, it is practically impossible for her to go out. On the other hand, when the children are at school or in college, the household is reduced to almost nothing; the husband always lunches on his own and in the evening any excuse is sufficient for dining at the club, so that many apartments now have only truncated installations, such as kitchenettes and dining alcoves. The home, in the old sense of the word, has had its day. At the same time, the idea of the family has not weakened, in spite of everything, and people who divorce generally remarry. An instinctive scruple, Puritan in tradition, condemns the idea of sexual relations unassociated with marriage, but it is accepted that people may remarry as often as they please. The family tradition remains, but it has lost its stability.

It is easy to understand the confusion which must arise in a country where the two essentially different conceptions of marriage, that of Catholics and that of Protestants, exist side by side. One periodical treated the question in the form of a sort of diptych: "What it means to marry a Protestant" and "What it means to marry a Catholic." The significance is, indeed, entirely different. In a Catholic marriage the priest maintains an interest in both the education and the conception of children, and if at the time of birth either child or mother must be sacrificed, the husband may fear that the priest will demand the sacrifice of the mother. Moreover, the sacramental tie once made must be considered permanent. People elsewhere fail to understand the inflexibility with which the Catholic hierarchy of the United States applies these principles. A Protestant marriage is completely different. The vows are more personal and possibly made with greater sincerity because they do not include any outside intervention, but fundamentally the partners will share only a restricted part of their lives, all the more so because they realize that they are not necessarily pledging themselves for their whole lives. There is less settling down. An American woman once explained to me that it is similar to the way in which the traveler will not unpack his trunks if he believes that he is going to change his room in the hotel.

This point of view explains the dual popularity of marriage and divorce in the United States. Between 1867 and 1947 the population increased fourfold, but in 1947 there were six times as many marriages and forty-four times as many divorces as in 1867; and for two million marriages there were 483,000 divorces, *i.e.*, 22.5%. While the spectacular divorce dispensaries of Reno or Las Vegas in Nevada are famous, it would be incorrect to consider divorce in America as a scandal. It is an institution which has become accepted as part of the normal course of marriage. The increase in the birth rate is linked with an increase in the marriage rate. The interest taken in the problem of union between the two sexes has never been greater, and in no country have professors, investigators, moralists, and statisticians ever studied the problem in such large numbers, or drawn from the masses of facts and figures assembled such a striking harvest of physiological, social, and moral conclusions. They are listened to, moreover, for America has faith in the expert.

II

These conditions directly influence the life and upbringing of American youth, but they suffer less from them than one might believe. When they are with their parents, the children share their life in an atmosphere of genuine familiarity. There is nothing of the English tradition (now largely extinct) where a trained nanny, not without a certain amount of ceremony, brings down her well-behaved little charges to see the grownups at a time decided beforehand. No, in America the child is there all the time, listened to rather than listening, never crossed, corrected, or put in his place, for, according to a doctrine that would have pleased Rousseau, the personality must be allowed to develop in full freedom. The child is allowed to join in all conversations and take part in decisions, and he warns his parents of the "complexes" of his young brother. He is not badly brought up, he is just not brought up at all. The European finds him unbearable, but this unrestrained freedom of conduct is, all the same, attractive.

This initial period, moreover, ends very early, for the child is sent to school when about six or seven, and thence to college. From then onward he visits his home only at rare intervals and thus becomes accustomed to leading his own life, to entertaining his own friends, who are rarely subject to parental scrutiny, and to paying his own visits to the movies, at least twice a week. Television may now keep him at home, but this is a recent development. As far as his parents are concerned, his upbringing is finished, so that divorce, frequent as it may be, does not always produce the ill effects which might be feared. To whom, now, does the child look for his education and general guidance, insofar as, in the European or at least the French sense of the term, he receives any? It is not to his father, who is away all day at the office and whom he treats with the barely respectful familiarity with which he might treat an elder brother. The father, if he has no authority, is devoted to his family and ready to undertake all sorts of humble tasks, such as pushing the baby's perambulator, a duty which in continental Europe has remained a female monopoly. In the United States the real power in the household belongs to the wife, whose influence, particularly on her sons, is predominant and survives the stages of their early childhood. Although American society relies more on the school, the university, and the church for its nation-building, this matriarchy, the prestige of which is clear to any observer, remains fundamental in the social life of the United States.

This upbringing, which allows the child the freedom of a runaway horse, produces curious and unexpected results. How is it that the American, once he has attained his majority, appears to us as the perfect conformist? It is, perhaps, because he has exhausted during his childhood and adolescence practically all his indiscipline and anarchy, so that he has no difficulty later in life in integrating himself into a collective society, which he himself fully accepts. But it must be borne in mind that, during the period of life in which the European exerts no influence, being considered as still in his swaddling clothes, the young American makes a considerable impression on a world dominated by demagogy and youth.

III

The American matriarchy reflects the power of woman, whatever age she may be. In her youth she is treated as a queen, sought after, showered with gifts, accorded all privileges by the stronger sex, and, from adolescence onward, enjoys complete liberty. She marries young, and the tendency is for the average marriage age, which was twenty-one in 1940, to become younger. The average age of the mother at the birth of her first child is twenty-two years, and at that time the American woman comes to a sudden realization of the duties, limitations, and hardship of married life in the United States. She has no more liberty, physical or moral, for, in the small towns at any rate, public opinion criticizes her narrowly. The good time is over. Then the young wife shows her capabilities as the organizer of the household, and in this she is far superior to the Englishwoman and in many ways similar to the Frenchwoman. She reigns over her house and children; every outing must be organized and planned beforehand, with the cooperation of baby sitters. Those who state that there is no family life in America are wrong, but it is true to say that this family life finishes sooner than elsewhere, and then the wife finds her liberty again. I do not know whether, in a home deserted by the children, the mother feels the kind of emptiness which Michelet describes in *La Femme*, but it is true that she often feels at a loss for an occupation, with her energy undiminished and eager to be utilized. Society women frequent cocktail parties, bridge parties, or country clubs. The intellectually minded in the provinces haunt local literary societies. The more serious, and these probably form the majority of women, make it their task, in the true Calvinist tradition, to work for the good of the community, in associations for social progress, religious activities, or in public life, where their influence is considerable. There are in no country so many women who devote themselves to the public good, concern themselves with social reforms; from this, since the whole country is imbued with a semireligious idea of service, comes a dangerous combination of morals and politics, as seen in temperance societies, in anticolonialism, and in numerous leagues in support of good government, the effects of which are not uniformly beneficial.

As long as his own interests are not imperiled, man submits to this ascendancy of the sex which has more leisure, more culture, and more energy for the quest of either pleasure or moral advancement. Society is indeed led by women. But men finally reserve for themselves a private domain where they are determined to remain masters, free from outside intervention. This may be their business, their club, or their sports. In brief, they prefer men's company, with the result that in social, professional, or intellectual life there is certainly less association between the sexes than in Europe.

If the system does not end in separation it at least brings about a dual claim for freedom, on the one hand between the two parents and on the other between the parents and their children. Youth claims independence of the older generation, which in its turn frees itself by a systematic practice of birth control. In the United States reproduction has become an act deliberately willed. It is an adventurous attempt on the part of humanity to substitute controlled birth for natural instinct. At one time it was believed that America was moving toward sterility. The baby boom has corrected this tendency, but it should perhaps be considered as nature's return to the offensive, which has coincided with one of the setbacks to civilization produced by war.

IV

If, thirty years ago, I had attempted to consider the various stages of life in the United States, I should scarcely have thought of speaking of old age. Then it appeared that existence ended with full maturity, after which there was suddenly nothing more. One had the impression that there were no old people, for, if they existed, they were never to be seen. The Chinese ancestor considered as the depository of all wisdom, the old man as described by Victor Hugo, *"on voit la lumière"* (in whose eyes light shines), or the European statesman full of experience and counsel, were all types unknown in America.

This is no longer true. The average age has increased from 17 years in 1826 to 30 in 1950, and there are now four times as many over sixty-fives as at the beginning of the century. There are now 43 million over forty-fives, compared with 13 million in 1900. In the decade 1940-1950, the over-sixty-five age group increased by 36%, and the forty-five to sixty-five group by 16.7%. There is, consequently, a whole category of elderly people who are conscious both of their age and of their existence as a group, who are determined to say: "We count!" It is a new and paradoxical attitude which has appeared in American social and political life since the Great Depression.

The problem for the elderly, in an economy where traditionally everything is dependent on employment, is to know how they can manage to live, particularly in a period when the purchasing power of the dollar is diminishing. In the over-sixty-five group three-quarters have pensions or are supported by their families, and one-quarter have jobs, these being more easily acquired since the war had the effect of extending the working life. But from the time of the large-scale unemployment of thirty years ago, the necessity of a policy toward old people has made itself apparent. Simply because of their numbers and their votes, the existence of elderly people had to be recognized and their demands taken into account. This situation has continued to exist, since the basic tendency of the population to age appears more permanent than the increase in youth due to the impetus given to the birth rate.

Since influence can be exercised only through organization, elderly people have organized themselves. Reference has already been made to the Townsend Clubs, which total five million members. The old California doctor has had numerous imitators. Among them mention should be made of the Allen brothers with their Ham-and-Eggs plan, Harry Jones and "Each Man a King," or the old Hollywood showman George H. McLain and his Citizens' Committee for Old Age Pensions; McLain, whose meetings end with prayer, speaks every week over twenty-two California radio stations. In the progressive Pacific states, where there is an abnormal number of old people, a whole policy has been developed concerning pensions. California legislation provides for seventy-five dollars a month for all persons over sixty-three years of age, with no disqualification if the recipient owns a house or a car. The state of Washington has instituted a similar pension scheme for people over sixty-five, which also includes free hospital service, rent subsidies, and cancellation of unpaid taxes. It is dubious whether these benefits can continue to increase, for they constitute an unwise overture to people who will be a greater charge to the community than an assistance in its development. Nevertheless, the problem has been considered, here as elsewhere, not only from the point of view of the beneficiaries, but also from the angle of the children who seek to be freed from the traditional responsibility of supporting their parents in their old age, parents who, indiscreetly or not, live much longer than they did in former times. Concern about insurance, whether individual or collective, marks a new stage in American evolution. I do not know whether the prestige of the elderly as such has increased, but it is an incontestable fact that they are there in evidence and are making their presence felt.

v

If, in comparison with Europe, I had to decide the factors that most greatly influence the formation of public opinion in the United States, I should say, I think, women and the young. Man in his maturity no doubt holds the levers that ensure command, and old age has learned to make its claims heard, but it is the feminine outlook, imbued with moral idealism and Protestant in inspiration, which colors the whole life of the country, while youth and even childhood, through a kind of out-bidding, gain the public ear by representing the future as opposed to the past, which is old age, and the almost past, which is maturity.

CHAPTER 25

Public Opinion

★

The United States is par excellence a country where public opinion plays an important role, inspiring, orientating, and controlling the policy of the nation. Nothing can be achieved or endure without it, and its veto is final. It is characterized by the fact that it is both more spontaneous than anywhere else in the world and also more easily directed by efficient propaganda technique than in any other country.

The essential problem to be studied here is the relative importance of propaganda technique and spontaneity in formulating American public opinion.

I

Among the influences that may sway public opinion, the one with which one first comes into contact is business. American business is a powerful organization, endowed with great unity. In thinking of American business one thinks instinctively of Wall Street, but one would have had more reason for doing so thirty years ago or particularly in the last century. Large corporations, like General Motors or Du Pont, now occupy first place, always provided that one should not really place in the first rank the influence of the average businessman of Main Street, the Chambers of Commerce, and the Rotary Clubs. The whole of American business, however, forms a closely bound bundle of interests, which express themselves in a way of life, of administration and government, and a certain attitude toward society, production, and exchange of goods, men's ways of dealing with each other, and international relations. According to the businessman everything in the state should be

226

planned with production in view, it being taken for granted that business interests and the nation's interests coincide. It was in perfect good faith that the president of General Motors, having become Secretary of Defense, could say: "What is good for General Motors is good for the United States." At every phase of this study we have met with this utilitarian philosophy, and it is in its name that business overrides the interests of the community to secure the lead in public opinion.

The Republicans are traditionally the business party, by reason of an outlook which is neither reactionary nor strictly conservative, but which puts production before politics, or rather considers that production and politics are one and the same thing. Babbitt boasts a good sound business administration, and the rank and file of the party scarcely find it astonishing that Eisenhower's first cabinet should have been composed of "eight multimillionaires and a plumber." The Democrats are not hostile to business, but they are less dependent on it; they find their main support elsewhere. Before Roosevelt's presidency it was said that the chariot of state could advance on Democratic tires, but that it would make more progress on Republican ones. It appeared that the prosperity of former years was a Republican foundation. Democratic prosperity was known under Truman, but businessmen feel more at ease with the Republicans. Powerful resources enable the business world to uphold by means of publicity, the press, and literature an optimistic atmosphere, which persuades people of the possibility of climbing to the top of the ladder, just as much today as in the past, showing them that the American system of free enterprise which offers such possibilities is the best in the world. A collection of the *Reader's Digest* presents a reflection of this propaganda.

The committees of action and social reform must be placed on at least the same level. The moralizing and reforming passion which descends from the Calvinist tradition and the philosophers of the eighteenth century, springs from sincere and selfless fanaticism. The conviction that one should moralize or convert the state to Christianity is not limited to believers. It penetrates the whole country, including Catholic circles, though the latter consider the question from a particular angle. The general conviction, however, has given rise to a whole host of leagues and associations which, even when they have no religious affiliation, remain nonetheless marked with the indelible imprint of Protestantism and Puritanism. The action of these groups is often inspired by passionate feelings, particularly as far as women, who play an important role in them, are concerned. This is also true of the pastors who, as we have already seen, often act as champions of the people, intervening unhesitatingly in public affairs. Hence the passionate character of some campaigns, such as that of prohibition, where fanatical supporters did not hesitate to borrow the most questionable weapons of the politician. It would be difficult to exaggerate the power of these pressure groups, whose technique has reached a kind of perfection. Not contented with stirring up agitation through the press, the radio, and conference campaigns, they make use of professional lobbyists, carrying out their plan of action in the lobbies of Congress. This lobbying has become normal in parliamentary life to such an extent that the Federal Lobbying Act of 1946 was introduced in order to restrain its operations. These groups have learned how to bring pressure to bear on candidates during election time, then to supervise the voting of the elected members, reminding them of their campaign promises through a harassing correspondence and finally by veiled threats which sometimes have an indefinable odor of blackmail. In this regime of public opinion the influence of the pressure groups is at least equal to that of the press and perhaps even more efficient.

The influence of the churches is seen behind these groups, even those which are of purely lay character. Their right to state their opinion on major political and social problems is fully recognized. Their intervention, which appears natural, belongs to a tradition as old as the nation itself. Some Protestant denominations are more politically minded, such as the Baptists or the Methodists, but the Catholic church has adapted itself very successfully and rapidly to this American custom. Certain religious bodies may even be criticized for paying more attention to social reform than to religious propaganda in the strict sense of the term, but in American Protestantism there is the tendency, as we have already seen, for social and religious aims to become merged. Catholic action is centered rather on the defense of the family, the moral discipline of the community, and the condemnation of divorce, birth control, and sterilization, which are in opposition to its doctrine. Protestant action is felt less in the family and for the family than in the community and for the community, which it seeks to reform, and in a spirit of progress, characteristic of Franklin and Jefferson, which considers, not without some degree of optimism, that man and society can be perfected indefinitely.

Idealism is placed before interests in this powerful moral current, but a moment is always reached when interests inevitably stake their claim. It must be borne in mind that, to the degree to which they are religious, businessmen give financial support to their churches, and they do not like to hear from the pulpit theories that might harm production. It is also possible that some national currents are not in line with authentic Christian idealism. Experience has shown that the churches lack the courage to oppose movements upheld by public opinion, such as warmongering, anti-Communism, national exclusivism, for fear that they will be bypassed, swamped, or left behind. Eventually a struggle arises between the different influences. When business, the lobbies, and the churches are on the same side their co-operation is irresistible, for interest and inclination are pulling in the same direction. A perfect example of this was seen at the time of the prohibition vote. Through a kind of confusion not surprising in a country of utilitarian civilization, the moral attitude can in good faith recommend increase in output, and it is equally in good faith that industrial egoism believes itself to be motivated by public interest.

The problem that remains to be studied is what happens when business and social action are in opposition. Then it is by no means certain that business will have the last word. Wall Street stands far from the ideological axis of the nation and looks at problems eccentrically, while in Main Street local pressure may compel businessmen to consider the religious point of view. Public opinion is sentimental; as far as it is concerned, interest is not always a decisive argument. In conflicts between workers and employers the problem is Roosevelt *versus* Wall Street. Business capital may control the press, money, and a wealth of sponsored literature, but the New Deal or the Fair Deal, handled by leaders expert in the use of broadcasting or the appeal of the physical presence of the whistle stop, can exert on public opinion an influence which it is powerless to resist. It is not certain, moreover, that the wage earner is inevitably supported by public opinion as a whole, which remains independent of political parties, social classes, and organization. And here I come back to the spontaneity of American public opinion, which struck me from the beginning.

II

The instruments that may be used to influence public opinion are no less powerful. There is, first of all, the press, the liberty of which is guaranteed under the Constitution. According to the Bill of Rights, Article 1, Congress shall make no laws abridging the freedom of speech, or of the press. This, to the United States, is an essential freedom.

Nineteenth-century tradition included a large number of newspapers, each of which expressed a certain local point of view. There were 2,226 newspapers at the end of the century compared with 24 in 1800. Under this system the press was essentially parochial in character, the papers were run by local men who were more or less personally known, and whose opinion was sought on day-to-day topics. The press then appeared as the normal expression of a life which was decentralized, familiar, jovial, and personal in tone. The charming book of William Allen White, *In Our Town,* gives an excellent description of a typical Kansas city and of its press fifty years ago. National problems aroused local reaction, which was expressed in editorials conceived and written locally, at the same time inspiring and representing a public opinion whose sources were largely autonomous. The second half of the nineteenth century saw the growth of a type of high-class newspaper like the New York *Times,* the New York *Herald,* the St. Louis *Post-Dispatch,* and the New York *World.* These were regional and almost national in compass and they greatly exceeded their predecessors in power, but they retained at the same time their tradition of personality, with men such as James Gordon Bennett, or more especially Joseph Pulitzer.

A new period was to begin with the twentieth century, an age which integrated the press in its turn into the general technical evolution. Following the approved methods of industrial rationalization, an attempt was made to produce news in the same way as any other product. Newspapers, organized in series like chain stores, had a tendency to follow the laws of mass production, and this meant that, with their increased avidity for clients and for publicity, they were logically condemned to conform in size to that of the great industrial enterprises. The consequence of this was that while an important paper with great personality like the New York *Times* could survive, the attractive and brilliant New York *World* disappeared, and the traditional local paper could scarcely be maintained in its old form. Facing the competition of rivals better equipped for mass production, it was controlled, bought up, or merely disappeared. These circumstances gave rise to an enormous increase in circulation, which rose from 24 million in 1909 to 55 million in 1951 (46 million for the Sunday press), but the number of papers published fell from 2,600 to 1,890; periodicals numbered 6,977 and Sunday papers 574. With the exception of the New York *Times* there is no paper with a country-wide circulation, but the press of the large cities, eventually taking precedence over the local press, extends its activities to whole regions and in some cases competition has been eliminated. In very large urban agglomerations two or more papers succeed in existing simultaneously, but in general there is a tendency for only one to survive; 40% of the dailies and 35% of the Sunday editions enjoy local monopoly.

As a result, the character of the editing surreptitiously changed, for, in spite of outward appearances of individuality, there is a tendency for the newspaper no longer to be edited on the spot. It often belongs to financial interests foreign to the town in which it appears and much of its material comes from outside, including, naturally, news received through syndicates, but, in particular, press association articles written by stars of national reputation for a whole chain of newspapers. This type of article, which appeared in the weeklies from 1875 onward, has now invaded the daily press. It is not surprising that under this system, in which news and publicity are more important than discussion, the old editorial has been reduced to a short paragraph. There is no question of the quality of the news having declined; on the contrary, apart from the temptation of sensationalism, the besetting sin of the Americans, it is of an excellent standard. The reporting, in keeping with the true genius of the nation, is lively, alert, full of picturesque, well-observed details, and filled with a wealth of realistic portraits, faithful evocations of the sittings of Congress and its committees. Miscellaneous news items, formerly rather intrusive, have now been relegated to their proper place. This striking progress in the presentation of the news has been paralleled by a weakening in political bias. The masses must not be discontented, while at the same time care must be taken to deal tactfully with powerful business interests, particularly those which supply publicity matter. This results in some measure of timidity in the editorials, which hesitate to go counter to the basic currents of public opinion, and discussion is largely limited to the "Letters to the Editor." It has been said that the editor sometimes writes these letters himself when he wishes to broadcast an idea for which he does not care to assume responsibility. It has also given rise to the use of the slogan, a publicity device, alongside argument, a discussion device.

At all events the full liberty of the press remains, and experience has shown that the existence of free newspapers, large or small, remains possible. What may appear disconcerting in the formation of public opinion is that the tide appears to have turned. Opinions expressed in the press no longer come from particular localities but are devised in a few specialized centers and then broadcast throughout the country as a whole. This is an advantage from the point of view of capital, which prefers to make use of the powerful instrument of the national press, and it also explains why the press is mainly Republican in tendency. But it must be borne in mind that the leading writers of the press association articles are free and that their lavish pay is a supplementary guarantee of their independence. It is, however, an indubitable fact that in this system the public is guided from above, and this is not a healthy method of forming public opinion.

Every citizen receives daily a mass of news which is far greater than anything existing anywhere else in the world. The smallest newspaper consists often of 24 or 36 pages and the Sunday papers of 60, 80, or even more. This represents an enormous waste of paper in order to produce editions of a size which cannot be put into one's coat pocket. The abundance of the news, moreover, defeats its own object; since there can be no question of reading everything, people in the long run are content with scanning the headlines. These, it must be admitted, are cleverly planned to give a summary of the news, but they offer only a lightning impact. It remains to be seen whether the press is really effective in its influence. This is doubtful, for the majority of the papers which appeared during Roosevelt's presidency were Republican and yet he was re-elected more than once. In 1952 most of the papers, even the Republican ones, upheld Stevenson and yet he was defeated. Is public opinion really formed elsewhere?

The radio, which has not replaced the newspaper and has even in certain cases incited the public to read it, has become a necessity. Everyone has one—in 1952 there were 114.5 million radio sets in use. Indeed, its use is more widespread than that of the telephone or the motorcar. When there is a need for economy, the man in the street will defend his radio passionately; it will be the last thing that he is willing to give up. News not only comes through more quickly by radio than through the press, but it also brings to its listeners the very voice of the orator, so that it is almost as if he were present. Roosevelt, Truman, Eisenhower, and Stevenson are there! The news commentator speaks personally to his listeners, his voice has become something familiar which one finds pleasure in hearing each day. It is a human contact which establishes an almost personal relationship, it comes easily, under conditions which insidiously make for laziness, for one has only to listen in a passive manner. In a regime which allows free discussion, the state has not made the radio into a privileged instrument of authority. It is federally controlled according to the interests, the needs, and the requirements of the public, and any propaganda is allowed fair use of it. For example, the use made of it by the "Radio Priest" is familiar to us. But there is no doubt that the radio has a tendency to divert the trends of public opinion into particular channels, and it thus plays its part on the side of grouping rather than individual development.

The widespread use of television is so recent that we are still at the stage of wondering what effect it will have on the formation of public opinion. We realize, however, that its effects will be, indeed already are, considerable. There are more than 33 million television sets in the United States and this number is increasing, even more among the humbler classes than among the wealthier. All political demonstrations of any significance are now televised. In July, 1952, on the eve of the two great party conventions in Chicago, there was still some doubt as to whether the delegates would submit willingly to being televised while carrying out their functions. But at the last minute the question was not even asked, since it was clear that refusal would have been universally condemned. The public is not content with hearing, it also wishes to see. This process of combining the two has created a contact which has the power to move the masses deeply. No declaration through press or radio would have been sufficient to put over the extraordinary defense of Vice-President Nixon at the time of his candidacy. Whatever the worth of his arguments, his appearance on television with his wife had a powerful effect, one which played exclusively on the emotions. It was the modern counterpart of the classical eloquence of the forum.

The effect of televising the proceedings of an assembly is extraordinary, for the viewer is really present, follows the ups and downs of the discussion and almost feels the atmosphere. As televised, the Senate investigating committee, in which Senator Estes Kefauver led the prosecution against political corruption, and the Senate committee hearings on the army and Senator Joseph McCarthy impressed public opinion in a way which articles in the newspapers or a simple auditory account on the radio would have been powerless to achieve. In this connection there is also the example of the two party conventions at Chicago in 1952 to designate the candidates for the presidency. One could see that the delegates were making an effort to appear to advantage, since their behavior could be observed. It was also possible to conclude that, since this was a question of news necessarily controlled, the television screen gave rise to mass reactions. "People who have told me about this event," a correspondent wrote to me, "have invariably said the same things about it and in terms which recalled the words used by the commentator." The reactions were all the more gregarious in view of the fact that at that time television was beginning to penetrate into the humblest circles. "A Negro charwoman whom I employ," this same correspondent wrote to me, "went back home to her family in Tennessee during the Democratic convention. She told me when she came back that she had followed all the ups and downs of it, as radio and television were used by almost everybody in her circle, even in the most isolated villages."

Doubtless the tacticians will continue to make decisive arrangements in the privacy of their hotel rooms, but in its main sittings the convention is carried out under the eyes of the whole nation. The task of the reporters is considerably eased by television; they are not content with watching the progress of the meetings, but may be seen from time to time going into the lobbies to see the televised image, since in this way, so they say, they can see certain details which escape them when they see the proceedings in the flesh. This news technique on the part of the professional is interesting, since it increases the scope of individual vision.

Television is, however, only a substitute, for one sees with a more intense sense of reality when one is really there. This is, moreover, the opinion of professional politicians. At the beginning of the presidential campaign it had been considered that television would relieve the candidates of the classic tours around the country, but by the end of the conventions, trains and aircraft were prepared, and Eisenhower and Stevenson erupted among the electorate, shaking everyone by the hand, embracing little girls, emerging in pajamas from their sleeping cars in front of enthusiastic supporters who were eager to see their hero in flesh and blood. There has been a change, however, for since the advent of television the American reacts to the sessions of Congress, any investigating committees, and any U.N. conference as if he had himself been present. I use the word react advisedly, for his opinion is formed less by intellectual judgment than by an almost physical impression of his senses. The sentimental and emotional character of the nation is finding once more its full outlet, under conditions of individuality and spontaneity, which are curiously contradictory to tendencies which might have been considered, unilaterally, in a unique sense as moving toward collective movements and standardization.

III

The problem that remains is how to unravel from these factors, which are on the whole contradictory, an explanation of the conditions which have led to the formation of American public opinion.

Since the eighteenth century and until the eve of World War I, the essential part was played by environment, by the occupations which made men what they were, by their family background, by the church which inspired them, by conversations in their bar or club, and by their local press. The democracy of the nineteenth century functioned under this regime which was handed down from the eighteeenth century and was founded on respect for private property, the pioneer tradition, local feeling, and slow communications.

Today the news system has developed to such an extent that the man in the street could know everything if only he had time to read the whole of his newspaper, hear all the broadcasts, and view all the television programs. His difficulty is one of judgment, of choosing between facts and discussions too numerous to absorb. Ideally he has the right to apply his criticism freely to all the information which is impartially offered to him. In point of fact he is provided with objective news to a lesser degree than that to which he is guided by slogans, in line with approved methods of publicity. His opinion is, therefore, formed under the influence of complex factors which in the long run are contradictory: personal or group interests; pressure exerted unconsciously on him by the press, the radio, and publicity; the traditions of the family background or the reaction of the temperament of the individual to facts, now increasingly multiplied by television. I have reached the contradictory conclusion that the American's docility leads him to follow passively the lines indicated by propaganda but that, when he is faced with facts or personalities, his reactions retain their spontaneity.

As far as his spontaneous reactions are concerned, the American retains for the whole of his life a certain measure of the license which he has known in his childhood. If anything makes an impression on him he will say so immediately without the least reserve or embarrassment, and if he pronounces a judgment he does so without the slightest apprehension, particularly if it is a question of condemning the foreigner, for moral reprobation pleases him. This is something exceedingly personal; yet, when it has been submitted to the steam-roller action of assimilation, it appears that individual reactions are curiously similar, to such an extent that a conversation with one's barber or taxi driver will invariably give one a fairly accurate estimate of general opinion. It is, therefore, clear that collective currents are formed which could be irresistible; the Government may orientate them, but cannot always stem them. We have already said that it is the women and the youth of the United States who count for most in its psychology. The same characteristics can be recognized in the formation of its public opinion—youthful, sensitive, and passionate.

CHAPTER 26

The National Spirit

★

It was for a long time believed that the United States had no solid national spirit, that the country was too large and particularly too diverse in its origins, that sooner or later it would split up, incapable of standing against trials. History has shown the contrary to be true; the national feeling has never been stronger than at present.

In its origins this sentiment sprang from a contrast and an affirmation of independence, a claim of independence from the old mother country. On the eve of the Revolution most Americans had no thought of being anything but English, but they wanted their own administration, their desire being for autonomy rather than for independence. A truly national spirit appeared when it became evident that no real autonomy could be achieved without independence. Thus, without being deliberately anti-British, their early patriotism became by the force of circumstances the opponent of an oppressive mother country. Curiously enough this hostility persists. It is upheld by the Irish element in the population, but it is to be found in a diffused form as a kind of inferiority complex as regards England, an inexpressible but persistent fear of being tricked by "perfidious Albion." An assertion of the independence of the American continent strengthens this attitude. America as a whole must be free from Europe and avoid all domination and all intervention from her. This is the foundation of the famous Monroe Doctrine, which is not entirely forgotten even now that Europe has been weakened. The Americans are conscious of the existence of a new world distinct from the old, the new world standing for liberty and boundless possibilities, the old world ap-

pearing by contrast a seat of despotism, persecutions, wretched-
ness, reactionary tendencies, and revolution. The two World Wars
have only served to strengthen this feeling. American soldiers who
came to fight in Europe returned more American than ever, in the
continental sense of the term. Paradoxically enough, the mass immigration of the nineteenth century served only to strengthen
the sense of patriotism among the newcomers. Grateful for the
welcome they received, anxious to become assimilated as soon as
possible, they became the most convinced of all Americans. Thus,
to the original patriotism, which was essentially Anglo-Saxon,
must be added a second, no less deep, in which the old fear of
English domination is replaced by a fear of attack from the old
world which the emigrants have repudiated.

II

With twentieth-century prosperity came a new strengthening of
the American national spirit. Owing to contacts made during
World War I, the nation became conscious, mainly by contrast,
of its great wealth, of the power which it gave, and of the privilege
which it constituted. The United States had a place apart in the
world by reason of its standard of living, and its industrial progress
made it the technical leader of civilization. In its continental isolation it felt sheltered from threats of invasion, far from the European bear garden or the Asiatic hell. The consciousness of a privileged position was not limited to the realms of big business, but
was extended to the worker or to any American, whoever he might
be. The outcome of this was a patriotism that was basically material and associated with a spirit of defense and, to a certain degree,
exclusivism, but also with extraordinary pride.

The pride was legitimate, particularly on the part of those men
who had worked to build up the national fortune; from this arose a
singular confusion between utilitarianism as inspired by Bentham,
a civic sense that was purely Calvinist in tradition, and a sincere
devotion to human progress. There is a tendency in some quarters
to confuse the national spirit with the production of wealth, and a
dual exclusivism is the result. The traditional America, which is
Anglo-Saxon and Protestant, is trying to defend itself against con-
tamination from the Slavo-Latin and Catholic element of the more

recent immigration wave, and the resistance is essentially politico-religious. But parallel to this there is anxiety to maintain the standard of living in spite of any competition or criticism coming from outside, and this attitude is to be found in all Americans. Reactions of this category have been in evidence since the nineteenth century, exemplified by the American Protective Association (A.P.A.) or the Know Nothing movement; but the attitude of the twentieth century appears different, defensive and exclusive rather than liberal and welcoming.

It is a question of nationalism rather than mere patriotism. It is expressed in a characteristically American way by local patriotism, where every citizen extols the superiority of his state, his city, his community, and is proud to make financial contribution to it, to help it by physical effort or by propaganda. The booster is convinced that his town is permanently growing, that it will become the largest and most beautiful of all, even if it is "the biggest little town in the world." He is by nature a "bull," and everyone agrees with him in condemning the disparager, a skeptic or possibly just a realist, who does not associate himself with the enthusiasm of his environment. It is the advice given to a group of children in Middletown:

> You must have community spirit. You must think that there is no finer town in the whole United States than this. There is no finer school than yours, no finer parents than yours, no finer opportunities anywhere than you have right here. . . . I tell you there's no lovelier place on God's footstool than this old state of ours.*

Sinclair Lewis describes as follows a convention in which Babbitt took part: "It chanced that all the delegates from Pioneer belonged to the Benevolent and Protective Order of Elks, and they produced an enormous banner lettered: Best People on Earth—Boost Pioneer, Oh Eddie!"

It would be wrong to mock at this, for the United States owes much to their boosting, and other countries might well envy them for it.

National patriotism, moreover, is orientated in the same direction. The Americans are all spontaneously and almost naïvely con-

---

* Robert S. Lynd and Helen Merrell Lynd, *Middletown*, New York, Harcourt, Brace, 1929, p. 487.

vinced of American superiority and, though they are encouraged by constant propaganda, one wonders whether that propaganda is really necessary. Here are a few examples given in *Middletown* * of this bluff:

"The United States is the best country on earth and should give her ideals to the rest of the world." (Extract from a sermon.)

"I want to see America first; then when I go abroad I can tell them all about America and what a fine place it is." (Extract from a Rotary Club speech.)

"We cannot read [the history of the United States] without the conviction growing and deepening that the hand of God had part in its writing and that a purpose more glorious than any yet attained lies in its development." (Extract from the Middletown press.)

"Because America has this government, the best government on God's earth, America can bring salvation to the world."

This propaganda involves a constant demand for enrollment among the different branches of civic activity of the community. Immediately after World War I there was a mad outburst of "days" and "weeks" inaugurated in this spirit. For example, here is the list offered by Middletown:

"Suburban Day"; "Home Sewing Week"; "One Hour Dress Week"; "Ice Cream Week," with a special essay contest on "Why I Should Eat Ice Cream Every Day"; "Truth Week," fostered by the Advertising Club and aiming to "build confidence through truth in advertising"; "Father's Day"; "Mother's Day"; "Boys' Day"; "Boys' Week," "a nation-wide movement to emphasize the fact that our boys are loyal"; "Thrift Week," with its "Own Your Own Home Day," "Savings Day," "Pay Your Bills Day," "Make Your Will Day," "Insure Yourself Day," "Live on a Budget Day," "Share with Others Day"; "Home Beautiful Week"; "Education Week"; "National Picture Week"; "Art Week"; 'Music Week"; "Odd Fellows Reconsecration Week"; "Joy Week," in which the ministers were asked to preach on "Does it Pay to Do Good Turns?"; "Week of Prayer"; "Father and Son Week"; "Mother and Daughter Week"; "Go to Church Sunday"; "Labor Sunday"; "Golden Rule Sunday," endorsed by the governor, who "would like to see the Golden Rule enshrined in every heart and believes it the solution for numerous situations"; "Saratoga Day"; "Clean Up and Paint Up Week"; "Child

* *Ibid.*, pp. 489-90.

Health Week"; "Tuberculosis Day"; "Non-spit Week"; "Hospital Dona-
tion Day"; "Tax Reduction Week"; "Fire Prevention Week"; "Courtesy
Week," with an essay contest on the value of courtesy; "Pep Week";
"Constitution Week"; "Defense Day"; "Buddy Poppy Day." *

This extraordinary combination of morals, progress, the church,
and business interests is the expression of a utilitarian idealism
which does not appear contradictory to the Americans and which
explains why this nation has become great. But one is also led
to understand why La Rochefoucauld's maxims are not appreciated there.

One must be a "joiner" and behave as such. An implicit code
requires any businessman who wants to succeed to be a member
of the Chamber of Commerce, of a church of good social standing, of the Republican party, of a country club, of a Freemasons'
Lodge, and of the committee of the Young Men's Christian Association (Y.M.C.A.). His wife will be a member of a fashionable club, of a country club, and a literary society, and she will
take her place on the committees of various social and religious
organizations. The pressure of local opinion is very strong and
very indiscreet; if one wants to succeed there must be no standing apart or failure to conform. Public opinion, organized and
controlled, forces conformity to accepted standards of respectability, and it is significant to note that this includes holding or not
holding certain opinions. Those who do not conform are boy-
cotted, they are not exactly persecuted but they are left to one
side and finally excluded. This is a far-reaching effect of the religious concept that sanctifies worldly enterprise and sincerely believes that such a view is possible. The Latin considers at heart
that life according to the Christian dogma is impracticable; rel-
egating saintliness into a walled enclosure, he declines to mix
heavenly with earthly affairs, and is readier for absolution than
repentance. We see here the Nordic outlook which has reached
a state of confusion between the affairs of man and God. Curiously enough, this sort of sanctification of civic life ends in the
suppression of man in the state and a sort of tyranny of com-
munal life, all the more serious in that it has divine right.

* *Ibid.*, p. 491.

III

Exclusivism was shown sporadically from the nineteenth century onward toward Negroes, the Chinese, and the Irish, but it appears true to say that the reversal of the traditional open-arms policy dates to the period after World War I and to the quota legislation of 1921-1924. Liberal elements show reserve in this matter, but a general defense policy has not in subsequent years ceased to meet with approval by the country as a whole. President Truman's veto on the McCarran Act of 1952 came up against a vote of two-thirds of Congress, which was thus able to impose the law. This attitude reflects a widespread fear of foreign influence. It is not a question of either anti-Semitism or anti-Catholicism, which were felt on numerous occasions before 1914. The growing feeling, particularly since World War II, is a generalized fear of Communism, of European agitators, and of leftism, a term used in a pejorative sense in the United States. In this sense there was an initial crisis of defiance after 1918, but the one that came after 1945 has been more general and definitely more emphatic.

The most spectacular of these movements is the Ku Klux Klan, a volcanic-like movement which erupts periodically, dies down, and then reappears. In its initial form in 1866 it was, following the methods of direct action, the protest of a secret society against the tyranny of Reconstruction, which was attempting to force the Negro on the South as an equal. When its action had been crowned with success it disappeared, or seemed to have, but it always existed below the surface like an underground lake. In 1915 it once more manifested itself in Atlanta, this time not exclusively anti-Negro but anti-Jew, anti-Catholic, anti-Irish, anti-foreigner, indeed against anything that was not national, Anglo-Saxon, and Protestant. From Georgia, whence it originally came, this second Ku Klux Klan, moving like an atmospheric depression, mounted the valley of the Mississippi and reached Indiana, whence the seat of its violence was dispersed in two waves, one moving northwest as far as Oregon and the other to the backwoods of New York State. Its program is one of Nordic nationalism and intensified Protestantism. It proposed a law to make the reading of the Bible compulsory in primary schools. It proclaimed that the principles of Roman Catholicism and monarchy are incompatible with American democracy, and considered that Catholics, since they admit owing obedience to a foreign pope, should have no right to vote in a Protestant country. It called for the exclusion of all Jews, who work against Christian society. It claimed that the right to vote should be reserved for those who had attended a public school for at least four years. It proposed a law forbidding the press to use any language other than English. Its procedure is reminiscent of fascism; whipping of opponents, auto-da-fé of books (Darwin, Karl Marx), mass processions, threatening posters, lynchings, and summary executions. All this was carried out in an atmosphere of mystery, with a hierarchy like that of the Masonic Lodges. The Imperial Wizard was at the head of the "Invisible Empire," the Grand Dragon commanded the "Realm," the Grand Titan the "Dominion," the Grand Giant the "Province," the Grand Cyclops the "Den," not to mention the Grand Monk, the Grand Turk, the Grand Scribe, and the Grand Chancellor.

Evidence of its obvious relationship with fascism and National Socialism, even though the Ku Klux Klan was an earlier institution, is that the social groups which spontaneously accepted the movement were the average businessmen and the lower middle classes in general, elderly workers of Anglo-Saxon origin, and Baptist and Methodist communities. In the South it recruited partisans among the Democrats, who were by definition anti-Negro, but elsewhere its adherents were mainly Republicans, who were hostile to Irish or foreign political officials. The outburst appears to have exhausted its virulence by about 1925 and it appeared that the Ku Klux Klan had ceased to exist.

It was still there all the same, like an underground stream, and it came to light again at the time of World War II, stimulated by a renewal of the same causal factors that had given it its former impetus. There was a hardening of the South toward Negro claims, which were increased by the fact that they had fought in the war and often had risen from the ranks; there was a renewed outburst of hostility toward Catholics, who had become increasingly hard to please; there was a defense policy against Jews; there was the California jealousy of the Japanese, whom they thought they had expelled but who had returned to their farms when their period of internment was over. This third burst of activity on the part of a movement now nearly a hundred years old did not display the same violence, though it was indicative of the same passionate feelings. In spite of everything, manners have become gentler, for we are in America not in Europe and practices which formerly would have been tolerated would now create scandal. But in the South at least, for elsewhere it has ceased to be an active force, the Klan maintains its tradition: "Keep niggers in their place and fight communism." From time to time one's attention is drawn to certain incidents, such as the punitive operations of the defenders of white supremacy. In Columbus County, North Carolina, in February, 1951, ten white men and three Negroes were dragged out of their homes by a group of armed men and horsewhipped to serve as an example. These vindicators of the moral law accused them of not going to church, of drinking too much and being seen together in places of debauchery. The perpetrators of these acts of violence cannot now be certain of impunity as they could formerly, for there are some judges courageous enough to condemn them. In July, 1952, Imperial Wizard Hamilton was sent to prison for four years, fifteen members of the Klan received prison sentences, and forty-seven more were fined. But this is a proof that the fire against which the country is fighting has not been completely extinguished.

It has been set ablaze again, in a less elementarily brutal but no less persistent form, by anti-Communism, which after all is only a new aspect of resistance to foreign ferments which might threaten national unity. It is not so much a political barrier against Russian supremacy as rivalry between two economic systems, both of which have been built up on semireligious convictions. What America defends passionately against the Communists is its doctrine of a free system of enterprise, which it maintains is inseparable from its standard of living, its civilization, and its Christian individualism. Its ideology, which has remained that of the eighteenth century, has rejected Soviet Marxism with a sort of horror, any Marxism in fact, including anything that might be suspected of leading to Marxism. It is in this sense that, if Communism is politically on the left, then all Leftism seems worthy of condemnation in the United States, and the right-thinking pursue it with the same horror as that with which the moralists cursed radicalism.

There was a first anti-Communist period after 1918. It happened then, as in France in 1848 or 1871, that people failed to make the distinction between trade unionist propaganda and a violation of common law; it is as if a Frenchman, even if highly placed, found himself surrounded by suspicion if he were reputedly "of the Left." This was characteristic of the administrations of Harding and Coolidge, but this tendency was reversed under Roosevelt, particularly when, in the struggle against Hitler, the United States found itself in the same camp as Russia. After a lapse of scarcely ten years, one remains astonished at the naïvety with which the President, his wife, and his most intimate counselors persuaded themselves that Stalin, succumbing to the charm of Franklin D. Roosevelt, had become Wilsonian. The awakening from these illusions may be dated with some precision to May, 1945, when, at the San Francisco Conference, the outlooks of Washington and Moscow clashed in such a way as to leave no possible doubt as to the authentic standpoint of Russia. Having adorned it with the most flattering colors, America decided overnight never again to see Russia under anything but the darkest tints.

The Communists, understanding that free discussion would get them nowhere with postwar America, adopted a policy of setting up cells, which was made all the easier by the immigration of large numbers of displaced persons. Rightly suspecting the widespread presence of spies in search of atomic secrets, public opinion was tempted to see them everywhere, particularly as a result of a number of spectacular cases of complicity which were more or less proved—that of Hiss for example—which contributed toward the development of a real obsession with regard to treason. Suspicion became retrospective, and the words, correspondence, and official reports of certain diplomats and civil servants were examined for anything that might indicate some Communist sympathy. Had I, in my innocence, dined ten years ago with a Russian, a denunciation might make me regret it.

This state of mind rose by a sort of crescendo to the Loyalty Order of 1947, the Internal Security (McCarran) Act of 1951, and Senator McCarthy's campaigns, which give rise to real terror through the latent threat they cause to hang over anyone. It has become difficult to penetrate into the United States, now pervaded by an atmosphere of police supervision, which American agents carry everywhere with them into foreign countries. They claim to purge libraries, to expel Communists and even Communist sympathizers from the teaching profession, to screen the Civil Service, and even to investigate the clergy from the same point of view. This is spoken of as the cold war but one could indeed justifiably describe it as an obsidional spirit. It must be observed that this is a crisis which is likely to die down after a time, but it nevertheless reveals a state of mind whose instinctive reaction is to defend the American system. Its initiative is to be found in public opinion rather than in the Government, which some people would even accuse of weakness in its resistance to foreign influences. Some groups which reach the highest Government circles are shocked by this attitude, which they consider nearer fascism or Communism than the liberalism of former times, but the general view is that liberty may be permitted only within the strictly limited framework of American institutions. One must accept them as they stand if one wants to live in the country. From this point of view the principles of the American Revolution are less universal in scope than they were in 1789.

I V

It may be concluded that in the United States the national spirit has attained an extraordinary degree of force and cohesion. It is all the more striking that the patriotism of the newcomers is no less sincere and passionate than that of the 100% Americans. "Near my house," wrote Marguerite Ann Stewart in *Who Are the American People?*, "is a big white plaque in honor of the boys of our community who gave their lives as soldiers in the last war. On it I find listed such names as John Brown, Patrick O'Reilly, Tony de Angelo, Tom Wing, Felipe Ortega, Joe Parsaghian. . . ."

What then is the common heritage of all these people of such varied origins? At first, among the people of Anglo-Saxon race and Protestant tradition, there was the question of the defense of an independence which they themselves had won, and which expressed itself in liberal institutions. This ideological factor is still present, for millions of refugees have found in the United States an independence which Europe had not given them. But now there must be added the consciousness of a standard of living which the New World alone can offer, a boon which is almost fiercely defended, since a glance at Europe shows only too well what they have gained by crossing the Atlantic. The formula "the American Way of Life" is relatively new, for I do not remember having heard it before 1914, and it expresses a combination of all these different elements. The idea is materialistic in its evocation of prosperity, political in its democratic significance, and moral by the Christian tradition of which it boasts. There is no longer a Protestant monopoly—Senator McCarthy is a Catholic —nor is there an Anglo-Saxon monopoly, for the Slavo-Latin is no less convinced than the Nordic American, but there is a spirit of attachment to a country and to a system which obviously brings its advantages. "Look at me!" says the American to the rationed European and the Asiatic who is dying of hunger. "How can one not want to be as I am?" He is sincere, but he makes the mistake of believing that the superiority of his standard of living gives him a general superiority.

However that may be, what a magnificent success it is! The United States is a nation and the most nationally conscious of all nations. But since it has passed from a welcoming attitude, and from defense to exclusivism, it is possible that a certain optimum has already been left behind.

PART V

POLITICAL LIFE

CHAPTER 27

Conditions of Political Life

★

The American conception of democratic government is directly derived from the eighteenth-century tradition. The American people accept its dogmas, with the invincible conviction that its institutions are the best in the world. The main ones include the representation of the people and the overruling decision of universal suffrage; presidential government controlled by Congress under a two-party system; the existence of a powerful federal executive which at the same time respects the sovereignty of the forty-eight states. In principle the Constitution is not open to discussion; everyone accepts it, trusts it, and upholds it, and yet at the same time the lessons of experience play no part in this loyalty, which is an expression of faith. It has often been observed that were the United States involved in international intrigue it might shake this extraordinary attachment to a regime founded in an age-old atmosphere of peace and security, but no such cloud has darkened the American horizon.

Complete confidence is shown in the capacity of universal suffrage to elect the most suitable candidates. The choice of the people has to be consulted about candidates for all kinds of positions; thus the most technical appointments are often made by popular vote: judges, administrators, and registrars of births and deaths. The highest administrative offices are entrusted to businessmen, without any question as to their former political experience, and they, having fulfilled their term of office, return to business. This is in keeping with the spirit of direct democracy, a legacy of the time of the pioneers when every type of office had to be filled without the aid of career officials. The aristo-

251

cratic idea of ability has given way to the idea of assignment, and when ability is required in administration it is considered that the two terms are synonymous.

This psychology has not always been apparent in the choice of candidates. In an initial period, which lasted from the Declaration of Independence to the middle of the nineteenth century, those elected were, as in England, generally gentlemen who considered it an honor to perform their duties in an unselfish manner. Washington and Jefferson were among these aristocrats. Then practical democracy became established with the "spoils system." This meant the establishment of the popular idea, Irish in origin, that positions belonged to the people, not as duties to be undertaken but as legitimate rewards for devotion to the party. This regime still persists to a certain extent, particularly in state politics, and patronage plays an important part in American politics as a whole. In the twentieth century, however, there arose a desire for an administrative machine that should have relative permanency, should be ready to serve the public interest and be endowed with a positive policy. There is, therefore, a tendency toward the formation of two separate domains in the American civil service, one remote from politics and the other dependent on political influence. The first, which is constantly increasing, depends on examinations or competitions for recruitment. In 1884 10.5% of the jobs were awarded on merit and 89.5% through patronage, but in 1951 these percentages had been virtually reversed, becoming 87.5% and 12.5% respectively. It appears astonishing to us that certain highly technical jobs should be considered as political and awarded as privileges to members of the Democratic or Republican parties— to the "deserving Democrats," according to the expression of William Jennings Bryan when he was Secretary of State. In this category come jobs which may be offered as election rewards—in the customs, income tax, or inland revenue offices, the offices of the Cabinet departments, and particularly in the postal organization. The chief organizer of a victorious presidential campaign is generally offered the appointment of Postmaster General, as was James Farley under Franklin Roosevelt and A. E. Summerfield in Eisenhower's Cabinet. The Senators make a particular point of controlling politically the favors distributed in their states and complain when the President acts without consulting them. On a high level, nominations made by the President, such as ministers, Supreme Court justices, and ambassadors, must receive the approval of the Senate, which thus participates in the executive branch of government, rather in the same way as the Roman Senate. The progress achieved in the constitution of a permanent civil service goes against this tradition. When the Republicans were returned to power in 1952, after twenty years of Democratic rule, they did not hide their disappointment at the relatively smaller number of jobs at their disposal with which to satisfy their numerous and impatient friends, while people who held jobs took their stand on the civil service regulations and refused to be dismissed in order to make room for more "deserving" Republican candidates.

It must be stated that in United States politics people who are elected do not enjoy very great esteem. Apart from Senators, governors of states, an elite among the Representatives, and possibly the ministers chosen by the President, recruitment is made from relatively humble social milieus. The tradition of the upper classes, who realize that true influence is to be found elsewhere—though since Roosevelt's presidency this point of view is open to discussion—is to turn aside from political careers. It is preferable to be served by politicians. Contrary to the practice of the French Third Republic, the Congress is not considered as the only true form of popular representation, or even as the principal one. Presidents and governors, who are elected by universal suffrage, consider themselves no less the representatives of the popular will, and in certain instances they have been known to pose as champions of the people against Congress. Several of President Truman's vetos were of that nature, a good example being the Taft-Hartley Bill. This is a very important point, since it emphasizes the significance of the element of referendum in the regime. The President and the governors of the states are by tradition popular leaders, but, unlike the Bonapartist tradition in France, they are not factious. Through legitimate election they carry out the executive authority with which they are vested and they receive the support of public opinion in so doing.

This recourse to the head of the state over and above the Congress is common to North and South America. The New World has been an innovator in constitutional history, for it has created the office of president, not a president who is a figurehead, as in France, but a president who governs, who is at the same time head of the state, head of the government, and leader of his political party. The French president is the guest of the Élysée and does not shoulder responsibility, but the occupant of the White House is a First Consul. In Latin America the president is generally a dictator without counterbalance, for there is no true parliamentary representation, nor any autonomous local administration, as "gate crashers" frequently displace elected governors; nor is there any conscious public opinion or any real respect for legality. In the United States there is certainly a counterbalancing element but, though this may be effective, it is nevertheless true that the executive is extremely strong. Its strength has, during the course of history, even appeared so great that it has been thought necessary to limit it. Did Washington, refusing to stand for election a third time, realize the full significance of his gesture, which by its tradition has dominated the whole constitutional evolution of the United States? For the country would be opposed to a man of dominating personality being installed in power, as happens frequently in South America. The lesson was learned after the triple re-election of Franklin Roosevelt, which, though in no way illegal, was contrary to the whole spirit of the system. Since then a limit of two terms of office has been constitutionally imposed.

The regime thus appears to be democratic and at the same time dictatorial, representative but not parliamentary, though authority is not considered a menace to democracy as it would be in Europe. There was a vast difference between Washington and Bonaparte. Nevertheless, the legal and effective powers of the President are enormous; he makes decisions alone, he holds all the sources of information, he is empowered to speak alone in the name of his country, he negotiates independently with the two houses of Congress and can hide information from them if he thinks fit, and, though he cannot make treaties without the Senate, he can make executive agreements or sign armistices. If he cannot declare war he can present the nation with a *fait accompli*. As commander in chief he decides the distribution of the armed forces. He has ministers who are solely his personal agents, and he can create offices at will and put them under the charge of men of his selection who need not be civil servants. Thus the White House is a seat of power comparable to the court of Louis XIV. It is there that jobs are allotted, that political orientation is determined, in an atmosphere which, owing to American customs, remains open to suggestion but which could nevertheless be subject to occult influences.

At the same time controls do exist; there are three which are essential and effective. Firstly, there is the sovereignty of the forty-eight states, which have independent legislation and administration: the governors of the states are in no way the agents of the President and receive no instructions from the White House; the nomination of "gate crashers" is not a North American practice. Secondly, there is the control of the two houses of Congress, which in a way are in closer contact with the voters than the President, since at all times a proportion of their number is more recently elected than he is. Since they have to be re-elected every two years, the Representatives live in a constant atmosphere of election campaigning. The supervision exercised by Congress is constant, detailed, and often niggling. Important nominations are submitted to the Senate for approval and, while it is admitted that the choice of ministers in principle devolves upon the President, though not without bitter discussion in certain instances, the appointments of ambassadors and Supreme Court justices are submitted to most meticulous scrutiny and are treated with great suspicion. For example, when President Eisenhower nominated the president of General Motors as Secretary of Defense, there was a debate before a Senate committee which lasted for several hours and insistence was laid upon the fact that he should give up all the shares that he possessed in the firm before taking office. A strong President, belonging to the type known as Lincoln Presidents, can impose his will, but a weak President, a Buchanan President, will be overridden. In the first phase of his presidency Eisenhower, who by contrast with Truman is essentially a peacemaker, attempted a policy of benevolent collaboration with Congress, acting as a sort of constitutional monarch in the English manner in his dealings with Senator Robert Taft, majority leader. This policy was not in keeping with American governmental tradition and it appears that with the death of Taft it has come to an end. Public opinion prefers executive power to carry its point. The third element of control, no less powerful than the other two, is the Supreme Court, which decides whether laws are constitutional. The nine justices, who are appointed for life, may invalidate any piece of legislation, and they do not hesitate to do so, being aware of the power which they wield and the reproaches which they would incur for not utilizing it. Their action is basically semipolitical, for while they discuss the legal aspects of a certain measure they are also concerned with discovering whether it meets with public approval, so that their jurisprudence has a powerful influence of orientation and, as President Roosevelt found, any other claims will fail against their veto.

This allotment of power is extremely effective. The President cannot dissolve Congress, Congress cannot overthrow him, and the executive is powerless before the Supreme Court. There is political unity, but in a more profound sense. If we examine the question more closely we shall see that we are dealing with a community rather than a state. The Roman concept of the transcendent state, which exists over and above the society which it governs and therefore may justify its *raison d'état*, has no place in the tradition or practice of the United States, at least up to the present time. The American state is no more than a body acting on behalf of the community, a community which may find other means of expression, directly—as, for example, by lynching—or more widely by the varied initiative of minority groups organized to bring about civic progress. The tradition is thus that of the Presbyterian community in contrast with the transcendental authority of the Catholic priesthood; that is to say, the fundamental difference between Anglo-Saxon and Latin countries. It therefore happens that in the United States one often seeks state action in vain. Particularly as far as the separate forty-eight states are concerned, there is no traditional civil service; after an election bringing about a change in the political majority all the personnel can be changed, from the governor to the hall porter and elevator boy. This forms a striking contrast with France where the hall porter can survive revolutions, evidence, in a country of ministerial instability, of the stability of the state. In the United States there is, therefore, no danger of state oppression as long as the regime operates under the above-mentioned conditions, but oppression arising from intolerance by the community of anything which opposes it is still possible. Liberalism is not the essence of the system.

It may be wondered whether these institutions, handed down from the eighteenth century, are compatible with the needs of the modern world where the existence of a strong state appears essential. The presidency as the executive power and the President himself as a personality occupy an increasingly important place. The powers allotted to the President have increased because of the two wars, and the questions on which he makes decisions have become more and more numerous. Radio and television enable him to have contacts with the people as personal and almost as direct as those of the assembly place of ancient Greece. Jean Jacques Rousseau believed that democracy was possible only in a very small state where the people could readily assemble and where each citizen could easily know all the others. All things considered, he did not see how the sovereign could in future maintain the exercise of his rights unless the city he governed was very small. This judgment has now been overruled by the modern technique of mass communications, and experience shows that the executive has never been more powerfully armed, though authority's gain has in no way become democracy's loss. Indeed, we observe that, in the period immediately following World War II, Congress asserted its control with as much jealous passion as it ever showed at any other period of American history.

This would not appear to be leading to a fundamental transformation of the regime but rather to the strengthening of the state itself. Questions which have to be dealt with on a federal basis, because their compass is not confined to a single state, are becoming increasingly numerous, and it is interesting to note that this tendency has been observed also in Switzerland. Thus, almost from necessity, the central administration has had to equip and arm itself for immensely increased functions, and paradoxically enough it is two Democratic Presidents, Wilson and Roosevelt, who must bear the responsibility for this infringement upon the rights of the forty-eight states. The symbol of this intrusion is the presence near each state capitol of a Federal Building which houses agents of the central government. In 1945 the Governor of California told me that in his capital, Sacramento, federal officials were more numerous than state officials. This was doubtless a legacy of the war and of the New Deal, but after each war the personnel established as a result of it shows a tendency to acquire permanency.

Another result of this situation is that the increasing complexity of the problems which have to be solved gives rise to the necessity for an increasing number of qualified officials, in whatever way these problems are considered. In the nineteenth century it was thought that specialists were unnecessary and that all that was required was that officials should be chosen by the vote of the people. Now increasingly greater recourse is made to the experts. For some time there has been a tendency to withdraw certain types of problem from the political sphere and place them in the hands of specialists, who are required to solve them objectively and to whom is given a power which is virtually arbitrary. This is the "positive policy" of Auguste Comte applied to matters of general interest, particularly when one is wearied of the intrigue of politicians. Such appointments put a brake on political corruption, but at the same time they reinforce the executive power, which controls the experts. Thus the presidential machinery is swollen to an extraordinary degree, to such an extent that the President himself can exercise his immense powers only through what may be termed the "presidency." The President's personal staff, which was formerly accommodated easily in the White House, has now overflowed into an Executive Office Building. McKinley had not even a shorthand-typist, Hoover had a staff of only 37, but Truman had at his disposal 325 officials attached directly to him, 1,500 office staff, and 61 autonomous offices which existed independently from the Cabinet departments.

Whatever the power of this bureaucracy may be, the American state has not become all-powerful, so that revolution in the European sense remains inconceivable in this country. It is too large and too much divided between the separate unities of the forty-eight states for a nerve center to be established which could command and dominate the whole. The concept of the community, to which the country remains attached, means that the state, however powerful it may become, is not a mechanism or an arm that can be seized by intrigue, plot, or force. If the Capitol were seized in a *coup d'état,* of what use would it be?

II

The political parties are the motivating force of the system, but one must make a distinction between them and the political organization from which they cannot be separated. The party is the organ for the development of a program, a tendency, a concept of government; it corresponds, as in Europe, to a political temperament. The political organization is a permanent institution run by professionals. It is only a means but, as so often happens, this means may become an end in itself. Thus it must be considered as an organization which has its own life and struggle for survival, but has no ideological initiative or personality. Its aim is to obtain and to keep power for its own advantage, that is to say, for the benefit of its members, under the leadership of a "boss" who often, without any official status, can succeed in dominating a town or a state. It must be realized that the organization is strictly passive and that it has no creative aptitude or even creative will. It should be likened rather to a recording apparatus, a sort of float which measures the fluctuations of public opinion, allowing for them and organizing itself in view of them. In his psychology the American politician is a realist. He observes the political horizon objectively, searching for the direction from which the wind is blowing, putting aside from his program anything that might prejudice it, taking his bearings from any group that might appear to be influential, such as banks, industry, the churches, social progress leagues, feuds, or racial feelings, and disregarding anything else. In this way, it must be admitted, he fulfills one useful function, that of sifting public opinion, passing forward certain requests or points unlikely to be disputed by the public, and putting aside what he considers to be impossible or premature. He may be a parasite, but the organization should acknowledge that he makes this initial differentiation between what is desirable and what is possible.

A whole procedure is thus necessary before any reform or measure can be carried out, whether it is of general interest or a personal matter. Application must be made to one of the two political parties, as though to a transport company, with a statement of the services required and a request as to the cost of carrying them out. The organization may thus be compared with a shell in which any creature can shelter, or with an omnibus in which seats may be reserved, it being borne in mind that since there are two rival companies it is prudent to take tickets with each of them. The public has become accustomed to this technique through long practice. The party offices are not highly esteemed; agents are dismissed after too extensive a term of service, though the reign of Frank Hague in New Jersey, for example, or Thomas J. Pendergast in Missouri, was of long duration. On the whole the public appears to accept, possibly through laziness or indifference, the use of this political machinery, paying the commission that the use of it entails. In doing this, nothing fundamental has been abandoned for, since the organization is passive, public opinion remains the essential motive force.

It is the duty of the political parties to interpret public opinion, but they have to operate within the restricted limits of the Constitution. "The right of revolution does not exist in America," states a manual for civics teachers in Middletown. "We had a revolution 140 years ago which made it unnecessary to have any other revolution in this country." And, "No man can be a sound and sterling American who believes that force is necessary to effectuate the popular will. . . . Americanism . . . emphatically means . . . that we have repudiated old European methods of settling domestic questions, and have evolved for ourselves machinery by which revolution as a method of changing our life is outgrown, abandoned, outlawed." *

In France there are men politically right or left who are hostile to the regime. If such men exist in the United States, no rights are accorded to them, and this limits considerably the field of discussion, for one can argue only within the limits of the system.

This self-criticism allows for a different outlook from each of the parties. Reformers or businessmen desirous of obtaining some advantage address themselves to either of the parties, acting purely from motives of opportunism and not from sentiment. But the

* Robert S. Lynd and Helen Merrell Lynd, *Middletown*, New York, Harcourt, Brace, 1929, p. 198.

attitude of the voters is different, for there exists a feeling of loyalty
to the party, which is handed down by tradition, and in which
sentiment plays a part as important as that of personal advantage.
Why are the voters Republicans or Democrats? It may be a question of temperament, of professional interest, of family tradition,
or of origin. Families which migrated from New England are Republican and those which came from Virginia Democratic. The
Irish are Democrats and the Scandinavians Republicans. Personal
interest is not the decisive factor. According to a survey undertaken in Middletown, a leading clubwoman said, "I have always
been a Republican and that's the way I always vote"; while another prominent woman said, "It seems perfectly natural for me
to be a Democrat. My family were always Democrats. . . ." And
in an editorial in the local press it was stated, "A man is a Republican or he is not, a Democrat or he is not, and the test of his
partisanship is the support he gives his party." * Important waves
of public opinion may upset this classification, such as at the time
of the Great Depression, but they reappear afterward, like deep
ruts in a lane.

III

To whichever party he belongs, the popular candidate is nearly
always of the same type. He must be straightforward, attractive in
personality and stature, devoid of pride, and always ready with a
winning smile. I read one day in a newspaper in the Northwest, in
an article entitled "A Doctor Talks of Health": "There is an interesting study by Gowin on a certain number of American leaders:
for example, he finds that bishops of the Episcopalian Church are
nearly 2 inches taller and 17 lbs. heavier than the average pastor
in the small town." This observation may be transposed to describe
politicians. And it should be added that the public insists on a
certain amount of familiarity from candidates seeking votes. They
should introduce their wives and daughters, or, failing them, their
sisters. The people like the General for presenting Mamie to the
voters, or Harry for presenting Margaret. What is asked of the
candidate is not so much ability but that he should be "one of us,"
"a real four-square American," a man whose feelings and reactions
are typically American. On the other hand, in a great cosmopolitan

* All quotes from *ibid.*, p. 415.

city like New York, for example, a candidate should be preferably Irish or Italian, with a name like O'Dwyer or La Guardia. Once one descends below a certain level, the politician is not in high esteem. People do not believe in his promises and treat him as a necessary evil. Serious people follow other callings.

Thus it will be seen that the main interest of the country is not political, but is concentrated on production. There is periodic excitement at the time of the presidential elections, as for a sensational match in the sports world. The presidential election is traditionally carried out in a sporting spirit and has a highly emotional flavor, but once it is over the voter returns to business, the fundamental reality of his life. It has not so far been the experience of the United States that the political game can influence the country's destiny by any decisive action. The experience is that of the past, but now circumstances and environment are changing. During the Great Depression the conditions which prevailed in the United States may be described as European, and economics in themselves were not going to give anxiously awaited solutions. Then World War II plunged the country into an atmosphere of international solidarity. There are Republicans who, like the French "ultras" of 1815, have learned nothing and have forgotten nothing. It is evident that they would like to return to the regime of Hoover and Coolidge, but this is clearly impossible. As for the masses, they know since the time of the New Deal what can be obtained from the state, that milch cow, the welfare state. But they fail to understand that the constraints of the European hell are henceforward thrust upon America itself. The man in the street still considers that he has the right to express an opinion upon anything whatever, and he finds it normal that his opinion should be taken into consideration. He likes a public debate on international affairs, carried on according to simple concepts derived from American political experience and animated by emotional arguments derived from the traditional mass reflex. Eisenhower's victory showed that in spite of the experts and their learned calculations, in spite of the over well-equipped party organizations, the American electorate remains simple, of a simplicity almost childish, which is motivated by sentiment.

The question remains as to whether this regime will change now that the position of the United States in world affairs has undergone such fundamental transformation. There is a permanent army, there is a diplomatic service which is endeavoring to establish its permanency, but, up to the present, political power has remained at the helm. No MacArthur has vanquished it. It must, however, be observed that if the regime has proved satisfactory for more than a century it is because nothing essential was ever debated, because any divergence was only on matters of secondary importance. When the really fundamental problem of slavery was under discussion, the resources of the Constitution were not sufficient to prevent civil war. The system will therefore be tested only when the parties come to grips on an issue of paramount significance; since that situation has not occurred, the regime carries on in its traditional way. In spite of the strengthening of the presidency, it remains subject to the control of Congress, which does not appear at all disposed to relax its hold. It is not a popular democracy but a Western democracy, that is to say, a true democracy because it is founded on respect for universal suffrage. If there is a danger to be feared, it is rather that public opinion may acquire too firm a grip on a state which is already too powerfully centralized and equipped. The Government can doubtless impose its policy by persuasion or by presenting the nation with a *fait accompli*. Twice, under Wilson and under Roosevelt, America has been implicated in a war in which she showed no desire to participate. But it is also possible that unfettered public opinion may impose itself irresistibly on the ruling powers, and in those circumstances, with democracy taking direct action, the braking power of prudence might be found insufficient.

CHAPTER 28
The Political Parties (1)

★

In the United States, politics are a mixture of seeking advantages, passionate feelings, and ideologies; while the proportion varies according to time and place, these three factors are always present. Men endeavor to protect their own impelling interests, if possible, within the framework of the party which would most naturally be expected to accede to their requests, but, if not, outside it. The election machinery is often rent by passionate feelings, which animate it with dynamic qualities but militate against its smooth operation through their uncompromising attitudes. Finally, ideologies cannot be separated from American life, for the United States is a country of ideologists, ever anxious to assert their principles and even to apply them.

It would appear difficult for a political organization to integrate into a coherent whole such dissimilar points of view. Indeed, it is not easy for a single political party to combine in its program, without any element of contradiction, the requirements of personal interests, emotions, and ideologies. Action is therefore possible only by means of coalitions which combine different factions and even opposing tendencies. Moreover, the immense size of the territory makes unity impossible. The Americans may have acquired, more than any other nation, unity in customs, manners, and comportment, but it is nevertheless true that the diversity of the various regions with their differing climates and geographical aspects makes it impossible for local interests to fall into line with an overall political program. The only possible progress is by means of compromise. The fundamental source of politics is local and must be sought in the different states, since federal policy is no more than a sum total or combination of heterogeneous elements. At the same time, the very reason which prevents unity within the party forces it into a national union, since no local or even regional group would be able to impose its point of view upon the country as a whole. The party program, reduced by necessity to a sort of common denominator, cannot therefore be satisfactory to all. But one must make the best of it if one wants to win the elections, and that is after all the reason for the party's existence.

If there are uncompromising members who refuse to fall in with such a hodgepodge of a program, then they break away from party solidarity and vote for the opponent, or else form temporarily dissident groups. It is only by taking into account these different attitudes that one comes to understand how these personal interests, emotions, and ideologies can exist within the framework of a single party, whose only unifying factor is its system of organization. The professional politician who handles this tool must be skilled in the use of it, and it entails on his part a sacrifice of principles which costs him scarcely anything, but which convinced party members will not accept without resistance. It is the duty of the party, in consultation with the experts, to judge to what extent, without harming the possibilities of success, the politician may retain ideological pretensions, agree to serve the interests of individuals, and allow passionate feeling to be displayed.

The American party system can scarcely be compared with that of France or the United Kingdom, and we find some difficulty in defining Republicans and Democrats, particularly in clearly distinguishing one from the other. Superficially they appear to resemble each other to an extraordinary degree, to be interchangeable in many circumstances, all the more so in view of the fact that the major laws are generally not passed by means of one party voting against the other. It is clearly wrong to judge American politics from the European point of view. The fact is that a long tradition, in a political atmosphere which involves a change of President every four years and congressional elections every two years, not to mention the regional politics of the different states, has led to the development of two distinct temperaments. Democrats and Republicans doubtless change with age and circumstance, but it seems to me that it is possible to define them by means of permanent features in their personality.

This definition cannot be made, however, without many distinctions and nuances, for each party contains left, right, and center elements, and the left of the more moderate party is often more to the left than the right of the more "advanced" party. Since there cannot be any homogeneity in these groups, which are, after all, coalitions, the problem to consider is where at any given moment the main axis of the group lies. The policy of the party has a completely different significance according to whether it veers toward the right or the left. The Democrats can appear almost conservative and the Republicans almost radical. It is, therefore, important to know the position of the President within his party. Grover Cleveland was a right-wing Democrat and Theodore Roosevelt a left-wing Republican. Truman, like Franklin Roosevelt, was at the left of his party, while Eisenhower is at the center of his.

In their present form, in spite of changes that appear fundamental, the two parties as at present constituted have been formed and recognizable as such since the Civil War. It was then that their basic principles were recognized and proclaimed. The deepseated change which was brought about in 1932, under the decisive influence of Franklin Roosevelt, has doubtless introduced new points of view, but these find their expression within the framework of the past. In considering as a whole the period which extends from 1860 until our times, it is still possible to speak in the present tense. I believe that, if one attempts to penetrate to the roots of the matter, the two temperaments have been in existence since the American War of Independence, though they were not then entirely in keeping with present-day definitions. The personalities of two of Washington's Cabinet members, Jefferson and Hamilton, correspond to the two political attitudes which may be considered most typical of the two currents of thought which have since been defined as Republican and Democrat. Hamilton, the English Tory, devoted to the principles of authority and efficient administration, is at the origin of the Republican outlook, which, democratic as it may be, is derived not from a reactionary point of view—indeed, this term has no sense in the New World—but from a spirit of conservatism. On the other hand, Jefferson, the amazing eighteenth-century ideologist, represents confidence in the People (with a capital P), that almost mystical concept of a sort of American left wing, closer in its outlook to the eighteenth century than to our own times. These are the two points of view that emerge alternately in American history, but neither of which is ever lost to sight. A quarter of a century ago, when Hoover was President, the Republicans were considered as the true expression of the national spirit, and the Democrats were relegated to the status of an opposition party which only occasionally came into power. After twenty years of uninterrupted Democratic victory, the Republican seems to be the exception rather than the rule. The truth of the matter is that the two currents continue their existence side by side, almost equal in force, easily distinguishable one from the other by the color and relative speed of their waters.

II

The Republican party was in power almost uninterruptedly from 1860 to 1932, a period of seventy-two years, during which Democratic Presidents appeared only as interludes. The party was formed in this period and in such a way that it was unable to evolve sufficiently when faced by the new circumstances brought about by the Great Depression.

In the first place the Republican party, using Lincoln as its spokesman, proclaimed the prime necessity of union and went to war to defend its point of view. It has maintained this outlook until very recent times, constituting itself the champion of federal power against the excessive claims of the states, at any time ready to secede. It is thus the party which upholds authority. It represents this point of view not only in the political field but also in the economic sphere, where it upholds the fundamental claims of industrial organization. Large-scale industry and organized wealth find in this party a natural champion. Bankers and important industrialists are in their natural element in it, but even more so are the average businessmen who frequent Chambers of Commerce and Rotary Club luncheons. The same is true of the society circles of the East, who are conservatives, snobs, and imbued with racial prejudice, and who hate the memory of Franklin Roosevelt and would consider it almost a scandal to vote Democratic.

It is significant to note that the flourishing period of Republican rule, which began with the presidency of McKinley in 1896, corresponds to a period of continuous economic prosperity, the sensational brilliance of which is reflected in the amazing progress achieved in the development of the whole continent and the fabulous increase in industrialization. Until the time of the Great Depression, which marked a turning point of greater significance than either of the two World Wars, the Republicans were the traditional representatives of prosperity; this gave them their best election argument in a society where merit is judged by material success. The loss of this monopoly seriously shook the Republican position at the time when the Democrats were able to boast of the amazing boom of World War II, which developed under the leadership of Roosevelt and Truman. Apart from the fact that in either case "you feel it in your pockets," according to the striking campaign slogan, Republican and Democratic prosperity are not alike. Republican prosperity is the result of the activities of great industrial and financial organizations, under a regime conceived in such a way that the economic field takes the lead.

This concept which subordinates politics to production is by nature conservative. It is also characteristic of a new continent where it is easier to produce than to share. Such a philosophy, which owes its birth to a kind of statutory prosperity, has remained today characteristic of the most authentic among the Republicans, those who may be described as real Republicans. Their program includes a social order in which the state upholds the producer without hindering him, intervening only in order to protect him, and militates against disorder within the country and competition from without. McKinley, who was elected in 1896 when he stood against the demagogue Bryan, proclaimed the necessity of a sound currency, and the outlook of the creditor toward the debtors of the West, who were instinctively inflationists. A sound currency presupposes a rational handling of financial affairs, a regime in which social disorder is held in disrepute. Today President Eisenhower holds the same policy.

Moreover, McKinley did not wait to be in the White House to

establish the tariff bearing his name, which remains even today a symbol of Republican protectionism. In the period of striking prosperity which followed World War I, first Coolidge and then Hoover remained faithful to this tradition. The trusts experienced a policy of benevolent neutrality, and leading industrialists were able legitimately enough to form the impression that the state was ready to serve them, and, moreover, that this was normal. But it by no means followed that during this period the masses turned away from such a party. Since there is no class consciousness in the United States, the workers listened to the Republicans when the latter affirmed that high tariffs formed the best way of guaranteeing them employment at a high wage. This reasoning influenced them just as much as a campaign for the lowering of prices, for in a way workers also reason as if they were producers.

Ten years of crisis, for which they were held responsible, followed by a renewal of prosperity for which they could not take credit, deprived the Republicans of a slogan whose efficiency in election campaigns had been shown to be decisive for a whole generation. Under the Democratic regime the country waged war against stagnation and unemployment, using means which were in opposition to everything laid down by Republican orthodoxy, while the return of prosperity coincided with inflation, the depreciation of the dollar, and state prodigality which was made almost a doctrine. Moreover, authority favored the workers rather than the employers. This was a situation calculated to perturb public opinion seriously, and, with a complete reversal, voters turned toward the Democrats for a period of twenty years. Thus a sort of reciprocal change occurred. Attending to the most urgent business, in the crisis and in the war, the Democrats, contrary to their former principles, had recourse to the power of the federal state, either to reduce unemployment or to organize the armed forces. This pleased them because of the election pull which this policy afforded them. Forgetful, for their part, of the doctrine which they had upheld since the Civil War, the Republicans protested against this attack on the rights of the individual states. Though they, moreover, had always upheld the intervention of the federal state by means of tariff protection, this same type of state intervention seemed to them a shocking policy when applied to relations between workers and employers. The employers, particularly medium-scale employers who were doubtless less well-equipped to defend themselves, considered intolerable this intrusion which resulted from a social policy entirely new to the United States. It is true that American industry had never had a liberal outlook; the liberalism which it unearthed was nothing more than a laissez-faire policy which held public authority at a distance when it had no need of assistance. This was the philosophy of the Republican party when it returned to power in 1952. An article in the *Wall Street Journal* advised the Government to confine itself to the maintenance of law and order but to abstain from directing economy. The American, if left to himself, would easily find a way of adapting himself to all necessary changes, as he had always done in the past when left free to do so by former governments.

It is in their relations with the workers that Republican employers felt the greatest bitterness, during the Democratic regime, toward the policy of social intervention, for which they were in no way prepared by precedent. During the decisive generations when national industry had been in procesas of formation, employers had enjoyed a regal independence vis-à-vis the workers. The labor force, which lacked conformity owing to the immigrants who supplied the greater part of it, organized itself in trade unions at a late date, and was never favored by the state. Then new legislation, which owed its birth to the crisis, contested the former supremacy of the employers, taking the side of the trade unions. Thus the Republican party, which continues to count the employers among its old guard, became with them a laissez-faire party, hostile to any new intrusion on the part of the authorities. It was a negative type of liberalism, and, moreover, the only one which the producers would admit. The Taft-Hartley Act, which was of Republican origin and was passed only in the face of President Truman's veto, symbolized a spirit of Republican reaction against the workers, which tended to reverse the progress of the trade unions during the Roosevelt period. It was Senator Taft, significantly enough nicknamed "Mr. Republican" by his party, who thus showed that the bias of the Republican party is to the right rather than to the left. In Republican vocabulary the epithets liberal, radical, and leftist have retained the disparaging sense which they had in former times in France.

Since they represented the principles of authority, organization, and national union as opposed to secession, it was natural that the Republicans should count for their main support on the ethnical element which forms the foundation of the American nation, that is to say, the Anglo-Saxon Protestant element. Thus they are more national, in the narrow sense of the word, than the Democrats, who number many people of mixed racial origin. Wherever the old-established racial element is strongly maintained, the Republican party finds its strongest support, that is, in the inland areas of New England and the Atlantic coast provinces, the medium-sized towns of the West where Chambers of Commerce flourish and where until recently men such as Babbitt lived, milieus of solid American family life which contrast with the great cosmopolitan cities, all this naturally with the exception of the South, which has remained politically different because of the Negro problem. This is the card played by the Republican party, one which is fundamentally racial. The support given to the Negroes during the Civil War and the pro-Negro interventions during the Reconstruction period made no difference, for, when Lincoln accepted the challenge in 1860 he was fighting for the defense of the Union rather than for the abolition of slavery.

When the Republican victors imposed on the South the famous amendments which incorporated into the Constitution the legal equality of the former slaves, they were dealing with a question which was on the whole foreign to them, since there were few colored people in the North. Ethnical liberalism remained, as far as they were concerned, purely a matter of theory. When during World War I large-scale migration filled the great cities of the East and Middle West with Negroes, the newcomers were correctly treated as far as their civic rights were concerned, but they were not admitted into white family circles any more than they were in the South, so that they experienced a feeling similar to that of the recent European immigrants, that of impatience to be accepted. Paradoxically enough they found the greatest comprehension of this attitude on the part of the Democrats, and Roosevelt and Truman ended by defending them in their civil rights policy. While it cannot be said that the Republicans adopted the opposite attitude, they appeared as the more strictly nationalist party, opposed to any kind of foreign element, whatever it was. Thus Eisenhower finally appeared more acceptable than Truman to certain diehards of the Deep South.

It is, therefore, not surprising that the immigration laws of 1921-1924, on the whole racially inspired, were the work of the Republicans, nor that the McCarran-Walter Act of 1952 bears the name of the Republican Walter. It is also significant that the Ku Klux Klan, Democratic in the South, took on a Republican aspect in the North when it spread to states as solidly Republican as Indiana and Oregon. The indignation of the Ku Klux Klan there was directed less against the Negroes than against the Catholic Irish and Italians. In the period that followed World War II the attitude represented by McCarthy did not originate essentially among the Democrats, though many of them were affected by it, but in Wisconsin, the state for which McCarthy is a Republican Senator. I believe that all Americans are anti-Communist, but in the presidential campaign of 1952 the Democratic candidate came second in proclaiming his anti-Communist attitude.

It is not enough to say that the Americans are proud of their country; they are all nationalists and nationalism is not a monopoly of the Republicans. The latter have, nevertheless, a traditional policy of imperialism of which at the turn of the century they made scarcely any attempt at concealment. It is to McKinley that one owes a new use of the formula "manifest destiny," to Theodore Roosevelt that of the "Big Stick," of which Taft's "Dollar Diplomacy" is simply a new edition, but the "Good Neighbor" policy is Democratic. When World War I had drawn the United States into the European whirlpool it was under Democratic responsibility; isolationism, a transposition of former exclusivism, developed preferably on Republican territory; it was Senator Henry Cabot Lodge, Wilson's opponent, who rejected the Treaty of Versailles, chiefly because it included membership in the League of Nations. The neoisolationism of World War II, represented by men such as Hoover and Taft, renewed this retractile attitude toward Europe, while in the Far East the Republican activism of MacArthur allowed the development of urgent resistance to anything international, not only on the part of the Democrats but in the left wing of the Republican party.

We have observed that in a country the size of the United States a federal party cannot be homogeneous, and obviously there must be deviationists. Theodore Roosevelt, who cannot be conceived of as other than Republican, advocated a social policy and opposition to the trusts, which might well be qualified as left wing. The old Senator Robert M. La Follette, who gathered together the farmers of the Northwest, protested against the domination of Wall Street. In each case dissidence arose, but without any consequences. It is significant to note that such secessions are always left wing, and this signifies that the party tends to lean toward the right. That is why in the exercise of their power, with all its responsibilities, Republican Presidents must maintain a "middle-of-the-road" policy. This has been the attitude adopted by Eisenhower, in which he was upheld by Senator Taft, the real leader of the party, whose premature death occurred only after he had shown his deep innate sense of government. The counterbalance was essential, for, after twenty years of opposition, the party came into power again with, to a certain extent, the outlook and the bitterness of the *"Chambre Introuvable."* *

* Name given to the reactionary parliament of 1815-1816 in France under Louis XVIII.

CHAPTER 29
The Political Parties (ii)

★

To define the Republicans implies also the need to determine the position of the Democrats. Their tradition is essentially to defend the nonorganized from organized interests, to protect the mass of the consumers against the cupidity of the producers, or ethnic and religious minorities and particularly immigrants against those overanxious for their speedy assimilation, and to champion the individual states against the Federal Government and the individual against the state. In the period between the Civil War and the Great Depression, that is, for nearly three-quarters of a century, the Republicans were almost continuously in power. Therefore the Democrats, even during the occasional periods when they were in power, acquired an opposition complex. They came into power when things were going badly, so that their programs were more concerned with reclaiming rights than with maintaining the privileges of those who had achieved success. They were capable of governing, even energetically, as well as their opponents, but could not maintain the nationalistic outlook from the moment that they made themselves the champions of those who, because they were discontented or merely because they were different, did not conform to the orders of those who were satisfied with the system. They therefore created a tradition which even their uninterrupted success from 1932 to 1952 has not completely obliterated. The Democratic party had become in an unexpected fashion a party associated with prosperity, but it remained the party that supported the claims of the people, opposed to the basic conservatism of the Republicans.

The geographical distribution of the Democrats is the result of this appeal to minorities, which, when added together, make an important total throughout the country. The tidal wave of Roosevelt's success temporarily swept over the whole country, but as it receded it brought to light the basic foundations of the party, that is to say, the South, the cosmopolitan and urban populations of the East and Middle West, and the agrarian West, which is unstable and in a permanent state of dissatisfaction. This is a group which has no homogeneity whatever. When Southerners, New Yorkers, and farmers from the West meet at Democratic national conventions, they would be from many points of view totally opposed to each other if the necessity of winning an election did not force them to agree on a common program. For several generations the color of the party was preponderantly that of the solid South, but when by their ever-increasing numbers the urban populations of the North began to occupy the predominant place in the Democratic ranks, certain fundamental characteristics of the coalition were modified. This modification was not carried out without resistance, and a latent crisis made itself felt in 1924 and 1928 over the personality of Al Smith; Roosevelt's dynamic personality obscured this during his presidency, but it still remains an unsolved problem.

There is, nevertheless, a Democratic tradition that has continued uninterrupted since the Civil War; it has the unity of a current, but it is the current of a river flowing through different regions with different climates. Until the time of Roosevelt a Democratic victory appeared impossible without the "solid South," which provided it with several unshakable strongholds. It was enough then to conquer a few pivotal states, such as New York, Ohio, and Illinois, and a majority of presidential delegates was won. It was, therefore, natural that the South should determine the center of gravity and outlook of the party. But in this part of the country there was one overruling question which eclipsed all others—that of keeping the Negro in his place. Considering any intrusion on this matter by the North as inadmissible, the South was logically led to affirm the principle of the priority of the individual states, a principle which, moreover, it had held before the Civil War. This legal liberalism, in a region which had long remained free from industrialization and was primarily an exporter of raw cotton, was paralleled by economic liberalism, characterized by the slogan, "Tariff for revenue only," a position on which it agreed with the urban consumers of the East, who were anxious to see a fall in the cost of living.

In order to uphold this policy, the Democratic leaders of the South demanded from their adherents a kind of sacred union. Since it would have seemed scandalous to vote Republican south of the Mason-Dixon Line, and also since Negroes were prevented by force from recording their votes, an unhealthy single-party regime was established, which forestalled the foundation of a left wing and made the whole of political life sterile. Only one army was mobilized and any element of dissidence in it was considered as serious as desertion. Thus in a poor region where the outcasts of fortune would have had claims to put forward, the outlook arrived at was narrowly conservative and even reactionary; in fact it was an area where the Democrats had a basically Republican point of view.

Owing to the industrialization of the South and the increase in numbers and proportional significance of the Democrats of the cities of the North, the Democratic balance was substantially changed in the period between the two wars. The South developed economically. The newspapers continued through the force of habit to preach free trade in their editorials, but on other pages which were no less read protectionist rights were shamelessly reclaimed for the factories which Yankee capital had established in North Carolina, Georgia, and Alabama, and before long in all the original rebel states. Then, in the campaigns for Al Smith and Franklin Roosevelt, the Democrats of the North became antiprohibitionist, socialist in tendency, and even (what a scandal!) pro-Negro. When Al Smith was nominated as presidential candidate in 1928, the South decided that this was going a step too far. Could they really vote for this Irish Catholic governor of New York State, whose program was presented as follows in a slanderous opposition pamphlet: "Alcohol Smith's platform. Alcohol Al for President! I stand for alcohol and bad government. My platform is wet and so am I. I owe my votes to the Catholics and the Jews. When I am at the White House I will lead the people and the Pope will lead me." Indeed, for the first time in the history of the United

States, seven Southern states—Florida, Texas, Oklahoma, North Carolina, Tennessee, Kentucky, and Virginia—forswore Democratic discipline and voted for Hoover. Roosevelt's prestige and success drew the party together again, but in 1948 there were again signs of dissidence. The Dixiecrats, rallied together under Governor J. Strom Thurmond, could not bring themselves to accept Truman's policy of civil rights, and perhaps even less his Fair Deal, and they enticed away four states—Louisiana, Mississippi, Alabama, and South Carolina. Faced with an essentially left-wing Democratic party, champion of the humanitarian rights of colored people, the loyalty of the South, which had remained so long unquestioning, wavered. In the presidential election of 1952 the Deep South supported the Democratic candidate, but Texas, Florida, Virginia, and Tennessee went over to the Republicans, while there were strong minorities to support General Eisenhower in Arkansas, Louisiana, and South Carolina. The South still remains essentially Democratic, but the single-party regime has ceased to exist there.

The axis of the Democratic party now passes through a line drawn between New York and Chicago, and its outstanding preoccupation is the mass of city dwellers who are tending to occupy an increasingly significant place in the equilibrium of the country. This element now supplies the Democratic battalions with their largest forces. Among their number new immigrants and first-generation Americans whose origins are still obscure are numerous —perhaps more numerous than Americans whose grandfathers or great-grandfathers crossed the Atlantic. There is no difficulty in distinguishing among them, without the aid of statistics, Irishmen, Italians, Poles, and some ten other European nationalities, often ill-assimilated. These cosmopolitan groups, not yet absorbed into the national environment, seek in the political party to which they are attached some sort of protection against the privileges of the old-established settlers, who are already equipped with the means to defend themselves. They are in need of resources which will enable them to enter the American community as members possessed of equal rights.

Meanwhile, they ask to be accepted as they are, with their foreign trappings, their inferiority, their lack of power of adaptation.

In the great Atlantic ports, it is the Democratic party which has assumed the role of protector of the uprooted, the weak, the isolated. They are not patronized, when they appear in its ranks, because of their race or religion, and this gives an amazingly refreshing impression in a society where the man who has achieved material success is only too ready to become pharisaical. Purists may wax indignant about the corruption of the political organization of the Democrats, but the opinion of the man in the street will not always share their indignation. They remember how they have been welcomed into the bosom of the party without any stage of Anglo-Saxon respectability being required of them. In symbolic manner the Irishman and the Catholic priest are two parallel forces in the Democratic army, neither of whom is entirely in the hands of the other, but who coincide in their interests, their reactions, and their tendencies.

In this same spirit the party defended the individual against the power of high finance, the customer and the worker against the producer, the consumer against the trust. It is, therefore, a partisan, if not of free trade—an English conception which never crossed the Atlantic—at least of the doctrine of lowered tariffs, acting as a brake to a rise in prices. According to Jefferson's tradition the rights of the People (written with a capital P) should never be sacrificed. There are in this all the elements of demagogy, but there is no question of a revolutionary policy; all these people, who have not yet made their fortune, hope that they will do so one day. They do not wish to overturn society, but rather to make themselves a place in it. Moreover, whether Catholics or Protestants, they are Christians, or at least profess to be so, since conformity is in keeping with the national background. They will, therefore, be content with finding places within the municipality, and, as far as the state is concerned, seeking protection for their rights as citizens or wage earners against the power of wealth.

This outlook has taken an increasingly important place in the Democratic program as industrial development became concentrated in the cities of the East, Center, and West, giving rise to a working population whose problems were in no way similar to those of the narrow conservatives of the South. When the country was stricken by the Great Depression, it was particularly by considering these groups that Roosevelt, himself a New Yorker, undertook the struggle against country-wide stagnation. Ethnic and religious rivalries paled before the scope of the problems which had to be solved—unemployment, poverty, rights of the wage earner—and all this in an atmosphere completely foreign to the United States, which hitherto had known only prosperity. For the first time a social policy, in the European sense of the term, became a necessity. It was at this period that the Democratic party became tinged with the Rooseveltian color, that of the New Deal, which it has kept ever since. While maintaining its original tradition, to which this evolution was only in apparent superficial contradiction, the Democratic party became through the force of circumstances one which put the federal state at the service of the mass of the population, whose right to be helped in times of difficulty and to be protected against the employers it fully recognized. In particular, the worker thus found his trade union protected, and he who had so many times voted Republican henceforth turned toward the other party, which had become almost officially the left-wing party. And that was the moment when the word "left" penetrated for the first time into the vocabulary of American politics.

As for the ordinary man in the street or the worker in the fields, he was not abandoned. Franklin D. Roosevelt spoke to him directly over the radio in his golden voice, assuring him that he would not be forgotten, that a policy of subsidies, public works, compensatory payments, and the creation of jobs would pour down manna upon him from a Democratic sky. We have already shown that this was not a doctrinal policy, in the strict meaning of the word, but a series of expedients undertaken at the maximum speed possible. It consisted of a lightheartedly extravagant form of opportunism, which was inflationary and which confirmed in the minds of the masses the feeling, which they had instinctively held for a long time, that the state belonged to them in all its various forms. Borne along on the current, the inspiration of which was the defense of the weak, President Roosevelt, followed in this matter by President Truman, was logically led to a policy of protection of the Negroes. But by seeking to impose a policy of civil rights the Democrats cut across the privileges of the individual states, as they had done earlier at the time of the New Deal, and this brought about the reversal which made them the champions of federal power.

The Republicans, mistaking their desires for reality, affected to consider the Roosevelt era as an interlude, after which the United States would return to its true tradition, that of an individualism in which each citizen relied above all on his own initiative and energy. There is reason to consider this as an illusion, for it is most probable that the Great Depression marked the end of the period of Republican rule, commencing with the Civil War, which lasted until the fatal year 1929, or, if one wishes, to 1932. The fanatical protestantism of men like William Jennings Bryan no longer represents the general tone of this new period in which the immigrant, the Catholic, and the worker anxious to keep his job represent another conception of society and the state. Al Smith, the precursor of Franklin Roosevelt, marked the turning point in this conception. In times of crisis it would be difficult for the Republicans themselves to avoid recourse to the weapons taken up by the Democrats, for they would be asked to do so, and indeed are, by members of their own party.

It results from all this that the Democrats cannot in any circumstances revert to narrow nationalism. Woodrow Wilson gave their foreign policy an indelible mark, as did Roosevelt, the United Nations Organization, and the Atlantic Charter. Care must be taken, however, not to exaggerate the importance of international ideology, which is doubtless sincere but which soon finds its limits. All Americans, the recently immigrated as much as the others, are jealous continentalists, who only allow themselves to be inveigled into international intrigues and combinations in spite of themselves, with great hesitation and many false starts. This is sufficient to explain why, whichever political party is in power, the orientation of foreign policy remains constant.

II

The two-party system has so far resisted all crises and has easily outlived all dissidence. European opinion, however, is surprised that no labor party has developed in the United States. In order to understand this one must go to the roots of the American conception of the relations between workers and employers. The American industrial system, as we have already seen, includes the collaboration of the worker in a productivity program from which it is taken for granted that he will benefit. To the European, who lives in an atmosphere of class warfare, this collaboration would appear suspect. It is not so, for it serves the worker without compromising the dignity of his position; but to believe this one must be to a certain extent familiar with American ways. This has given rise to a current of misunderstanding all the more difficult to move against because, at least from the French point of view, there appears to be in the American labor movement an indefinable lack of spirit.

With his high wages and a standard of living which provokes his sympathy for ours in Europe, it does not occur to the American worker to contest the principle of the capitalist regime under which he lives. From this angle he is conservative, whether as an egoist he hopes for personal success within the existing framework, whether he lacks the imagination or the idealism to conceive of anything else, or whether this capitalism has evolved sufficiently to satisfy him. Even a lawyer as progressive as Oliver Wendell Holmes, the Supreme Court justice, wrote in his correspondence with Professor Harold Laski that it was humbug to believe that capital was robbing labor, and that he suspected despotism on the part of those who wished to overthrow the system. Laski replied that the two different points of view were due to the differences between the two civilizations. The Americans lived in a society where the classic principles of capitalism still function successfully, but he, Laski, lived in an environment to which the capitalist machinery was no longer adapted. It is a case of two entirely different backgrounds, between which no comparison can be possible.

There have been revolutionary movements in the United States, such as the International Workers of the World at the beginning of the century, but they have never spread, doubtless because of the absence of class consciousness. The protests on social matters of the left-wing European workers, whose noble motives we can appreciate, have no equivalent in America. There is an effort to improve the position of the wage earners to the maximum, but within the existing framework. The problem thus stated becomes simple and above all materialistic, idealism paling before practical achievement. The American argument, "Look what I have obtained!" is realistic. The European argument, "Look what I wish to obtain for my class, something beyond pure material achievements," savors of dreams and mystical devotion to a cause. The weakness of the American propaganda in this field, when addressed to Europeans, is its failure to understand that, when it has discussed the question of standard of living, there yet remains something to be said. When the French worker meets his transatlantic opposite number, he finds not a member of the proletariat or an exploited worker, but a man whose social position is discussed in the unions on equal terms with that of his employer, a worker who generally goes to the factory each day in his own car, who wears gloves to work, and who in the evening is scarcely distinguishable from his employer. When representatives of capital and labor meet, the atmosphere is that of a business conference. The workers' delegate also arrives in a Cadillac and doubtless stays at the best hotel. Wages, pensions, conditions of work, and recruitment policy are discussed as they would be in Europe, but there does not appear to be any underlying revolutionary spirit. Certain advantages obtained by the workers may challenge managerial control, but there is no thought of establishing a principle.

The uncompromising positions taken should not deceive us, for they in no way mask the quasi-political "will to power." When John L. Lewis imposed himself on the coal-mining industry, he may have achieved for the workers greater advantages than they could have acquired under nationalization, but it is significant that he does not seek nationalization of the industry. When the port of New York was condemned to remain in a state of stagnation owing to the longshoremen's strike, there was not the latent revolutionary movement that would be feared in a similar case in either London or Marseilles. Discussions are carried out as between businessmen, or sometimes as between gangsters, but on the whole the gangster is less dangerous to the social order than is the apostle of revolution. One would hesitate to describe as apostles the leaders of the American Federation of Labor or the Congress of Industrial Organizations, but from the viewpoint of sheer achievement their policy is efficient. During the period of prosperity which followed World War I, leading industrialists were generally anti-trade union or paternalist. The indubitable advantages which they conferred were generally "bestowed," in the manner of Louis XVIII's charter, rather than granted as part of a worker's contract. But this phase has now ended. The great development of the American Federation of Labor and the Congress of Industrial Organizations has brought into being powerful bodies, capable of imposing their will upon employers and of exercising an influence upon the Government and Congress. Roosevelt and Truman, who upheld these organizations, benefited from their support, as did Adlai Stevenson. At the same time no workers' movement ever appears to have considered constituting a political party. It would appear that they attach importance to the avoidance of taking their stand on matters of principle, and remain voluntarily in the realms of practical achievement. Claimants as far as discussion is concerned, the trade unions collaborate in matters of execution.

This is probably where the deepest psychological difference between the Old and New Worlds is to be found. In Europe, the worker is skeptical of the advantages that an increased output of the factory might achieve for him. If the firm in which he works tries to make its own publicity on this subject, the employee smiles, and if a worker accepts and endorses the employer's reasoning he is said to have been hoodwinked. If I myself speak of it, I am suspected of some sort of collusion. In America this type of propaganda neither astonishes nor shocks, even if it is put forward somewhat indiscreetly. As a European, I become somewhat annoyed by the systematic optimism of the employer describing the amazing results of a productivity reacting on the worker, but what he affirms is in the main correct. At times there are articles on this subject written by workers; if we are tempted to doubt their good faith, we are wrong. We must become accustomed to the idea that in the United States propaganda is not necessarily bluff, even when it has that appearance.

Faced with these results, the militant socialist or Communist, if he is honest, cannot fail to be impressed, but at the same time there is something lacking as far as he is concerned, probably because his own plan of campaign contains other objectives. The

French worker has his history, his tradition, his human values, and his spiritual wealth. His representatives feel a subtle nostalgia when their American opposite numbers speak to them only of the material advantages they have achieved. They have no mystical feeling of class consciousness, no revolutionary apostolate, scarcely a human apostolate, but merely the vocabulary of businessmen. Our idealist feels that in this rise in the social scale, brought about by material success, there is no place left for protest, for principles, or for some indefinable hope of a promised land.

CHAPTER 30

The Return of the Republicans

★

The year 1952 marked a turning point of great importance in the history of the United States, the greatest, even taking the war into consideration, since 1932. After twenty years of Democratic success the Republicans returned to the White House. The question which now remains to be considered is whether this reorientation is decisive.

I

No election campaign had been as sensational as the one which terminated on November 4, 1952, in the triumphal election of General Eisenhower. No campaign had aroused more interest, as was confirmed by the unusually large number of voters, or inspired more passionate feelings. It was also the most picturesque, both because of the part played by the personal intervention of the candidates and because of the new technical methods employed, notably the use of television. Never, unless it were in 1860, had the stakes seemed so important. Europe awaited the result with passionate interest, realizing that on it her destiny also depended. It should be added that the experts have rarely been so far wrong in their forecasts; they had not excluded the possibility of the General's success, but none of them had dreamed of such an overwhelming victory. In order to find similar excitement and passionate feelings it seems to me that one must go back to the election of McKinley in his campaign against Bryan, or especially to the election of Lincoln, which brought about the Civil War.

When the campaign opened in July, 1952, the Democrats had been in power for twenty years. Five presidential elections in which they had been victorious had led to the impression that they were permanently established in the White House, and there was a tendency for the Republicans to appear as the party which was always defeated (see fig. 1).

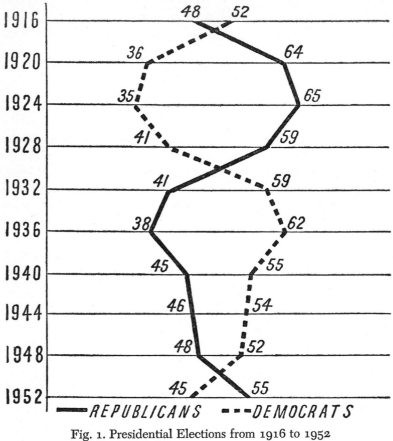

Fig. 1. Presidential Elections from 1916 to 1952
(percentage of votes)

During this period the Democratic majorities had always been substantial and sometimes overwhelming. In 1932 Roosevelt had obtained 22,821,857 votes against 15,761,841 in favor of Hoover, that is, 59% of the votes as against 41%. In 1936 the vote in favor of the President broke all former records, since he obtained 27,-476,673 votes against 16,679,583 in favor of his Republican opponent, 62% against 38%. Democratic majorities were maintained in 1940 and 1944, though less decisive than before: 27,243,466 votes against 22,304,755, and 25,602,505 against 22,006,278, or 55% against 45%, and 54% against 46% respectively. This tidal wave, Democratic or pro-Roosevelt, covered the whole country to such a point that in 1936 the Republicans retained majorities in only two states, Vermont and Maine. In 1948 Truman still obtained 24,105,812 votes against Dewey's 21,970,065, or 52% against 48%, so that the Democratic advance was maintained in spite of the disappearance of the party's amazing leader, whom a unique exception had maintained in office for four consecutive terms. The voting combination which had assured the success of the party for twenty years included the Democrats of the East—essentially the working populations of the great cities—the conservatives of the South, and the farmers of the West. But in addition to these main groups a whole host of people who benefited by the welfare state made their contribution to Democratic victory.

It is true to say that from 1940 onward the Republicans gained ground, since in that year they found strong reinforcements and their voters exceeded twenty-one million. Geographically speaking they regained to a large extent their former main positions, New England, the Middle West (Indiana, Michigan), the Northwest (Iowa, the Dakotas, Nebraska, Kansas, Colorado). If Roosevelt had not been the Democratic candidate in 1944 they would probably have been victorious, and they felt certain of success in 1948. It may even have been this false sense of security which brought about the defeat of Dewey by Truman, the latter being a very able man who put much more effort into the campaign than did his opponent. It can, therefore, be considered in the long run inevitable that the pendulum should swing back in favor of the Republicans. This reasoning applied even more to 1952 than to 1948; but it must be appreciated that the Democrats held powerful cards, particularly owing to their social policy, which was approved by the people and coincided with outstanding prosperity.

When the campaign was about to open, what were the respective positions of the two parties, considered independently of the two candidates whom they were about to choose? We have shown that the strength of the Democrats lay in their hold on the working classes, and their weakness lay in defaulting in the South owing to their civil rights policy. On their side, the Republicans could count on the ruling classes and the middle classes of the East and the Middle West, so long as they were not recent immigrants. It was possible, however, to distinguish within the ranks of the party two diverging centers of attraction. In the Middle West, grouped around Senator Taft of Ohio, the Old Guard was stronger, with its policy of protectionism and its pledged resistance to the claims of the trade unions, and, as far as foreign policy was concerned, of neo-isolationism allied with mistrust of Europe and the predominance of Asia, in that order of preoccupation. But a more liberal group, under the leadership of Governor Dewey and Senator Lodge, made their influence felt in the Atlantic coast region; they, in effect, supported President Truman's foreign policy. The Old Guard described them as internationalists, using the term with pejorative intention.

There was thus, on each side, a strange combination of strength and weakness. The Democratic advantage resided mainly in the enormous popularity of Roosevelt, which was to a certain extent passed on to his successor. Experience had shown that the social courage of the New Deal and the Fair Deal was compatible with the return of prosperity, and moreover with war and rearmament as well. The people were in favor of the policy of the welfare state. "If you vote for the Republicans," announced the Democratic propaganda, "your benefits will no longer be guaranteed, nor will the prosperity which has become your prosperity." Nevertheless, too long a period of power had, in spite of everything, exhausted the party. The reign of some of the most powerful local leaders had become out of date and the party had yielded to the temptation of an ultrapartisan policy, even one based on subsidies and the creation of employment. The result had been a certain amount of corruption, not really deep-seated but superficial and widespread, and this had given rise to small scandals, even in the entourage of the President.

The Republicans made use of this weapon and handled it all the better because their organization was superior to that of their opponents, for they were well-provided with money and received the support of all the leading financiers of the nation. Although they were in a chronic minority in the elections, they were in a huge majority as far as the organization of industry and commerce was concerned. Therefore, a large number of the public considered that they were better qualified to administer the country. It was, nevertheless, impossible not to recognize the fact that their successive defeats had estranged them from the masses. As the opposition party they had become increasingly conservative, even reactionary in the proper sense of the term, for they wished, like Louis XVIII, to "renew the chain of time." Twenty years of grudges stored up had made them bitter, narrow-minded, and excessively impatient to participate once more in the benefits of power. It is particularly as far as the Old Guard is concerned that these reproaches were justified. There was even among the ranks of the party itself a feeling that Taft, whatever his qualities as a candidate might be, would have no chance of success.

II

It is in this atmosphere that the two conventions opened which were to choose the two presidential candidates.

In the Republican camp Senator Taft had been preparing his campaign for a long time, eagerly supported by the professional element in the party. Nobody represented tradition more than he did. He represented tradition in its most narrow form, he, who had inaugurated the famous Taft-Hartley Act. The real Republicans were justified in nicknaming him "Mr. Republican." He, then, was sure of the support of the orthodox and regular members of the party.

But another candidature was called for, not so much by the ranks of the specialists in election campaigns as by the mass of the people—the victor of World War II, General Eisenhower. He had been made president of Columbia University in New York and had then been nominated by President Truman to create a European army, and so had remained aloof from politics, though he had in no way indicated that the idea of contesting the presidency would displease him. He had, at times, made political speeches, but had always confined himself to generalities. He was a member of neither party and it was not generally known whether he was a Republican or a Democrat. The Democrats had even considered him as a candidate, and President Truman had sounded him out. Because of his high military office he had considered that he should not take any part in politics and had always replied that he would not make any move to stand as a candidate, but that if public opinion clearly requested him to put forward his candidature he would consider what he should do. Then a rising wave of public opinion in his favor made itself felt, and within the Republican party itself an Eisenhower party was constituted under the inspiration of Governor Dewey and Senator Lodge. The professional politicians considered them as amateurs, but the movement gathered increasing strength. When, in the early months of 1952, the names of the eventual candidates had to be put forward in the primary elections of the Republican party, the name of the General appeared almost everywhere, with a powerful and largely spontaneous utterance. His candidature before the Republican convention was therefore brought about by a sort of plebiscite. He accepted the invitation and, having resigned his post in Europe, returned to the United States. At the time of his nomination there was an impression that if he succeeded, it would be by reason of a sort of plebiscite over and above the parties, which would have a national rather than a partisan significance. This is, moreover, what finally occurred, but before the convention the choice took the form of an impassioned contest, revealing in the opposition party two hostile groups which it was later difficult to reconcile in a common effort for victory.

The Republican delegates met at Chicago from July 7 to 12 and found themselves in the presence of a solid organization which had for a long time worked in favor of Senator Taft. The nomination of the Senator seemed probable. Though less well-equipped from a professional point of view, the supporters of the General had the advantage of a wave of public opinion in their favor. It appears that the specialist politicians did themselves harm by the excesses of their technique in maneuvers. By the end of the first roll call Eisenhower was in the lead with 595 votes as against 500 for Taft, 81 for Earl Warren (governor of California), 20 for Harold Stassen (former governor of Minnesota), and 10 for General MacArthur. On the first ballot, a series of withdrawals amounting to an avalanche gave the General an overwhelming majority of 845 votes as against Taft's 280, which meant that Taft was cast aside. The delegates at this convention were practical; they had estimated that the Senator would not attain the presidency, and the popularity of Eisenhower, which was enormous if somewhat vague, did the rest.

On the Democratic side passions ran less high, because, since Truman had decided not to run again, none of the candidates made convincing claims, whether it was Vice-President Alben Barkley, a follower of Truman, or Averell Harriman, representing the "liberal," that is, left-wing, elements of New York, or Senator Estes Kefauver, a spectacular champion of the struggle against corruption. The initiated circles were in favor of a man little known to the public in general, Adlai Stevenson, who had made his name as governor of Illinois, but who did not wish to stand for the presidency. President Truman had asked him in vain and when the convention opened at Chicago on July 21 he still resisted. He received votes, however, from the first ballot, and on the third ballot a majority of 617 votes against Kefauver's 275 forced him in a way to accept the nomination and stand as Democratic candidate. A member of Chicago society, an intellectual, and a first-class orator, with a personal distinction which gives him an indefinably English appearance, he took the lead solely through his personal superiority, which, as events were to show, was by no means a trump card. He was an authentic Democrat but belonged to the moderate wing of the party, and seemed anxious not to be too blindly a follower either of the outgoing President or the professional organizers of the party.

Thus on each side amateurs had triumphed over professional politicians. This was an indication of the inner feelings of public opinion, though the campaign was to show later that recourse to the professional organizers was necessary in order to reap success. Eisenhower was to succeed, making perhaps too many concessions to them; Stevenson was to fail, refusing to put himself into their hands.

III

It is impossible to imagine two candidates more dissimilar than the General and the Governor. The former, a professional soldier, knew Europe but was entirely ignorant of American politics, though he was at the same time nearer than his opponent to the outlook of the average American. He was born in the Southwest and was one of the people in his deportment, his reactions, and his social origin. Stevenson, who had acquired solid political experience as governor of a state, belonged to a higher stratum of society, had been well-favored by fortune, and was an intellectual by taste and upbringing. All this is well known now, but at the beginning of the campaign the electorate knew very little about either candidate. General Eisenhower had a world-wide reputation, but he was a legendary figure whom very few people had ever approached; while Governor Stevenson, who was popular in Illinois, had scarcely been heard of elsewhere.

On this account a number of problems arose. It was uncertain what would influence Eisenhower and in what direction he would orientate his campaign. He had been supported by the "international" groups, and, since he had carried out a European policy, it was generally assumed that in matters of foreign policy he would have an outlook similar to that of the Democrats, that is to say, he would be a liberal. At the same time it was by no means certain, since he would need the help of the professional party organizers and could scarcely do without the support of the Taft faction. It therefore remained to be seen whether he would stick to his position as representative of the amateurs, or whether he would allow himself to be absorbed by the diehards. There was the same element of incertitude about Stevenson. He had been nominated without having committed himself to any promises, but it was also doubtful whether he, a newcomer in the field of federal politics, would be in a position to do without the assistance of the professionals. It was also a matter for speculation as to what factions the struggle would really be carried out between. As far as their parties were concerned, each of the candidates was in the middle of the road, so that it appeared that the general tone of the campaign would be moderation. This was indeed the intention of the candidates, but behind them there were Truman and the Taftists, neither of whom shared this moderate outlook. These were vigorous combatants, imbued with strong partisan feelings; they had accumulated deep-seated grudges through mutual opposition carried out over a long period of years, and they had not been brought up in the academic atmosphere to which it was assumed that the two official champions belonged. Behind them there were the professional political workers, determined to give no quarter, with all the injustice of partisans.

In the first phase of the campaign, the candidates appeared to be seeking each other out. The supporters of Taft, who were very bitter, held themselves aloof, and one wondered whether they would bring themselves to collaborate with any degree of efficiency. The liberal group, for its part, did not appear to exert any decisive influence on Eisenhower, who, comparatively isolated in his headquarters in Denver, was contented to make vague declarations which were something of a disappointment to his supporters. One journalist went as far as saying, "Ike is running like a dry creek." As for Stevenson, he established his headquarters at Springfield, Illinois, with the intention of remaining independent of the professionals, and notably of the most eminent among them, President Truman, whose advances he met rather ungraciously. It was necessary for the tenant of the White House personally to take the lead. "I myself shall be the key to the campaign," he said. Stevenson, through his talents as an orator, compelled recognition on the part of connoisseurs, but he had no popular appeal. Thus neither party moved forward.

In September, in a second phase, the position became clearer. At a historic breakfast in the president's residence at Columbia University, the General renewed contact with Senator Taft and the two leaders formed an alliance, in which the Senator finally put the powerful organization of the Republican party at the service of the campaign. Posing with set smiles before photographers, the two men declared themselves in agreement, with a few reserves in the matter of foreign policy. The price which had to be paid remains a secret, but the center of gravity of the campaign was slightly altered. When he resumed his tours the General visited the South, where he received not only a cordial but almost a triumphant welcome. His speeches remained vague, directed against Communism and the mess in Washington, but his presence played an essential role and he attracted crowds who surged up to him as he went by, and this was an indication which he was soon to take into account. Meanwhile Stevenson continued to make himself known and appreciated. He used precise arguments and his speeches sparkled with flashes of biting wit. People listened to him willingly but did not flock in crowds to hear him, and he did not stimulate curiosity. The professional politicians were roused by this distinguished but restricted atmosphere. They requested President Truman to intervene, and Stevenson himself, doubtless influenced by the poor results of his first move, resigned himself to accepting their support.

At this juncture a significant incident happened, the Nixon affair, which was to do a great deal toward orientating the campaign in the direction which it was finally to take. The Republican candidate for the vice-presidency had received from a group of adherents, in his functions as a Senator, a subsidy of $18,000. Was this permissible? When the matter became known, passionate discussion immediately ensued, even within the Republican party itself, which was far from being unanimously in favor of the Senator. Eisenhower was greatly embarrassed and was a long time taking his stand. Was he to dissociate himself from Nixon in order to continue his campaign against political collusion without being compromised? Or was he to follow wise advice and offer Nixon the support of his moral authority, in order not to change horses in midstream? While he was postponing his decision, Nixon, in a nation-wide television program which cost the party an enormous sum of money, addressed himself directly to the public with an appeal to sentiment which won them over through the courage which it demonstrated. His cause had been won. There remained only for Eisenhower to give him a spectacular slap on the back as he disembarked from his airplane, and to say, "Dick, you're my boy!" There were practically no arguments, just the presentation of a picture which was in keeping with American taste. Appeal to the emotions had come into the campaign and was henceforth to dominate it completely.

Then began the third and decisive phase. Ike, and let us deliberately call him by his familiar nickname, had found a plan of campaign. He does not really succeed in great political speeches, but he is excellent when he has recourse quite simply to the mere fact of his presence. What he says matters little, and he appreciated that. He came to realize through experience that it was enough for him to appear and, putting aside the notes prepared by his advisers, to speak to the people as an honest man who would be able to solve problems, an upright leader in whom the people could have confidence. Had he not emerged victorious in battle in North Africa, Normandy, and the Rhineland? In the same way he would win the battles of peace in the future. The procedure was fully successful and the crowds surged to see him pass. In some places more than 100,000 people went out of their way to see him drive by with his procession of cars filled with his supporters. During his whistle-stop tour great waves of humanity swept into the stations where he halted. People came to see him rather than to hear him, and when he presented his wife, Mamie, the enthusiasm was delirious. Conscious of the success which he thus obtained, he did not show himself difficult about making concessions. He consented to appear on the same platform as McCarthy, the nationalist Senator from Wisconsin, and the no less antiliberal Senator William E. Jenner of Indiana. His original supporters, who had hoped that he would lead a liberal campaign, free of Republican partisan servitude, recognized him no longer, and Senator Wayne Morse of Oregon, who, it must be admitted, was something of an *enfant terrible*, split away from him ostentatiously. But elsewhere, with an instinctive feeling for public opinion, the General declared that he would not go back on the social policy of the New Deal. In truth, his program was not at all clear, and the only thing which was evident was that public opinion was being swept off its feet in his favor.

The Democratic party was concerned about this wave of opinion, which was not helping their almost too-distinguished candidate. They appealed to the President, as an experienced politician, to move the people. He set out eagerly in full fighting spirit on one of the famous whistle-stop tours, in which the campaign train goes from station to station to meet the voters at home, by means of personal contact. Truman is a fighter and he remembered that four years earlier he had in this way beaten Dewey, whom everyone expected to be elected. He bore a grudge against the General, who could have been his candidate and who was now unhesitatingly criticizing his administration. He was even less considerate in his attack, describing Eisenhower as a war hero with no political ability, prisoner of the diehards, a reactionary who would endanger the social benefits acquired through twenty years of Democratic rule, a fascist who did not hesitate to become involved with a man such as McCarthy. Some of the more delicate-minded shuddered at this violence, which they considered as incompatible with presidential dignity. The general impression, however, was that he made headway, and the professionals engaged on sounding public opinion came to the mistaken conclusion that Stevenson would rapidly regain the advance that his opponent had won over him. In point of fact, Truman's campaign probably did more harm than good.

At the beginning of the fourth phase the Democratic argument in favor of prosperity seemed to be winning the day. "When one thinks of the Great Depression, the Republicans must bear the responsibility for that! Do you want to see it return? We never had it so good. Don't let these Republicans take our prosperity away!" The Republicans in their turn grew anxious. The argument about corruption hung fire. The moral severity of the Republicans was largely made up of aversion, but could one be sure that they would do better? The anti-Communist policy was more efficient, and touched a very deep-seated anxiety on the part of the public. But it was necessary to find something else. It was then with an inspiration of genius that one of his advisers prompted the General to make his sensational declaration: "I shall go to Korea!" Public opinion interpreted this as signifying: "I shall go to Korea to end the war." This was a decisive discovery and won the day, Eisenhower being considered in the light of a *deus ex machina*.

This analysis remains cold and cannot bring out the extraordinary atmosphere of a traveling circus which characterized the campaign. The Americans followed its up and downs with the same freshness of approach and the same childish joy that they would have shown a century ago, when the result would have had no international consequences. This responsibility vis-à-vis world politics scarcely appears to have troubled the interested parties, and this is a proof that man develops less rapidly than do situations. One might have imagined that one was back in the legendary nineteenth century, when attempts were made, by means which savored of the fairground, to catch the votes of the pioneers of the West. This nineteenth-century atmosphere survived, paradoxically enough, with the most advanced twentieth-century technical equipment—radio and television. The candidates could be seen and heard by the whole country at the same time. Without the emotional appeal which he was able to make on television, Vice-President Nixon would probably not have been able to extricate himself from the unwise move that he had made, and the smile of his wife, who remained loyal to him through his troubles, certainly moved a public no longer given to reasoning. The campaign appealed to the emotions and that is the clearest explanation of it. Stevenson's qualities were no less than those of his opponent, but, to quote La Rochefoucauld's maxim: "Our merit wins us the esteem of honest men, our stars that of the public at large." *

I V

The voting on November 4, 1952, came as a surprise, particularly to the experts in forecasting. They had doubtless expected a Republican victory, but one with a small majority, and in this it will be seen that they were not entirely mistaken. But there was a real landslide and a whole avalanche of votes in favor of Eisenhower. He obtained thirty-three million votes as against twenty-seven million given for Stevenson, 55% of the votes cast compared with 45%. His substantial majority is all the more striking when one considers the proportion of the electoral votes, for there were 442 Republican votes against 89, and that meant that the victor had a majority in almost all the states; all the electoral votes of a state go to the party which has the majority, even though that majority is very small.

In 1936 Roosevelt had obtained an even more sensational victory with 62% of the votes against 38% and 523 electoral votes against 8, but never had such a large total number of votes been cast in favor of a President. Roosevelt had obtained 27,476,673 votes against 16,679,583 in 1936, but Eisenhower had six million more and, even taking into account the increase in population, the result is striking. It must, moreover, be added that Stevenson with twenty-seven million votes obtained more than Truman did in

* *"Notre mérite nous vaut l'estime des honnêtes gens, et notre étoile celle du public."*

1948. The conclusion is that the result was Eisenhower's victory rather than Stevenson's defeat. I believe that it was one of the Democratic leaders who hit the right note in this commentary:

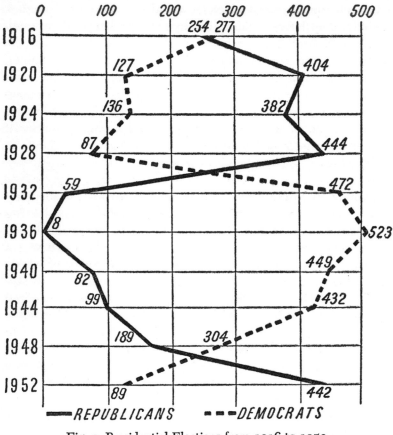

Fig. 2. Presidential Elections from 1916 to 1952
(number of electoral votes)

"We have been beaten in a popularity conquest but we have not undergone political defeat."

The observation is all the more pertinent in view of the fact that Ike's personal triumph was not matched by a corresponding victory for his party. After the election for the House of Representatives in November, 1952, there were 221 Republican members and 213 Democrats. In the Senate, after the renewal of one-third of their number there were 48 Republicans, 47 Democrats, and one dissident Republican, Senator Morse. These precarious majorities, always at the mercy of someone's death, underline the fact that while the country voted for the President in a kind of plebiscite, it did not show a similar preference for the Republican party. In truth it did not condemn the Democrats in any decisive fashion, nor the policy which they had upheld for twenty years. There is reason to believe that, had the contest been between Truman and Taft, a Democratic President would have been elected, for it must be realized that Truman was very popular.

Looking at the trends over a long period it is clear that since 1936 there has been an instinctive move toward a balance between the parties. After the exceptional enthusiasm shown that year, one which seemed to sweep over the whole country, there was observed a progressive return of the Republicans toward their former position held before the Depression. Hoover had obtained 59% of the votes in 1928 but, having touched a minimum of 38% in 1936, the party obtained 45% in 1940, 46% in 1944, and 48% in 1948. Similar gains were made in Congress. There were only 18 Republican Senators in 1936, but their number had risen to 38 in 1944 and 50 in 1946; they fell to 42 in 1948 and rose again to 49 in 1950. In the House of Representatives the Republicans, who numbered only 89 out of 433 in 1937, rose to 246 in 1946 but fell to 199 in 1951. Everything pointed to a Republican victory in the presidential election of 1948, and it may have been accidental, due to Dewey's insufficient campaigning, that it did not occur. In considering the party and not its exceptional President, it must be concluded that the Republicans have achieved an election victory, but without triumph.

It is interesting to study an election map. In 1936 Roosevelt was successful in all the states, with the exception of Maine and Vermont. In 1948 the Republicans had won over New York, Pennsylvania, New Jersey, Indiana, Michigan, Oregon, North and South Dakota, Nebraska, Kansas, New Hampshire, Delaware, Maryland, and Connecticut, but President Truman was nevertheless elected. Then in 1952, by a tidal wave similar to that which swept the country in 1936 but in the opposite direction, the Republican candidate gained the whole of the East, Middle West, Northwest, Southwest, and Pacific coast, while his Democratic opponent was victorious only in the South, and even there he lost Texas, Florida, Virginia, and Tennessee. This partial defection of the old "solid South" appears even more striking when one considers that for the first time substantial minorities voted for the Republican candidate in the other Southern states, as many as 44% in Arkansas, 47% in Louisiana, and 49% in South Carolina.

In the light of this campaign, which we can now observe with a certain amount of perspective, it is possible to decide which arguments carried the day. The Democrats had counted on prosperity, for which they considered themselves, not altogether justifiably, to be the guarantors, but the electorate did not appear to fear the loss of prosperity in voting Republican. They were going back, moreover, to an old tradition. Stevenson, and more particularly Truman, had even put people on their guard against a reactionary policy which might deprive them of the ever-popular advantages of the New Deal and Fair Deal. They had thought that they could count on the vote of all the trade unionists, but it appears that a number of workers, even though they were firm adherents of trade unionism, voted for Eisenhower. It is also believed that many recent immigrants, large numbers of Catholics, and even substantial numbers of Negroes deserted the Democratic cause. The Republican candidate had pledged himself to maintain the social legislation of the Roosevelt era, so that the vote was not given on social grounds. The electorate paid more attention to the Republicans when they advocated changing a governmental team exhausted by too long a period of power, and even more when they aroused national, or rather nationalist, feelings against Communism. McCarthy is more representative than one might care to admit of a deep-rooted feeling on the part of the American people.

The response of the public to these appeals largely explains the Republican victory, but other explanations must be found before one can understand the power of the tide which swept Eisenhower to the White House. For this one can scarcely find any solution other than the personal arguments of the General. It was not Eisenhower's program, vague, unstable, and even contradictory, which swept all before it in an irresistible wave, but the extraordinary radiance of his whole being, though he is not outstanding physically. This radiance was expressed in his smile, his contact with people, even in the simple fact of his presence. He appeared to the Americans as one of them, belonging to that Texas and Kansas which from the moral point of view are now, rather than New England, the heart of the country. Even more as his campaign developed the masses saw in him a leader who, by his destiny, his honesty, and his simplicity, would govern and administer better, settle national and international problems better, quite simply because he was himself. Thus his promise to go to Korea transformed what already promised to be a fine election victory into a triumph. It was essential that sooner or later he should bring the war to an end. And perhaps this was the only real campaign pledge that he made.

But the General did not sweep the whole of his army to victory with him, for if he entered the White House through a wide doorway, his supporters penetrated the Capitol with only a slender majority over their opponents. The exceptionally large presidential majority was due mainly to a great number of habitual abstainers whose votes swelled the number but were independent of party discipline. The significance of their votes is not political, or at any rate not partisan. This has given rise to the state of affairs where, from the presidential point of view, the candidate elected holds almost an open mandate, while in Congress the nominally victorious party has only a slender majority. In several states votes were given for Eisenhower but not for the Republican nominees for Senators, Representatives, and governors. For example, in the South those who voted for the President voted for him personally rather than for his party, and basically the Democrats remain the masters in this territory. In the same way, though the farmers of the West voted for Ike, it would be incorrect to suppose that in so doing they were repudiating the agrarian policy of Roosevelt or Truman.

v

If, in considering the return to power of the Republicans in 1952, we attempt to sum up the situation, we are obliged to recognize that there are still to be found among them the two distinct currents evident at the Chicago convention. It is as if there had been two parallel elections. Once he had been elected, the President showed himself again to be the man whom his first supporters, the liberals of the party, had considered him. If he is indeed a Republican in his instinctive conservatism and his consideration for the businessman, he is in no way a narrow nationalist, a fanatical protectionist, or an isolationist. The attitude of the Republicans elected to Congress is completely different. They are real Republicans of the active right wing, who display all the passionate feelings of nationalism, isolationism (or at least neoisolationism), and the most unwavering protectionism; and it is possible that the Republicans in Congress represent more authentically the true spirit of the party than does the occupant of the White House. It had been thought that Senator Taft was the perfect representative of this outlook, but when he was leader of the Senate, during the few months which preceded his early death, he made a point of ranging himself with the President in the center of the party. This proves that the responsibilities of power inevitably bring those in authority into a political orientation which is always the same.

CHAPTER 31

Political Personnel

★

The twentieth century has brought undoubted progress in recruiting political personnel. Ability is considered more than in the past, and the upper strata of society do not stand aloof from politics as they did formerly. At the same time the general level differs in municipal, state, and federal politics.

In municipal politics mayors and councilmen are often of humble social standing. In the large cosmopolitan cities the men holding office are generally foreign in origin and often Catholic. It is the traditional sphere of Irishmen, who have more recently been joined there by Italians and Poles. Nothing prevents a man born outside the United States from reaching the top in a political environment such as New York or Chicago. In New York, as has been said, a party ticket to be acceptable should contain an Irishman, a Jew, and an Italian, and in the future it might well be a Negro and a Puerto Rican. It should also be mentioned, though care must be taken not to exaggerate on the subject, that on the lower fringe of municipal politics in some of the largest urban agglomerations collusion exists between politicians and gangsters, and the latter have easy entry into the whole field of gambling, low-class bars, and prostitution. A European comparison with this situation may be found in certain Mediterranean ports, which are equally cosmopolitan. The party organizers are quite at home in these shady quarters, and at times businessmen do not hesitate to make contact with the members of this underworld in order to be assured of their neutrality. Some trade unions enter into similar contacts in order to be left in peace; for example, the American Federation of Labor had to disown its New York longshoremens' union for this reason. Thus the situation arose whereby in New York State a union official in the building trades, who had been sentenced to prison for shady dealing, was approached in prison between 1948 and 1953 by important political leaders who came to ask him to use the influence which he had still retained to quell strikes and appease labor conflicts. The supporters of good government succeed from time to time in cleansing these Augean stables, but it is not certain that the interested parties always prefer to undertake the administration; with honest men one cannot expect to come to an understanding when one is in the wrong, but it is always possible with the politicians of less strict conscience.

In the states, the members of the legislatures are highly representative of the population, that is to say, very ordinary men, while the governor may well be outstanding, since the regime favors personality at the executive level. The governor is generally a citizen of the state who has made a name in his profession, as a lawyer for example, or in some secondary political role in which he has displayed civic courage. An attorney, elected public prosecutor, if he has had the occasion to distinguish himself in some spectacular trial which has shown that he fears neither gangsters nor politicians, may well be destined to become governor. Governor Dewey of New York State was a good example of this.

For the election of a member of the House of Representatives or a United States Senator, the question of the candidate's personal links with his constituency is important. Too close a foreign connection would be a handicap, except in the very cosmopolitan eastern states where Italians or French Canadians are acceptable, or in the North Central states where it is preferable to be Scandinavian. At the same time the rapid assimilation of the immigrants is permitting increasing numbers of men who are not of Anglo-Saxon or Protestant origin to arrive at the top, that is, to become members of Congress. But it should be observed that, while names of obvious Latin or Slav origin are quite frequent in the House of Representatives, they are less common in the Senate. In 1952 I noted that while there were several Senators with German names, there were only three that were, from an

American standpoint, foreign—Henry C. Dworshak of Idaho, John O. Pastore of Rhode Island, and Dennis Chavez of New Mexico. The list of the Presidents of the republic is particularly interesting to analyze. Many of them were formerly governors of states, for example, Grover Cleveland (New York), the two Roosevelts (New York), Calvin Coolidge (Massachusetts). Some were former members of Congress, Lincoln being Representative for Illinois, McKinley for Ohio, and Truman Senator for Missouri. Generals, such as Washington, Grant, and Eisenhower, also figure, and sometimes Cabinet members, for Hoover was formerly Secretary of Commerce and Taft Secretary of War. The classical career is from attorney to governor of a state and from governor to President, for by that route men can acquire political experience and put themselves in the public eye. Presidents who have not followed this way are seriously handicapped.

As far as social background is concerned, it is very significant that all the Presidents have been Protestants, with the exception of Jefferson and Lincoln, who did not belong to any church. There have been nine Episcopalians, including Franklin Roosevelt, six Presbyterians, among whom were Cleveland, Wilson, and Eisenhower, four Methodists, including Grant and McKinley, four Unitarians, including Taft, two Baptists, Harding and Truman, and two members of the Dutch Reformed Church, one of whom was Theodore Roosevelt. Fifteen of them were Freemasons. It does not appear possible, even today, for a Catholic to be elected President, and the parties hesitate to propose one even for the vicepresidency. The experience of Al Smith provided a lesson which the professional politicians will not easily forget. The Presidents, then, have all been Protestant, and 27 out of 33 of them Anglo-Saxon in origin; the remaining six belonged to the Nordic races, the Roosevelts and Van Buren being of Dutch origin, Jefferson Welsh, Hoover Swiss, and Eisenhower of distant German descent. As far as their professional status is concerned, there have been 22 lawyers, for the law is indeed a school for politics, several generals, one mining engineer (Hoover), and one professor (Woodrow Wilson). The earlier Presidents came mostly from the South, later they were recruited from the East, but in most recent times they have hailed from the West; Truman is a native of Missouri and Eisenhower of Texas. It would appear that this tendency is likely to continue, since the center of the electorate is definitely moving west, particularly as far as presidential elections are concerned. In early times the Presidents were drawn from the upper classes, but since the middle of the nineteenth century they have been mainly recruited from the middle or lower classes, Lincoln, Coolidge, Truman, and Eisenhower being examples of this. It remains exceptional for the President to belong to society circles, as did the Roosevelts and the nonelected candidate Stevenson.

The personnel appointed by the President varies considerably according to his character and political opinions. The entourage of the White House is completely different in atmosphere, according to whether Franklin Roosevelt, Truman, or Eisenhower, whether Democrats or Republicans, are in power. The following picture was given in an outstanding report by William S. White in the New York *Times*. In Roosevelt's time, the typical man encountered in the corridors of the White House was a Harvard graduate, legally minded, and decisive in manner. Important matters were discussed at aristocratic breakfast parties, held at a late hour at the President's bedside. Matters of policy were also discussed at Roosevelt's residence at Hyde Park. Businessmen were received by the President but were not admitted into his confidence, and the idea of attending a Rotary Club luncheon seemed to be outside the scope of this group of university aristocrats. During Truman's period of office the professors disappeared and it was the time for the politicians, professional local political workers, and Democratic "friends," whose claims the loyal President never betrayed. It was not "My country right or wrong" but "My party right or wrong," and the loyalty of the President to all those who at the given moment helped him touched the depth of the peoples' hearts, even though a few profiteers mingled in the crowd around him. Truman could also be found in some quite simple hotel in Kansas City, though it was not at the gatherings of the Rotarians or the Lions that his followers found themselves most at their ease. The general atmosphere was like that of the best of mid-nineteenth-century politics. With a complete reversal of outlook, Eisenhower filled the White House with businessmen, for the President believes in the capacity of such men to administer the state, but his choice is leading industrialists rather than average businessmen. His Cabinet, composed of "eight millionaires and a plumber," is in this respect typical. For the State Department he chose John Foster Dulles, a famous lawyer specializing in business litigation; for Secretary of the Interior, Douglas McKay, head of a super-automobile agency; for Secretary of the Treasury, George Humphrey, a banker with steel interests; for Attorney General, Herbert Brownell, a well-known lawyer; for Secretary of Defense, Charles Wilson, president of General Motors; for Postmaster General, A. E. Summerfield, an important estate agent with interests in the oil and automobile industries; for Secretary of Agriculture, Ezra T. Benson, a leading agriculturist; for Secretary of Commerce, Sinclair Weeks, banker and company director; and finally for Secretary of Labor, Martin Durkin, the president of the plumbers' union in the American Federation of Labor. The last-named resigned in September, 1953, realizing late in the day that he had been mistaken, but his companions did not say, as they would have done in France, that he had been "sold." Eisenhower thus chose six businessmen, two lawyers, and one workman, conceiving the Government as a large-scale business to be placed in the hands of those who should show themselves to be most efficient. Moreover, only Dulles and Brownell in his Cabinet had had previous political experience. It is certain that this choice did not please the professional politicians, who felt that they had been deprived of office, but it is certain that the President acted in a typically Republican manner, putting economics first. The White House is now characterized by efficiency; this includes early rising, and the discipline of the staff is military, Cabinet meetings opening with a moment of silence which has rather the effect of a prayer. By contrast with this, Franklin Roosevelt appears a sort of Alcibiades.

One striking feature of the recruitment of all political personnel is that there is no permanency beyond elections. Even eminent Cabinet members fall back into oblivion when their patrons relinquish power. There have been great administrators, but they have usually been businessmen who have returned to their business at the end of their period of government office, and great industrialists find it quite natural to leave industry temporarily when called on to serve in the national interest. There is a stable diplomatic personnel, but it has not been achieved without difficulty and without a number of retrograde steps. A typical incident remains in my memory. In 1899 I visited some municipal baths in Boston. The manager, who was showing me around, appeared extremely interested when, in reply to his question, I told him that I came from Le Havre. He asked me what the climate was like, whether there was a pleasant social life there, and whether the housing was comfortable. As I expressed surprise at this curiosity, he told me quite simply: "If the Democrats win the next election, I shall be made consul at Le Havre." The American diplomatic service has never entirely freed itself from this tradition. A praiseworthy effort has been made to build up a permanent and efficient staff, which is remarkable from many points of view, but it remains an acknowledged fact that a great number of posts, and notably the most important, should be given to nonprofessionals in recognition of election help given to the winning party. When a new President comes into power it is not only the Secretary of State who changes but also heads of departments and even sections within the State Department. It must also be added that the suspicious attitude adopted inside the State Department and in foreign posts by the secret police of men such as McCarthy discourages young men from entering a career still pervaded to such an extent by the political errors of the past. At the same time definite progress has been made and my baths manager at Boston definitely belongs to another age.

The general impression is that there has been a definite improvement in the recruitment of political leaders since the nineteenth century. Fifty years ago society members would turn away from politics with a kind of disdain, and Theodore Roosevelt stood out as an exception. It is no longer extraordinary to see members of the leading families turning to a political career; in addition to the Roosevelts, there are Henry Cabot Lodge, Jr., John Kennedy, and Frederic Coudert, Jr. There is also the fact that the responsibilities are different from what they were in the past. During the long period of British hegemony the English political leaders were drawn from the upper classes and it would appear that the United States is moving in the same direction.

PART VI

EXTERNAL RELATIONS

CHAPTER 32

American Economy in Its World Relationships (1)

There are few historical examples of a similar transformation of a continental country into a country with important exterior relations; of a country independent from the economic standpoint into a country henceforth bound by principles of external solidarity; of a country without responsibilities into a country charged with world-wide responsibility; from a merely autonomous economy into a leading world economy. This amazing expansion is a normal consequence for a nation which has grown up on a new territory, but its progress has been speeded by two wars which have brought victory, though they have not been the essential influential factor. The general balance of the United States has undergone a change because of them, but at the expense of a world disequilibrium which has resulted in former positions having become unrecognizable. It should be added that, if international conditions have changed, American psychology has not developed at the same pace; there is a time lag between the actual position of the United States in the world and the attitude of the American people toward intercontinental problems. The relations between American economy and world economy are one of the twentieth-century problems yet to be solved.

I

Before World War I a balanced system of trade had been established between the United States and the rest of the world, particularly as far as Europe was concerned. This equilibrium in-

311

cluded a favorable American balance of trade, in which imports amounted to barely 80% of exports. The system was complementary, for the excess of exports went to pay the interest or dividend on capital placed in the New World by Europe, which remained a sort of sleeping partner. The excess of exports appeared as a normal feature, and the Old World could easily obtain the dollars she needed. Moreover, the question was not even raised, since relations of Europe with the rest of the world had reached a degree of stability which looked as though it would be permanent. On the circumference, and considered as such, the United States was only one element in the world circle of which Europe formed the center.

The year 1914—not 1940—marked the end of the period of world equilibrium which had characterized the nineteenth century. A fundamental change in relationships arose at that period, and the period between the two wars did nothing to correct the balance, though an effort was made at adaptation. World War II accentuated the measure of disequilibrium and now it has all the appearance of a chronic illness, of a deep-seated vice attacking the trade system of the twentieth century. The relative position of the United States in the world has changed. A gigantic America is facing a ruined and declining Europe, an America strong by reason of its size in comparison with the little peninsula of the Asiatic land mass, now deprived of the vastness of Russia. The consequence of this is that there can be no complementary trade system, no reciprocity; what remains is a disproportionate system with one economy predominating. How has this disruption occurred? While Europe, in spite of strong efforts, has not yet succeeded in regaining its former rhythm of development, the production capacity of the United States is demonstrating unimaginable progress, exceeding all the records already established and even ceaselessly beating its own records. Since America needs help from no one and certainly none from Europe, she is not becoming a large-scale importer, except for raw materials found outside Europe, though by reason of international needs of materials which she alone can supply her exports are constantly increasing. Until 1914 she was still a debtor country because of the foreign capital invested; she has become a creditor country and creditor in respect to Europe, who is now in the normal way of things incapable of discharging her debts. There is, therefore, a lack of proportion between the two continents, and no complementary system of trade bearing any marks of a healthy economy has succeeded in becoming established. The balance of trade is on one side excessively favorable and on the other pathologically in deficit, allowing for a type of balance of payment which can be settled only by temporary expedients. This is the great twentieth-century crisis.

While the two World Wars, and particularly the second, have had the effect of breaking Europe's back, they have on the contrary given impetus to America. At first neutral, the United States derived profits from its position as supplier to the belligerent nations. Then, when it entered the war, it did not fight on its own territory, and its potential resources are such that the trial which proved catastrophic for Europe was for it an opportunity for technical progress and large-scale reorganization of production from an over-all point of view. Had there been no war, Europe would doubtless have continued to develop in the same way as before 1914—possibly not as quickly as America, but a sense of proportion between the development of the two continents would have been maintained. This has not happened.

Between 1938 and 1952 the over-all production of the United States has tripled: taking 1948 as 100, the index for 1938 is 46 and for 1952, 114. Agricultural production has increased by one-quarter, from 74 in 1938 (base 1948 = 100) to 114 in 1952. It must not be forgotten that the United States is comparable to a continent rather than a country, and that it is, as the United Kingdom has never been, both an industrial and an agricultural country. Its extraordinary capacity for exuberance is coincident with an almost complete independence of anything outside. Its exceptional financial position enables it to import without any difficulty anything that it does not produce, so that it is not only the leading world producer of a number of products but has also become since 1914 the largest world consumer. It is a well-known fact that the United States, which has 6.4% of the land surface of the world and 6.2% of the world population, consumes 64% of the world's oil supply, 61% of the rubber, 63% of the iron ore, 44% of the manganese, 50% of the zinc, 48% of the copper, and 48% of the lead.*

Europe, and more particularly the United Kingdom, had filled this role of leading world producer and consumer before the United States, but because of its limited area and its particularly high population density it had to import a large proportion of its foodstuffs and raw materials, and this was the basis of the economic relationship between Europe and the rest of the world. The American position is completely different. Gigantic machinery has been set up in North America to absorb the raw materials and certain agricultural products. It has a fantastic appetite, and, running parallel with imports, the national production is showing itself capable of supplying an increasing proportion of its needs. Certain materials, such as iron ore, are becoming exhausted and have to be obtained from outside, though Canada should not really be considered as "outside"; while others, on the contrary, such as rubber, are freed from dependence on imports by the development of the synthetic product. The American nation is thus well on the way to returning to her old tradition of maximum continental independence. If there is, under such conditions, a tendency for continental overproduction, Europe, in spite of its needs, has not the purchasing power necessary to acquire the surplus. Since the surplus is continental rather than national, however, the United States is in a position to absorb it. There is the basic will to do so; the country is used to relying mainly on its home market, which rarely fails it, so that its economy feels a natural temptation to autarky. No psychological attitude toward international trade has developed, as it did with the United Kingdom, a country dependent on imports as well as on exports. "Self-sufficient giant!" commented the *Economist* of January 26, 1952. The principal source of the trouble which brought about the world crisis of the twentieth century lies there, just as much as in European ruin.

II

Since World War II imports have by no means developed at the same pace as exports. Taking 1936-1938 as a basis, the export index increased in 1952 to 250 by volume and 514 by value, while

* 1950 figures taken from the *Paley Report* (*Resources for Freedom*).

imports reached only 151 by volume and 437 by value. Before 1914 American imports remained at a figure just below two billion dollars and in 1938, after the boom of the war years and the period immediately afterward, they still remained at approximately the same point, reaching 1,960,000,000 dollars. They rose after World War II to 4,159,000,000 dollars in 1945, 10,967,000,-000 in 1951, owing to the boom in imports caused by the Korean War, and 10,717,000,000 in 1952. These figures are high in themselves but they represent only a small proportion of the total national product: 4.3% of the gross national product in 1929, 2.4% in 1938, 3.4% in 1951, and even less in 1952.

The United States is thus not a country of large-scale imports, and its substantial imports consist to an increasing degree of raw materials. It is both interesting and symptomatic to follow the transformation which the types of imports have undergone since the last century.

Imports by Main Groups
(% of total imports)

	1875-1879	*1921-1924*	*1952*
Raw materials	26.7	53.1	51.3
Foodstuffs	41.3	24.8	29.3
Manufactured goods	30.0	21.1	19.4

These figures illustrate how the United States, in becoming more and more industrialized, has been obliged to import more raw materials, while it has become increasingly able to do without imports of manufactured goods. This is the normal evolution of any country in the process of industrialization. It is true that, particularly since World War II, the raw materials imported have been upward of 24% in the form of semifinished products, and the same tendency holds for foodstuffs. Raw materials receive more and more their first processing in their place of origin, either because of cost of production or because of local national feeling.

The United States normally imports, either as raw material or semifinished product, rubber, wool, mineral oils, hides and skins, nonferrous metals, timber and wood pulp, vegetable oils, and fertilizers; also, as far as foodstuffs are concerned, coffee, tea, cane sugar, fruit, and vegetables, cacao and alcohol. At the point of development which it has now reached, America can no longer feed its industry without importing raw materials, some of them in large quantities; but, with the exception of a few exotic products, it could live very easily without food imports, without having to fear any blockade; and, finally, it could cut off all imports of manufactured goods without noticing it. At this very moment when its imports are increasing, its intensified research on the subject of synthetic products is a step in the direction of increased autonomy.

In view of its needs the United States logically turns for its imports to countries which produce industrial raw materials or foodstuffs, but, apart from luxury articles, quality goods, or specialized articles, the main industrial countries do not figure among its main sources of supply. It is only to be expected that the place of Europe as a source of American imports has continued to decline. Europe still provided 46.6% of the total imports in the period 1911-1915, but this fell to 30.4% in 1921-1925 and 18.6% in 1951; the heavy drop came immediately after World War I, but this tendency was accentuated by the second war. On the other hand, the American continent has come to take the first place as the source of United States imports, the proportion rising from 35.0% in 1911-1915 to 38.6% in 1921-1925 and 53.1% in 1951. Had it not been for World War II Asia and Oceania would have shown similar evolution for they contributed 16.9% of America's imports in the period 1911-1915 and 28.9% in 1921-1925, but the proportion fell to 22.9% in 1951 because of the unsettled state of the Far East. Africa has not proved of great interest as a source of imports, for it provided only 1.4% of the total in 1911-1915 and 2.1% in 1921-1925, but it is a source of raw materials to which the United States has given more consideration since the war, for African imports were 5.6% in 1950 and 5.4% in 1951.

The list of the countries which supplied the United States with her imports in 1938 reads, in order of importance: Canada, Japan, the United Kingdom, Malaya, Cuba, Brazil, the Philippines, the Dutch East Indies. In 1951 the order had changed to: Canada, Brazil, the United Kingdom, Malaya, Cuba, Colombia, Australia,

Mexico, Venezuela, India. With the exception of the United Kingdom, all these countries are exporters of industrial raw materials or unprocessed foodstuffs. Brazil and Colombia supply coffee; Canada, Chile, Mexico, and Malaya nonferrous metals; Canada paper and wood pulp; Venezuela, the West Indies, and Colombia mineral oils; Malaya, Indonesia, and Siam rubber; Australia, Argentina, and Uruguay wool; Cuba and the Philippines cane sugar; Canada, the Benelux Customs Union, France, Sweden, and Germany iron ore or pig iron. One can see the complementary trade system thus involved, though it is not with Europe, from which the United States is increasingly turning away in favor of the New World, Asia, Oceania, and Africa. The countries which are a source of dollars are now outside Europe, and this is one of the most serious aspects of the European crisis.

III

The exports of the United States exceed the imports. Before 1914 the average level of exports was 2,500,000,000 dollars and World War I increased this to some 5,000,000,000-8,000,000,000, but because of the crisis it dropped to 2,378,000,000 in 1931, rising to no more than 3,057,000,000 in 1938. The stimulus of World War II brought exports up to 9,589,000,000 in 1945, 15,032,000,000 in 1951 and 15,191,000,000 in 1952. In comparison with the immediate prewar period, the volume of exports has risen by 50% but the value has almost quintupled. At the same time, in spite of these enormous figures, the proportion of the national output exported is not only insignificant but actually declining, for while exports counted for a little under 10% of total production in 1938, they are now no more than some 5%. The United States is thus a country dependent essentially for its prosperity on the home market, and exports do not play a decisive role in the economy.

Nothing emphasizes more the transformation which the American economy has undergone in the last three-quarters of a century than the changes in the percentage and composition of the exports, as shown in the following table:

Exports by Main Groups

(% of total exports)

	1875-1879	1911-1915	1921-1925	1952
Raw materials	39.4	46.15	39.9	24.0
Foodstuffs	44.8	23.15	23.6	14.0
Manufactured goods	15.8	30.70	36.3	62.0

The place occupied by raw materials has substantially declined to the advantage of manufactured goods, and that of foodstuffs to an even greater degree. The increase in the exports of manufactured goods is even more striking if to the finished manufactures one adds semifinished products and foodstuffs which have undergone the initial process of transformation. Semifinished products, which are included in the raw materials group, account for 10.8% of total exports, and partly processed foodstuffs for 4.8%, so that articles which have undergone some process of transformation account for 77.6% of total exports. These statistics reflect the increasing tendency in world trade to export materials in at least a semimanufactured state, and also the striking industrial expansion which the United States has undergone.

In 1890 three-quarters of American exports consisted of four nonmanufactured products—raw cotton, wheat, mineral oil, and meat—but today these form no more than about one-fifth of total exports. America doubtless remains, as far as total amounts are concerned, the leading world supplier of raw materials and foodstuffs, but in future what the world will seek to purchase from the United States will be manufactured goods, particularly all kinds of machinery and, in general, mass-produced articles. The United Kingdom, leading exporter of the nineteenth century, sold cotton goods and iron and steel products. The United States, leading exporter of the twentieth century, also sells textile manufactures, but the engineering products which it supplies have developed in infinite variety: pipes and sections, hardware, oil-drilling machinery and cracking units, road-construction equipment, excavators, textile machinery, sugar-extraction equipment, internal combustion engines, and refrigerating machinery down to machines for the cigarette industry, the whole range of machine tools, sewing machines, typewriters, printing machinery, calculating machines, cash registers, all agricultural machinery, vehicles of all sorts, motorcars and spare parts, trucks, motorcycles, aircraft, electrical machinery including radio sets, refrigerators, batteries, electric motors, and all types of household goods; and all these in steel or nonferrous metals. We are now in a century which is no longer one of steel and cotton but one predominated by artificial textiles, chemical products, and nonferrous metals, and the representative par excellence of the present century is the United States.

The logical consequence of the present tendency would be for the United States to cease exporting raw materials and foodstuffs. Practically speaking, coal, iron ore, corn, and raw wool are no longer exported and already at the beginning of the century the country was absorbing an increasing proportion of the meat and wheat produced. The two World Wars have reversed this tendency of home consumption as far as wheat is concerned and the second war made the United States for a short while a source of European coal imports, but the basic tendency is in the opposite direction, and one even wonders whether in the long run American cotton will continue to be sold in the world market. The balance of trade between the United States, Europe, and the other continents has undergone a fundamental change in the last fifty years and this appears to be permanent. The table below, giving the destination of United States exports by continents, is a striking illustration of this transformation:

Destination of United States Exports by Continents
(% of total exports)

	1875-1879	1911-1915	1921-1925	1951
Europe	81.0	64.0	52.7	26.9
America	14.6	27.1	31.2	42.3
Asia and Oceania	3.8	7.8	14.5	16.5
Africa	0.6	1.1	1.6	3.9

A lengthy commentary is not necessary. The decline in exports to Europe, particularly after World War II, is striking, and it is the remainder of the American continent, the only one intact after the upheaval, which has become the important market for United States goods. Had Asia not been devastated by the war it is possible that it would have tended to replace Europe as second continental customer.

These trade tendencies are the logical consequence of the stage of economic development of the areas concerned. Europe, traditionally more industrialized than the United States, required from the latter supplies of raw materials and foodstuffs, but not manufactured goods because it made them itself. But the two wars, in particular the second, completely upset the balance of the system for, still needing cotton, cereals, and even at times coal, Europe also required industrial equipment (to replace war damage), mass-produced goods, and armaments. We are no longer considering the relations between a highly industrialized continent and a young economy, but between an aging continent and a young giant, now powerfully equipped. Moreover, vis-à-vis continents other than Europe, the United States fills the role of the industrialized country in its relations with relatively primitive economies, which are in the process of acquiring industrial equipment. The United States occupies from this point of view the place which Europe held fifty years ago, for it is to it that the nations eager to enter into a manufacturing career all come; and all the nations show this desire. They are being equipped according to the American plan, finding in the United States the twentieth-century equipment which they are so impatient to acquire. It will doubtless be possible for Europe to recapture some of these markets, but it will never regain its monopoly of them, or even occupy the first place.

These differences in trade relationships are clearly reflected in the list by order of importance of the United States' main customers in 1938 and 1951. On the eve of the war they were the United Kingdom, Canada, Japan, France, Germany, the Netherlands, Argentina, and the Philippines; in 1951 Canada, the United Kingdom, Mexico, Brazil, Japan, Cuba, Germany, India, Italy, Venezuela, and France. The countries that are now in a position to buy—for all really need to do so—are those who sell raw materials on the American market or are simply neighbors of the United States in the New World and thus acquire the necessary dollars. New commercial currents have thus arisen in the world and they pass at a great distance from Europe.

CHAPTER 33

American Economy in Its World
Relationships (II)

★

It was normal before 1914 that America, a debtor country, should have a favorable balance of trade, for it was borrowing capital and paying through exports. But as a creditor country it should logically be orientated toward an unfavorable balance of trade, combined with a policy of foreign investment. After 1918 the experts awaited this reversal of its economy, but it did not occur during the period between the two wars; moreover, the position became aggravated in the period which immediately followed the second. The result has been a chronic lack of dollars in Europe which reflects the lack of equilibrium in commercial relations between the continents. One is tempted to say that this is an effect of the war, but one ought perhaps to consider it rather in the light of something more serious, the displacement of the world center of gravity. This appears to be the real source of the twentieth-century economic crisis.

On the eve of World War I, United States exports exceeded imports by about one-third. The excess increased to 50% during the years 1914-1918, but after the war and until 1939 the balance remained constantly favorable, showing an excess of exports over imports of 25% in 1928 and 28% in 1939. This favorable balance continued after 1940 and increased to the point of becoming definitely unsound. In 1939 exports amounted to 3,177,000,000 dollars and imports to 2,318,000,000, leaving an excess of 859 million dollars, but in 1944 the favorable balance rose to 10,330,000,000 dollars, with exports at 14,259,000,000 and imports at 3,929,-

000,000; this disequilibrium continued after the return to peace, though in a less exaggerated form. The excess of exports over imports was 5,646,000,000 dollars in 1945, 4,796,000,000 in 1946, 9,585,000,000 in 1947, 5,529,000,000 in 1948, 5,429,000,000 in 1949, 1,423,000,000 in 1950, 4,065,000,000 in 1951, and 4,474,000,000 in 1952—the last figure on a total of 15,191,000,000 dollars of exports and 10,717,000,000 of imports. The total favorable balance accumulated between 1940 and 1952 was 700 million dollars.

Such a situation was easily understandable during the war when the United States was an important source of supply for the belligerent countries and, though belligerent itself, did not have to fight on its own territory. It has become abnormal and unhealthy, however, through its prolongation into the peace period, but the reasons for this are only too clear. Europe still needs the help of the United States for its reconstruction program. The countries outside Europe require American industrial equipment and manufactured goods for their current needs, while basically the United States has no need of outside help, and all its former traditions lead it jealously to guard the privilege of this autonomy. Before 1914 the element of invisibles in the balance of payments corrected the lack of balance in its trade. These were the interest on capital invested in the United States, the amounts spent abroad by American tourists, the remittances sent by immigrants to their families remaining in Europe, and international "services" which Europe was almost alone in carrying out. Today, interest on capital invested appears as a credit item in the export column, and if the "services" and the tourist expenditure appear on the debit side, the corrective element is far from being sufficient to restore the balance. In 1951, for example, the excess of exports over imports and the interest on capital invested, less "services" and tourist expenditure, still left a credit balance of five billion dollars. The truth of the matter is that Europe was devastated by World War II before it had completely recovered from the effects of the first war, and that the peace which followed the second war has brought nothing but an atmosphere of cold war. The world is still endeavoring to restore its balance. Nature always provides this balance, but at what price? For, according to

Philippe Berthelot, speaking as a European, "Everything comes to an end, but ends badly."

II

The characteristics of American trade since 1945 reflect to a great extent the economic problems of other countries. The latter, in capital debt and without any remaining reserve, can pay for their imports only by means of exports and, inasmuch as they fail to export, they lack the dollars necessary to pay for their purchases. Thus there is no real balance, no reciprocity, and recourse to expedients is necessary in order to settle payments. How can the importers of American goods settle their debts? It was done in the first instance by consignments of gold, so that the gold stock of the United States, which was only 1,526,000,000 dollars in 1914, rose to 20,083,000,000 in 1945 and 23,255,000,000 in 1952. The United States absorbs this gold and returns practically none of it. Europe also acquits itself by liquidating all its credits. "Everywhere a creditor, nowhere a debtor," the economist Neymarck said proudly of France in 1914. At that time the United States had a debt of just over one billion dollars, but now it is everywhere a creditor. The proportion in which other countries pay their debts to it is reflected by the transfer in its balance of payments of capital interest from the debit to the credit side. The importer then has to rely upon the good will of the exporter, and one has to have recourse to expedients such as delayed payments, investments by the exporter, and acknowledged or disguised grants, such as the Marshall Plan or UNRRA. This really means that part of the American exports are not paid for. It is estimated that in 1951 the surplus exports and services paid for by these expedients, that is, in reality, not paid, was 6,142,000,000 dollars: 4,501,000,000 by various grants, 163 million by government loans, 412 million by private agreements, and 1,066,000,000 by investment. If one also takes into account payment in gold of 442 million dollars, it means that 5,700,000,000 dollars or 38% of the exports and services were not paid for by normal means of settlement.

Thus the paradox of this monstrously favorable balance of trade ceases to appear entirely as a paradox and it can be said that, taking into account grants, loans, and delayed payments which change the character of part of the exports, there is a tendency toward equilibrium. There is nothing in this which should appear surprising, for in the long run nature has a balancing mechanism which operates according to infallible rules. There is thus being established in the world a series of exchanges which, when it has taken on its final form, liberated from the expedients of the immediate postwar period, will no longer resemble the nineteenth-century system founded on the supremacy, or rather the monopoly, of Europe. It would be an illusion to think that the restoration of European economic capacity to its former level would bring about a restoration of the pre-1914 trade system, or even that operating before 1939. The new, fundamental factor to be considered is the position of the United States in international commerce as a creditor country without an element of counterbalance in her trade relationships. The dollar crisis is not only a consequence of the war, but also a general tendency of the century.

Commercial exchanges between the United States and Europe have, since World War I, lost any reciprocal element or any idea of reciprocity. Europe may require American goods but it lacks the dollars to purchase them, because the United States does not buy European goods and is accustomed to give without receiving, or to lend without any serious hope of reimbursement. America has acquired the mentality of a benefactor or a trustee in bankruptcy, and the extent to which it will continue is mainly a matter of politics and not of commercial interests, though the latter are more important if relationships are to be economically and morally healthy. The debtor also runs the risk of losing any sense of reciprocity, either by holding out his hand to receive, consenting too easily to remain in debt, or showing a reluctant gratitude for services which he considers to be anything but disinterested. Since they cannot develop their exports in an unwilling American market, the European countries are constrained to find sources of imports and customers elsewhere.

If there is to be in the future any really reciprocal exchange system, it will be between the United States and countries outside Europe who supply her with raw materials and foodstuffs.

The latter have dollars with which to purchase United States manufactured goods, so that it is not only a question of source of imports, but American exports also are directed toward countries such as Angola, Afghanistan, Australia, Bolivia, Ceylon, Chile, Colombia, Ecuador, Indonesia, Malaya, New Zealand, Nicaragua, Nigeria, Pakistan, Siam, Uruguay, Venezuela, and the Belgian Congo, not to mention those two important customers, Canada and Brazil. It is only to the extent to which Europe controls some of these foreign economies that she can benefit from their capacity to earn dollars; the sterling area and the French Union thus profit from the terms of trade marked, in 1950-1951 for example, by a spectacular rise in price of colonial products. During the nineteenth century Europe played in the field of world trade the centralized role of a suction and forcing pump, absorbing raw materials and producing manufactured goods. Today the United States has taken Europe's place. It is not difficult to see how the problem of the relationship between America and countries outside Europe will be solved, but the continued European lack of balance remains the unsolved problem of the free world.

III

What would be required for the world as a whole to revert to a stable position? It is obvious that Europe must adapt herself to a new situation, but it is equally important that the United States should be equally ready to do so, by adopting a creditor mentality, which would involve a policy of foreign investment, increased imports, resignation to a deficit in the balance of trade, and renunciation of a long tradition of protectionism. The lack of balance in world trade is in the main about forty years old, but the Americans have, as far as their international reflexes are concerned, remained to a large extent the same as they were before 1914.

It was not that the leaders of the country's economy failed to realize immediately the change that had come about and the reversal of attitude which it would necessitate. In the period 1920-1930 Wall Street was well aware of the fact that a country which changes from debtor to creditor should change its financial and commercial policy. People well-versed in economic matters held the point of view that the excess of exports over imports should disappear from 1925 onward, and that this would be beneficial to American economy. It was, moreover, admitted that an increasingly larger percentage of national investment should sooner or later be directed outside the country. That indeed is what the experts thought and said, but their opinion was not followed. The American, who has not changed much, does not like investing his capital abroad, as did the Englishman and the Frenchman before 1914. There is still so much scope within the United States, under such favorable conditions, that he is not tempted to search elsewhere in countries for which he holds an inveterate mistrust. If capital is voluntarily placed abroad, it would be in Canada, which, it is important to understand, is not considered as a foreign country; or possibly in South or Central America. The American does not feel at his ease anywhere else. He tides over difficulties because he is rich and powerful, as is the dollar, but he contrasts strongly with the nineteenth-century Englishman, who knew how to cut his losses and had a long tradition of commerce and colonial trade. American investment prefers large-scale operations, such as the complete transfer of an industry or the complete organization of some service; the result is that the operations are not carried out sufficiently quietly and, in spite of a widely advertised anticolonial policy, they arouse more hostility than the traditional British investment policy.

In 1925 American capital abroad, which was estimated at 10,405,000,000 dollars, was invested 40% in Latin America, 27% in Canada, 24% in Europe, and 9% in Asia and Oceania. In 1950 private investment was estimated at 11,804,000,000 and that represents only a very small increase; as much as two-thirds of it, or 8,200,000,000 dollars, is invested in the American continent. Notable items in other parts of the world include 840 million in the United Kingdom, 726 million in Persian oil, 285 million in France, 198 million in Australia, 140 million in South Africa, 149 million in the Philippines, 40 million in Egypt, 58 million in Indonesia, and 38 million in India. The investments which are, properly speaking, industrial are made in the United Kingdom, France, Brazil, and Australia, but the largest-scale investment of American capital is directed toward the development of Canada. But one could not really maintain that the last-named is, in fact, foreign investment, except to humor a certain Canadian sensitiveness, for North American unity is a continental reality which makes itself increasingly felt and goes beyond the narrow national limits of the past. American investment has also shown an interest, similar to that shown in Canada, in investment in oil mining, particularly in western Asia and Venezuela. If one considers this dual development which is being actively carried on, United States foreign investment must doubtless now reach some fifteen billion dollars. It is striking how small the investments are in the regions classed as underdeveloped, those of the famous Point Four of President Truman. American capital is very little drawn toward this type of investment, about which the destined beneficiaries themselves are somewhat reticent, as if they feared the introduction on their soil of too powerful a partner. Thus, at least up to the present time, with the exception of a few investments which are geographically limited, America has not taken the place which England so brilliantly occupied in the nineteenth century, seconded by France.

If the United States has not learned its lesson as an investor, it has done so even less as an importer, and it is in this field that its attitude and reflexes are characterized by congenital protectionism. This protectionism seems to me to be continental rather than national, characteristic of a continent which, as soon as it acquired political independence, wished to be economically and industrially autonomous. We have already pointed out that such a program of autarky, unattainable and, moreover, stupid for a country of limited size, is completely conceivable for a continental economy. It can be understood how in the long run there can arise from it a state of mind in which Cobden's free trade policy appears as a foreign doctrine, English, alien—giving the word its pejorative sense.

It is true that with the twentieth century powerful industries have developed which, unbeatable in their costs of production and beginning to overproduce, showed a tendency toward liberalism, and were more anxious to conquer foreign markets than to protect home ones. A new preoccupation was thus being felt in American customs policy, and this, after appearing in 1890 in the reciprocity clause of the McKinley Tariff, inspired the Trade

Agreements Act of 1934. A few large-scale industries, the New York banking industry, and the consumer generally speaking are orientated toward a certain relaxation in the rigidity of tariffs, but this must give rise to no mistaken conceptions, for industry as a whole, particularly the medium and small-scale, remains deeply and even savagely protectionist. Dependent on the home market, the industrialist of a medium-sized or small township watches jealously over imports, ready to ask immediately for an increase in the tariff if he feels the pressure of foreign competition. He then says that foreign goods owe their lower prices merely to the starvation wages paid in foreign countries with a low standard of living. The argument invariably carries weight, particularly since these complaints are heard at once in the House of Representatives and even more easily in the Senate. From the political point of view Main Street triumphs over Wall Street. Even the Democratic party is only moderately liberal. Its tariffs, which are in principle mere fiscal devices, are in fact protectionist, and its reciprocal agreements contain an escape clause which gives the President a key with which he can at any moment lock the door in the face of the would-be importer. As for the Republican party, it is by tradition, doctrine, and temperament a partisan of the high tariff policy. President Eisenhower, whose personal tendencies would be on the whole liberal, but who has no popular support for this outlook, has only obtained from Congress the renewal for one year of the Reciprocal Trade Act. Any hope of a relaxation of tariff policy under the Republican government is vain. Such a relaxation would only mean that the imports would come up against a second line of defense even more redoubtable, that of the administrative regulations of the Customs, which have the power to annul any concessions allowed elsewhere. There should be no mistake about the fact that it is under implicit directions that the Customs practice this inflexibility.

Europe can clearly be diagnosed. It has become a chronic debtor and is deprived of its former reserves, so that it knows that it cannot balance its transatlantic trade unless it is allowed to pay by means of goods. If the United States insists on Europe organizing itself and is willing to assist, it is absolutely necessary that America should open its doors more widely to imports from Europe, that there should be "trade not aid." It must be admitted that American opinion, particularly under Republican guidance and in spite of warnings from a government which appears to have understood the situation, is scarcely orientated in this direction. It is not instinctively disposed either to a policy of foreign investment, to a lowering of tariffs, or to the acceptance of an unfavorable balance of trade, which it would envisage only with pessimism. There seems a basic tendency to prefer a system by which profits are made on the home market and that part of the exportable surplus is disposed of by means of a sort of dumping.

The American nation is far from understanding that the excess of imports over exports is in reality a sign of wealth. The American's reflexes are not international and his first care is to maintain the privilege of a home market, the absorption capacity of which he considers to be limitless. Basically he does not consider that he needs the help of the outside world in order to maintain a prosperity which must be defended against the competition, which in his eyes is unhealthy, of countries with low wage levels. At the least threat of unemployment an outcry compels the raising even higher of the Great Wall of China which surrounds the country.

From the standpoint of economic wisdom these ideas are false. If one has lived in the United States, however, one understands why they are held, considering that one is dealing with a continent whose unexploited resources are extensive, and with a home market the purchasing capacity of which, limitless by reason of this fact, grows with every new step forward in the production price. The American economy in this period immediately following World War II has adapted itself to a regime in which part of its exports are not paid for; it is a sort of dumping, political in aim, but which has also a function in maintaining the full operation of the system as a guarantee against unemployment. The essential thing is that the machinery should function.

In the nineteenth century the world achieved economic balance, but no solution has yet been found by the twentieth century. In the nineteenth century the balance was maintained by England, in the twentieth the lack of balance is concentrated around the United States.

The economic exploitation of the whole world and world trade showed real unity during the nineteenth century. On leaving the shores of Europe one entered a sort of international mercantile republic, operating under British direction and, on the whole, functioning according to the practices of British free trade, or, more properly speaking, fair trade. Goods were exchanged without too many obstacles and men could travel freely. It must be borne in mind that, between 1840 and 1914, forty million emigrants left Europe to settle overseas. But the essential fact to be noted is that the United Kingdom had a permanently unfavorable balance of trade so that all the countries of the world had, or could obtain, sterling; this observation is also true for all the important countries of western and central Europe. The United Kingdom was the great importer of the world, but her entrepôt trade accounted for the redistribution of vast quantities of different products. The trade deficit was compensated either by services, though these too may be considered as a trade commodity, or the income from capital which the United Kingdom and Europe invested abroad on a large scale. These facts are well known and even banal, but the present century is in difficulties because it does not possess an equivalent system.

England in particular and Europe in general had large adverse trade balances because they needed imports from outside Europe, that is, because their trade relations with other continents were of a complementary nature. England needed wheat, meat, textile raw materials, and minerals. South and even North America, Asia, Africa, and Oceania needed manufactured goods, services, capital for investment, that is, the products of the technical knowledge accumulated by a civilization which from the industrial point of view was more highly developed than theirs. Since currency was freely interchangeable, the use of sterling was universal, a London credit being the equivalent of a credit anywhere else in the world.

Today North America has replaced England as the key to economic international relations, but the situation is not at all the same. First of all, an enormous, impenetrable continental bloc, that of the U.S.S.R. and China, stands outside international trade relations. But interchange of goods is scarcely freer elsewhere, for economic nationalism has surrounded every country with barriers which often cannot be penetrated. These barriers do not consist so much in customs tariffs or import quotas as in an inextricable network of formalities and administrative annoyances, ranging from exchange control to passport visas and vaccination. It gives the same impression as an engine whose transmission system has seized.

But I come back again to the essential point. The trade balance of the principal party, the United States, is favorable, and this means that no country holds dollars and that, in so far as countries may hold sterling, it is worthless since it is not exchangeable with dollars. The American balance of trade remains favorable because there is no reciprocity between the United States economy and that of the rest of the world. Great Britain is an island, Europe is "a little headland of the Asiatic continent," but the United States forms a large continent. England has always needed to import wheat, meat, cotton, and mineral oil, but the United States has always possessed all these products within her own territory; only in recent years has she felt some shortage of raw materials indispensable to her industry.

Opposite this America, whose very independence may be considered as a perturbing element, there is only a reduced Europe, thrown out of balance in spite of her attempts at recovery. Trade, after all, implies a certain measure of equality among the traders, and this equality is nonexistent as far as Europe and America are concerned. No really satisfactory balance has been established, either, between the United States and the other continents, for though the American buys rubber and now even mineral oils, he needs neither wheat, meat, nor cotton.

There is then a fundamental and disturbing difference between the two systems which we have just compared. The European system was a natural development, founded on reciprocal exchange, in a century blessed with international peace. The American system, equally natural in its origins, has become because of the war an economic leader whose too rapid ascendancy in comparison with other countries has not so far permitted the establishment of a world system compatible with a healthy economy.

CHAPTER 34

The Foundations of the Foreign Policy
of the United States

★

The conditions under which the foreign policy of the United States is decided come from an initial contradiction.

The American by tradition is continentally minded. He became so from the political point of view as soon as his nationality was constituted as separate from that of the Englishman, through the voluntary separation from the Old World. He is continentally minded from an economic outlook because his country is self-sufficient in natural resources, and also by reason of the home market on which American prosperity is founded. In his attitude toward the outside world this psychology, which is liable to survive the circumstances which brought it into being, appears to be an ever-flourishing source of congenital isolationism.

But this same American's interests are universal, and this is shown in different ways. In the first place by his Protestant moralizing, which is characteristically British, he looks at all problems from the moral angle and reserves for himself a privilege which gives him great satisfaction, that of passing judgment on others. If other people do not comport themselves according to his ethical standards, he reproves them as if they had committed a sin. It is a legal type of moralizing which shows the American's sincere attachment to certain principles handed down from the eighteenth century; they include an optimistic conception of human nature, faith in democracy, respect for international law, condemnation of conquest and particularly colonial conquest carried out overseas; if it is carried out on land, it is merely expan-

333

sion. But economic interests have in the end compelled the Americans to look at things from the world standpoint, for, since it has become an importer of raw materials and an exporter of manufactured goods, the United States wishes to have its share of the world's natural resources and the international market. It has spread commercially and politically beyond the bounds of its continent and therefore has been forced to take an interest in anything which goes on in the world.

Two factors have entered into play here and each implies this idea of contradiction. The American interest is both isolationist and expansionist. As for public opinion, the motive power of the regime, it is instinctively hostile to all compromise with foreign powers, but cannot help taking part, even in affairs which are not its concern. Accustomed over a long period to be able to interfere with impunity, it does not realize that circumstances have changed. Personal interest and passionate feelings are so intermingled in this attitude that it is often impossible to disentangle them.

It is not within the scope of this study to describe the foreign policy of the United States, but merely to determine on what it is founded. I believe that its psychology and inspiration have remained the same since the nation's early days, but the face of the world and the position of the United States have changed in a way which amounts to upheaval rather than to evolution. The pivot of this revolutionary movement should be fixed at 1914, or perhaps even as far back as the Spanish-American War of 1898. There is first of all a traditional doctrine inherited from the eighteenth and nineteenth centuries; then, in the period between the two World Wars, a crisis in this doctrine; finally, since World War II, a new orientation which would appear to have become established.

I

The traditional doctrine is based on certain main assertions and certain dependent secondary considerations.

The main assertions are the maintenance of independence vis-à-vis the old mother country in particular and Europe in general, if necessary in opposition to them. The American nation came into being because of a revolt and, in its political sentimentality, it guards the memory of this. The revolt alone was not enough, for the American continent must still be defended against any new European aggression. The past remains the past, to be accepted, or rather tolerated, inasmuch as former colonial empires are concerned; but there is no question of accepting further conquests, or even armed intervention on American territory, which, from the American point of view, means not only the United States but the whole of the Americas. The whole history of the United States is, therefore, permeated with a condemnation in principle of any nondemocratic political regime, or even those which are in opposition to the particular principles of American democracy. It is not solely a question of moral disapproval; the United States refuses to recognize, or recognizes only with the greatest reluctance, governments established by violence or imposed from without. It is obvious that the Americans have often maintained diplomatic relations with regimes with whose principles they are not in agreement, but at the basis of their doctrine there is the idea that recognition implies tacit approval, which is in opposition to the policy of nonintervention. It is one of the instances, so frequent in the United States, where ideology and diplomacy are mixed, and this confusion reigns in the American mind whenever there is question of a *do jure* recognition.

Now let us study the secondary considerations. American policy claims the liberty of sea communications. This is not a primary consideration for an economically autonomous country, but rather an aspect of its independence, all the more so when one considers that in the nineteenth century the United States had a large fleet of sailing vessels. There is a similar claim with regard to international sources of raw materials, a matter from which the United States is increasingly unable to stand aloof. It is the same where access to world markets is concerned. While American exports were confined mainly to raw materials, her markets scarcely needed to be safeguarded, but the position is no longer the same now that they consist of increasing quantities of manufactured goods. Thus grew up the doctrine of customs policy, which was to remain a permanent characteristic of the United States: without claiming a privilege, to protest against any regime which carried with it discrimination against American exports.

Though a protectonist at home, the American speaks the language of liberalism in international economic discussions. This is the traditional American standpoint.

There exists, on the other hand, a whole series of aims or precautions to which the United States remains indifferent, to the point of not understanding them when held by others. This includes, for example, the acquisition of territory. Once their national territory had been established—by conquest, moreover, as they are only too ready to forget—they declared themselves satisfied, all the more so because, since they did not lack space, territorial extensions had no real value for them. How many times was not Europe persuaded during the nineteenth century that the United States would annex Canada or even Mexico. This opinion showed a fundamental misunderstanding of the American mind, satiated by the area of this continent where, unlike Europe, there was room for everybody. The acquisition of colonies must come under this same category. American colonial expansion has taken place, but it has been carried out not overseas, but by the swallowing up of a continent, as happened also with Russia. To Americans Algeria is "colonial," but neither Texas nor California is; nor, in the triumphant eyes of Stalin in 1945, was Mongolia or Manchuria. They are in completely good faith about it, considering themselves to belong to a colony which has been liberated, and therefore from a sentimental angle hostile to all colonial powers and pledged to support all movements toward liberation. The spontaneity and the depth of this anticolonial feeling are generally misunderstood, and if the United States Government is forced to disregard it, or even to contradict it, it can do so only in a hypocritical fashion. Finally there is one thing which America has accepted only in spite of herself: that is to undertake the responsibilities of world leadership. It is not that the United States was not, before 1914, imperialist in her own manner, for indeed she was and did not attempt to hide it; but her expansion was limited to her own continent. When the Americans found themselves faced with world domination, they sincerely recoiled before the encumbrance of an empire; if destiny has finally imposed this responsibility upon them, it is against their wishes, unless, as the old saying goes, *"L'appétit vient en mangeant."*

The primary importance of the geographical factor of this continental isolation which gives rise to such a great measure of security is clearly visible in the initial stages of the development of American foreign policy. But of no less importance is the ideological factor, the sincerity of which cannot be doubted, and the free expression of which has for so long been strengthened by its impunity. The whole policy is impregnated with a persistent flavor characteristic of America and the eighteenth century.

The American outlook up to 1914 and almost up to 1939 has been inspired by two fundamental speeches. In his farewell message at the end of his second term of office as President, Washington said:

Europe has a set of primary interests which to us have none, or a very remote relation. Hence she must be engaged in frequent controversies, the cause of which are essentially foreign to our concerns. Hence, therefore, it must be unwise in us to implicate ourselves, by artificial ties, in the ordinary vicissitudes of her politics, or the ordinary combinations and collisions of her friendships or enmities.

And in his famous message of December, 1823, President Monroe stated:

. . . the American continents, by the free and independent condition which they have assumed and maintain, are henceforth not to be considered as subjects for future colonization by any European powers. . . . We owe it, therefore, to candor and to the amicable relations existing between the United States and those powers to declare that we should consider any attempt on their part to extend their system to any portion of this hemisphere as dangerous to our peace and safety.

The moral authority which these speeches have retained for more than a century is enormous, almost Biblical in flavor. Their significance is clear. The United States, freed of former colonial bonds, was saying to Europe, "I am not interfering in your affairs; don't interfere in mine." It was the attitude of the New World addressing the Old. The consequence was at once clear; the United States would take no part in any European quarrels, having no feeling as to which party should triumph or which be defeated. There was no feeling of solidarity, and this same outlook is maintained even today, for the American still considers himself a being apart.

But this lack of interest which breeds neutrality must not be applied to the American continent, which the United States considers as a kind of private hunting ground from which all intruders must be repelled; this, by an extension of the Monroe Doctrine, leads to a temptation to claim the right of intervention. There is no feeling of neutrality, either, as far as the Pacific is concerned. If a kind of current of feeling exists which carries the American away from Europe, this same current bears him westward and impels him to take an interest in Far Eastern affairs, and sometimes to intervene in them. In each of these cases there are a latent imperialism and an irresistible instinct for expansion, which is like a biological development which is particularly well illustrated by the expression "manifest destiny." But the dominant note is the attitude of defense against Europe, a defiant reaction, the deep-down reflection of the disdain of a bygone age. Until the time of World War I the Americans remained provincial, separated by an ocean from the political hub of the world, mainly busy with the development of their continent, lying outside the main axis.

II

The crisis which United States policy underwent in the twentieth century had as a fundamental cause the extension of the American horizon. From the end of the nineteenth century the country had begun to move toward a new economic balance; because of its striking industrial development it became an importer of raw materials and an exporter of manufactured goods. The former isolationist attitude remained, but certain groups began to turn increasingly toward foreign countries. The political horizon was equally enlarged, the turning point being the victory over Spain in 1898. The United States became established in Cuba, Puerto Rico, and the Philippines, in several Pacific archipelagos, and shortly afterward, in 1903, in Panama. With the opening of the Panama Canal in 1914, the Caribbean route became an essential part of American sea communications. Indeed, from the beginning of the twentieth century onward, American political interests were conceived on a world-wide scale. Europe had hitherto considered the United States as a secondary power, to which only ministers were accredited, but henceforth ambassadors were sent. The Washington government had attained equality with the greatest in the field of international power.

The American political psychology had not changed, however, and in 1914 the initial reaction of the United States was well in keeping with former tradition. Preferences were doubtless felt in the West for Germany and in the East for the Allies, but neutrality appeared to be the only possible attitude and nobody at all imagined that the country would be dragged into the war. The *Suave mari magno* of Lucretius expresses very well what was in the Americans' inmost hearts. Yet three years later America entered the war. If one asks the Americans why, they will reply that the Allied cause was a just one, and that, since they recognized it as such, they came to their aid, without any other interest in the conflict. Thus the American people led a crusade. This explanation may be taken at its face value as far as individuals are concerned, for they were certainly inspired by the ideology of the righteous cause, but the direct cause of armed intervention in 1917 was the impossibility of tolerating any longer torpedoing by the Germans. The freedom of the seas was being flouted, as it was in 1812 by England, and this freedom is one of America's political principles, so that the moment arrived when abstention became no longer possible without losing face. I, moreover, believe that many Americans have confirmed the truth of the point of view that the fundamental cause of the intervention was political. America could exist in harmony with a world balance of power founded on British hegemony, which guaranteed the predominance of the English language, a common bond between Englishmen and Americans. But the extension outside Europe of German domination, under a system founded on entirely different principles, a completely different ideology, would have signified for the United States the rupture of a system with which they felt bound up, and they considered that it was worthwhile going to war to defend it.

This attitude showed not merely a change but a complete reversal of all former tradition, though contemporary Americans, who were not aware of it, honestly believed that they would subsequently be able to revert to their former position. We have already shown what fundamentally contradictory elements were involved in this universal ideology mixed with an isolationist temperament. Exceptional circumstances served to make open demonstration of this, provoking what in illnesses would be called the crisis. Wilsonian ideology was certainly, as far as international politics was concerned, representative of the deep-seated American attitude to things, but an instinctive tendency was dragging them in the opposite direction. Though they are internationally minded from the doctrinal point of view, they certainly are not from the temperamental.

It is thus not surprising that after the Armistice and particularly after the Treaty of Versailles a powerful reactionary instinct forced the United States to adopt once more the isolationist attitude shown by Washington and Monroe. There was, moreover, the illusion that the aims of the war had been fulfilled, that by this completely exceptional intervention America had been protected from any outside threats, that the Anglo-Saxon system had been consolidated and that, as Wilson expressed it, the world had been made safe for democracy. A page had been turned. Thus America, repudiating the logical consequences of its intervention, refused to sign the Treaty of Versailles or to become a member of the League of Nations or the International Court of Justice, persistent in its avoidance of official collaboration in the reconstruction of Europe. With the Fordney-McCumber and Smoot-Hawley tariffs it returned to a continental superprotectionism, and finally, through the legislation of the Neutrality Act of 1935-1937, demonstrated its firm resolve never again to be drawn into a European war.

The Republicans, following the Democrats who had led the country to war, had officially no feeling of solidarity with Europe, yet at the same time it became customary to intervene, not as allies and on an equal footing, but as arbitrators. In point of fact America remained in Europe. By means of observers and experts it was able to play a leading role in conferences at which it considered itself officially absent, while American public opinion took sides with passionate feelings, reserving for itself the right to judge, approve, or condemn, from a superior moralizing point of view. France was militarist; Germany after all deserved pity, and perhaps after all she was not wholly responsible for the war. The American program was to maintain peace in Europe, to prevent the development of any imperialism there, to bring the nations together, to uphold the League of Nations without becoming a member of it; this some Americans did with religious passion. In theory if not in practice this policy claimed to be following the traditional outlook, but a "manifest destiny" henceforth imposed upon the Americans a policy of intervention, even more outside Europe than within the Old World. In America there was the "Dollar Diplomacy" of Coolidge, in China the "Open Door" of Stimson. Commenting on this new position, the London *Times* published an article in 1921 at the time of the Washington Naval Conference to the effect that for the first time in the course of history the United States had felt the necessity of having a world policy in the full meaning of the term. They had passed with practically no transition from the position of a straightforward commercial power to that of a leading power controlling world finance, and they had come to realize how this change must re-act on their relations with the rest of the world. For the first time America had come to understand the full meaning of world communications, that is to say, the importance of having a commercial fleet and a navy, safe sea routes, coal and coaling stations (though it would be oil today), submarine cables, and all that in accordance with their own national interests.

III

Monroe was virtually outdated and the crisis of the totalitarian threats was to bring this fact into the open. The principles of international law upheld by Wilson were flouted in Manchuria by the Japanese and in Ethiopia by the Italians, and the League of Nations was powerless or afraid to intervene. Mussolini and then Hitler set up regimes wholly contrary to democracy, aggressively proclaiming themselves as such. Their success and their claims once more threatened British hegemony, bulwark of the Anglo-Saxon system. A drying East wind blew persistently over Europe and its evil breath attacked Western liberal civilization with corrosive action. This time the United States was moved by a spirit of solidarity. The approaches to the American continent for the first time seemed vulnerable, for since Lindbergh's symbolic flight across the Atlantic in 1927 the ocean no longer appeared as a total protection. Public opinion was aware of what was happening but did not draw any immediate conclusions; it turned toward the past rather than toward the future, and its principal aim was to prevent the country being drawn into another European war. "You won't have us a second time," it seemed to say, and the Neutrality Act arose out of that point of view.

The attitude of American public opinion was orientated in this way, but the Government realized that a new threat was appearing on the horizon, if not directly aimed at the United States at least against the principles which it represented, and even against the outposts of American security. Not without much hesitation, uncertainty, and retrograde steps, President Roosevelt's administration, which had been in power since 1933, drew from these circumstances the severe lessons which they contained. It was essential to take a stand against totalitarian regimes, encourage those who fought them, and, if necessary, give them support. The common defense program for the New World must be strengthened by a good neighbor policy, exempt from imperialism and working in the direction of Pan-American union. The approaches to the American continent must be guarded and these must include not only Greenland, Iceland, and Newfoundland but even Lisbon and Dakar, since it had become a matter of importance to know who controlled these bases. Was the security of the United States then a question of protection of the high seas? The truth of the matter was that while England ruled the waves there was no threat to America, but the position would not be the same were Germany master of the Atlantic.

The 1930's appear as a turning point in American policy. Until that time the United States had always advised the Allies to adopt a gentle attitude toward Germany, and had taxed France with militarism because it continued conscription and wished to maintain a powerful standing army. Henceforth the attitude was to change and America was to counsel firmness, resistance, and, if necessary, armed intervention. This happened with regard to Manchuria, sanctions against Italy, and Munich. Formerly France had been reproached for its army and now it was blamed for not rearming sufficiently, and it was almost accused of cowardice when it retreated before the abyss of the war. It was merely a question of exhortation and pressure brought to bear. We were told, "Sacrifice yourselves to the last man!" Part of American public opinion, violently antifascist, adopted a tone of moral combativeness which cried shame upon the Europeans for their cowardice, but the official policy was one of neutrality, an almost aggressive neutrality. Nevertheless, a stronger current was bearing the country in the opposite direction, and it was by virtue of inescapable logic that we witnessed them participating for a second time in a European war.

Why should the Americans have entered World War II? It was for exactly the same reasons that drew them into the first, with the slight difference that antitotalitarian ideology played a part which it had not played in 1914. If American security had been put into danger by the threat of a German hegemony, the National Socialist aggression was in direct opposition to democracy. It is, however, not at all certain whether, without Pearl Harbor, the Government would have taken upon itself the responsibility of involving the country in war. Had not the President said "again and again" that he would never send American boys to fight in foreign wars? The Japanese aggression transferred the "foreign" conflict into a war for the defense of the American continent. Sentimental attraction toward the Pacific then came into play and, of the two theaters of war, Europe and Asia, it is indubitably the latter which took first place in popular sentiment. It was a national conflict, while the former was merely political. Among these motivating factors there was no element of imperialism. Possibly later their appetite grew with eating, but it must be recognized that the Americans were not eager to establish themselves as world leaders.

IV

The year is 1945. America is once more victorious and has shown herself capable, not only of setting up a powerful army, but of using it on the battlefield in a war which was both heroic and administrative, which displayed to the full the diversity of its qualities. Nevertheless, the goal was no more attained than it had been in 1918. Germany had been conquered and National Socialism laid low, but the former threat reappeared, transposed and in the even more dangerous form of an equally expansionist Russia and a left-wing totalitarianism. The world was most decidedly not safe for democracy, at least not for the Western democracies, which henceforth must be distinguished from the so-called peoples' democracies.

After the illusions of Yalta, which were quickly dispelled, the American Government realized from April, 1945, at the San Francisco Conference that a new adversary was appearing on the horizon, even more powerful than the former, and in evidence both in the East beyond the Elbe and in the West beyond the Bering Straits. There are only two world powers left in opposition, not only through division of influence but in their conception of production and of ways of living. The fundamental source of their difference is ideological. For the American, imbued with the doctrine of free enterprise, Communism is not only harmful but to be condemned from a moral standpoint as being incompatible with democracy, and thus arises the tendency to fight it in a crusading spirit. Politics, interests, and passionate feelings are inextricably mingled.

The object to be defended, for the third time, is the Anglo-Saxon world and even Western civilization, but under transformed and almost reversed conditions. Formerly the British and the French formed the front line and the Americans left it to them. Now America is in the front line and England is no more than a "good second." The responsibility has shifted to the United States. The Americans must be present in full force everywhere, ready to bear the military, financial, and political burdens of the free world. There is no first-class power standing between America and Russia, and the United States has become the guarantor of the whole of Western civilization, for the façade of the United Nations Organization deceives nobody.

Thus there is no longer any question of the Americans shutting themselves up in their continent, sheltered by two oceans now shrinking like Balzac's *"peau de chagrin."* Isolationism can no longer be defended; it must be borne in mind, however, that complete isolationism has never existed, and that the mental attitude of the isolationist still survives. What was formerly called isolationism was the wish to have as little intercourse as possible with Europe, but this exclusiveness did not include either Asia or the remainder of the American continent. Today nobody will deny that America's responsibilities cannot be limited to the American continent, but the neoisolationists think that Asia should come uppermost in external considerations, and they are known as "Asia firsters." If they envisage the defense of Europe, they are tempted, like Hoover or Taft, to picture a sort of peripheral resistance, with air bases in Scandinavia, the Iberian Peninsula, and the British Isles. The "internationalists," who include the Democrats and the left wing of the Republican party, accept the protection of Western Europe with the military defense of the Elbe, and financial aid in a reconstruction program destined to restore its autonomy. America is hesitant before these two conceptions, though it moves instinctively toward the first. A peripheral defense program requires an effort in air equipment and atomic weapons, but it allows for a limited contribution of manpower. For a considerable time it appeared that the Government was adopting the international policy, but major changes effected in the Pentagon in the high command seem to be pointing in a different direction. A peripheral defense policy against the U.S.S.R. is being established, whether the theater of defense be Europe or Asia, the Atlantic or the Mediterranean, the Indian Ocean or the Pacific.

In defending the main sea routes against the advances of a European or Euro-Asiatic hegemony, the United States must support England and to a large extent replace it. Successively against Russia, against Germany, and even against Italy, United Kingdom policy has traditionally undertaken to keep free the Suez route to the Indian Ocean and the Far East. It is now Russia, in its enlarged aspect as the U.S.S.R., which must be prevented from infiltrating into the Mediterranean, the Indian Ocean, and the China seas. America must, therefore, uphold all the states in a line from Spain to Japan which might serve as barrage, buffer, or support.

It is a heavy and overwhelming task, and any other nation would crumble under it. It is in Europe that it appears the most difficult. One must have no illusions about the fact that it is a purely negative interest which keeps the United States on the continent of Europe. The Americans are there merely to prevent Russia from overrunning as far as Brest the countries which are still free west of the Iron Curtain. With this aim in mind and with no economic motives or desire for domination, America, the protector, undertook, notably by the Marshall Plan, to support the reconstruction of an autonomous Europe. We have already shown how the part played by European exports and imports in American trade is steadily decreasing. As Europe exists it must be defended, but were it to disappear under the sea like Atlantis, one may be sure that America would consider it as a relief.

It is true that Europe and overseas territories over which it exerts an influence appear to the United States as a heavy charge, an old-fashioned legacy of the past with which it refuses to acknowledge its solidarity. American public opinion is almost 100% anticolonial and it is urging the Government to take away from Europe the colonial bases of European powers which it is to its interest to uphold. This contradiction emphasizes the extent to which American policy depends on sentimentality. It is spontaneously anti-French in North Africa and Indochina, anti-English in India, anti-Dutch in Indonesia; if this attitude in the long run is contradicted by imperious logic, it can be done only in a hypocritical manner, since the Government does not admit it to the people. Although it is a matter of the preservation of Western civilization and the maintenance of its work in the world, America refuses to admit that there is any question of common defense. It is determined not to be classified with Europe by the countries which the latter has dominated. And what do these countries themselves think? They observe the United States proclaiming the independence of Cuba or the Philippines, but they cannot believe that there is no American intervention in Cuba, the Philippines, Panama, or the Pacific islands. They consider that America is today the successor in the expansion of the white races, a nation that must be mistrusted. Their liberty nevertheless remains limited, for it would be difficult for them not to take sides between American and Communist influence.

There are, in practice, only two political systems existing in the world and opposing each other over the heads of Europe. Part of American opinion, including most of the Democrats, the more liberal-minded of the Republicans, and the Government itself, feeling able to work together on this issue, have adopted a policy of repressing Communism. Others, more impatient in face of an adversary whose provocations are often difficult to bear, tend toward pushing it back. America has demonstrated by its resistance in Korea that there is a limit beyond which it will show no toleration of transgressors, but before that other limit, total war, it stopped, refusing to take the risk that men like General MacArthur or Admiral Radford would have accepted. The American Government, faithful to an illusion which it previously held in 1918, had thought that it could leave the defense of Europe to Europe, and proceeded to large-scale disarmament. Its position as pioneer in atomic warfare seemed sufficient. When in 1950 it observed that what it had thought to be a nuclear monopoly was no monopoly at all, its policy changed to one of rearmament for defense and, if necessary, for attack. This took place before developments in Korea.

Finally, as Russian progress in the atomic field became clearer, President Eisenhower proposed in 1953 a world agreement on nuclear energy. America, in truth, feels daily more vulnerable to atomic attack. In September, 1953, the Civil Defense Administration drew up and made public a list of 193 cities which would be likely to serve as targets. It is possible that the Government sees in civil defense a means of large-scale expenditure which might be capable of preventing a depression at one time or another. It is also possible that it is intentionally exaggerating the danger to arouse a singularly unmoved public opinion. Indeed, a Gallup Poll taken in 1953 showed that only one-third of the people questioned believed that their city could be threatened by atom bomb attack; this means that two-thirds of the population continues to live in the traditional illusion of continental security. It is not that no effort has been made to inform them and keep them alert, for this has been in progress for a long time, but to them must surely be applied the saying of the preacher, which is fundamental: "We know that we shall die, but we do not believe it."

War seems inevitable to some, probable to others, possible to all, but what is the real reaction of public opinion to this possibility? It is clear that it is essentially different from the European attitude. When Americans turn toward the past and recall the terrible events of the past twenty-five years, the Great Depression rather than the war comes uppermost in their minds, for it probably caused more suffering among the people of the United States than did the war. Measured in terms of its influence on the attitude and reactions of the American people, it should be grouped with the Civil War as one of the two outstanding happenings since Independence. By comparison, the 1940 war is only a secondary experience, suffered by the combatants and indirectly by their families, but for others it is associated with a period of full employment and disappearance of the crisis in the dynamic progress of renewed production. Galbraith expressed this opinion in his *American Capitalism*. By this it must not be thought that the Americans want war. They talk of it as men who have without doubt fought heroically, but outside their own country. Samuel Lubell, in *The Future of American Politics*, makes these troubling statements: "If there must be a war, let us finish with it," or "Let us prepare ourselves to fight Russia, alone if needs be, for it is inevitable." It is the attitude of men who believe that things will be the same a second time. I know scarcely a single European west of the Iron Curtain who would use the same language, for, as far as we are concerned, war is death and the end of everything. The picture of it held in the United States, even considering the threat of atomic warfare, does not seem to be at all the same. It is certain that America does not want war, but many Americans in all classes of society are capable of speaking of it with *sangfroid*, as a thing which can be envisaged. This more than anything else shows the difference which has grown up between Europe and America. As La Rochefoucald said: "One cannot look directly at either the sun or death." * That is how we Europeans consider war.

* *"Le soleil ni la mort ne se peuvent regarder fixement."*

CONCLUSION

CHAPTER 35

The United States and Western Civilization

★

Europe, the white race, and Western civilization were only recently synonymous terms. Today the leading sectors of the white race are no longer in Europe and Western civilization has spread beyond the limits of the Old World, though there is a part of the Old World which no longer forms part of it. Not so long ago Europe and the West could be superimposed upon each other, like two identical geometrical figures. One now begins to wonder where the center of gravity of the West will lie in future. If it is to be in America, then surely Western civilization will follow a new path where Europe will no longer be able to recognize its former self, and this is the problem that has arisen ever since the United States and the U.S.S.R. became the leading powers of the world. When one speaks of the United States, one is tempted to do so as if one is merely dealing with a power which in its turn has achieved political hegemony; but it must be considered as a continent, a civilization, a stage of human development. Any other view of it is too narrow, and it is only in this way that the American problem can be seen in its full perspective.

The United States, like Europe, belongs to the Christian tradition, to the democratic humanism of the eighteenth century, and finally to the Industrial Revolution. The American conception of knowledge, of the individual, and of techniques is the same as ours. At first sight, therefore, the Americans appear to be doing no more than continuing, by expanding it on a large and magnificent scale, a line of development which has its source in Europe. It is indeed these foundations which give personality to our common civilization—which one could not say any longer of the

351

U.S.S.R.—but it is the combination of these elements in their due proportions and in a new order which is making of America a new world, different from our old one not only in dimensions but in quality.

Christianity and humanism may have crossed the Atlantic, but the same cannot be said of the classical tradition of Greece and Rome, which is characteristic in the formation of Europe. Contact with the Mediterranean is a reality for us. The originality of Europe resides to a large measure in the well-matched association of the Anglo-Saxon spirit, which is synonymous with efficiency, and the Latin spirit, which is expressed in individual intellectualism, a combination of the practical with the critical approach. This balance has not been transmitted to the United States, though peoples of Mediterranean origin are numerous among its inhabitants. The Italian, Spanish, Portuguese, Greek, and Romanian immigrants who have settled in America come mainly from the lower social strata, and have had no other desire than to repudiate their past and become assimilated as quickly as possible into this essentially Nordic society. The culture of the Latin countries is no longer known and understood except in specialized university circles, and this contact is solely by means of books.

Thus the critical spirit, which is by its very nature individualistic, has decreased in importance as compared with the collective practice of high output. Culture in the true sense of the word, with all its personal aspects, is tending to be increasingly eclipsed by technical progress and the prestige of high-powered equipment. The result of this is a society orientated more and more toward achievements which depend on collective action, where the individual acting alone and thinking alone is reduced to powerlessness. Mass man has triumphed over the anarchic individual, for the necessities of modern production have so willed it. Emphasis is placed on the importance of science, the amazing progress of which astonishes the world of today and will probably astonish even further the world of tomorrow. Technical considerations are considered as all-important, and it is believed that their infallible methods can be applied to anything whatever. The man who really counts is the expert, before whom everyone must bow.

It is possible for an equipment megalomania to exist, in which the means becomes an end in itself. One sometimes gains an impression of this in certain universities, which are almost too well equipped. A radio set in every room, television, moving pictures, too much material comfort, all breed mental laziness. Megalomania of technical progress can also exist, and this is possibly felt in certain methods which are used to excess in medicine and psychiatry. This is merely a question of proportion, for no objection would be felt if a proportionately sufficient place were allowed for culture, that is, for man himself following the tradition of ancient Greece and of Europe. Man is considered less as a being who can think than a being who can act, like Theodore Roosevelt who, according to Henry Adams, was "pure act"; since action requires specialized ability, there is the risk that excessive recourse to the specialist will bring about a lack of balance.

II

Western civilization, in its European form, had attained full spiritual maturity before technical progress, born of the Industrial Revolution, penetrated it and tended to dominate it. This tendency, which cannot help increasing, will doubtless transform the destiny of the West. It is at work in full swing in the United States, and the brake which held it back in Europe cannot operate effectively in the New World.

Education in America is becoming increasingly characterized by technical considerations. The humanities have practically no place as compared with a French *lycée* or an English public school. Secondary education is carried out in the high school, which gives to all pupils, without selection, an excellent practical education with only a scanty academic background. Real culture is to be found only in the universities, but classical education is found only as a kind of accessory. Where a study of the humanities exists it is generally relegated to a subsidiary section which is suspected of being reserved for the aesthete and to which a large proportion of foreign students are attracted. In religion a similar judgment is often passed on the contemplative, who is clearly out of his depth in this country of action.

It is clear that the conditions under which a spirit of humanist culture is formed are very different from those which require the training of a worker to be efficient in the realm of collective action, whether one is considering industry, surgery, or social work. The specialist, who is well trained in his speciality, therefore becomes a necessity, and he must be given technical training, not general culture. There is thus everywhere the need for selection, from secondary education onward, for the special skill that will be required either for large industrial enterprises or for the army or for the navy. Once admitted, according to the rules of planned vocational guidance, the candidates are taken in hand, enrolled and followed until they enter into the practical sphere. They will have learned much and will have been given extensive information on facts and figures, but nobody will have opened the window for them on the major problems of the mind.

In this the American appears to us as Germany's star pupil, and it is not the first time that we have made this observation. He has inherited from Germany, in addition to efficiency of organization, an almost fanatical respect for method, for objectivity, for science and everything which may claim kinship with it. The conscience (*Gründlichkeit*) and the objective spirit (*Sachlichkeit*) of the Germans are found in America, but with modification due to Anglo-Saxon common sense which German lack of proportion has never possessed. The result is efficient; it consists more and more of a complicated and perfectly planned framework in which the individual is required to classify himself. Education is essentially a preparation for this classification. For example, in examinations for the selection of personnel there are generally a large number of very simple questions, put in writing, to which the candidate must answer "yes" or "no." It is indeed a system very similar to that of intelligence tests. The examiner merely has to verify that "yes" and "no" appear in the right places and the total, if the numbers are very large, will be calculated mechanically as in the compilation of statistics, or, if we are to believe Sinclair Lewis, in the totaling of the number of conversions in religious revivals.

The system produces competent people but it does not guarantee that they should be cultured. The pupil is given plenty of meat, but no effort is made to see that he chews it and assimilates it. Cocteau's counsel seems pertinent here: "The mind should have strong teeth. Chew things with strong teeth and do not let them become merely the ornament of a movie star smile." The assimilation of things of the spirit is the real lesson offered by the study of the humanities, but America appears to consider this old-fashioned. In an examination for the recruitment of administrative staff, 80% of the questions were on scientific and technical matters, while the 20% reserved for general culture were allotted not to literature or philosophy but to sociology—a very significant replacement. There is a whole new conception of life there, and it is one toward which our century is moving, with the United States in the vanguard. Are we wrong to look backward, like Lot's wife?

III

In this regime, where technical training is of primary consideration, some men, either behind the times or forerunners of a new age, are nostalgic for something different. At Harvard and the University of Chicago the need is felt to give to the study of the humanities a place of some significance, for there are men alert enough to wonder whether in the long run excessive specialization will not dry up the deep, creative springs of the national mind. The Committee on Social Thought of the University of Chicago has undertaken to wage war against the abuse of quantitative information, against the rigid divisions in which knowledge is pigeonholed and shut away. It is seeking, on the other hand, the realization of the type of interchange of ideas which constitutes real knowledge. There are certain signs which, indeed, should make one think. Since the rise of Hitlerism and World War II the creative source of American science has come largely from scientists from central or eastern Europe, who have been cast out of the Old World through persecution. One is tempted to wonder whether the Anglo-Saxons, by reason of their tendency to specialize, their propensity for giving sport a place of honor in university hierarchy, have not neglected the development of highly cultured personalities which form the very soul of a civilization. This would imply, in the long run, condemnation of a type of society where equipment and the instruments of applied technique are all-important, where the tool itself has become more important than its function.

The New World is in no way hostile to the general idea used as a source of inspiration, but, though the American feels in spite of everything that there is an empty space to be filled, his response is not that of the classicist. He is more tempted to consider educating "specialists in general ideas," that is to say, another class of experts. In everything he seems to be interested in methods rather than things themselves. Renan wrote: "The Greeks created masterpieces, and then they believed that one could formulate rules for creating a masterpiece." The Americans should meditate on this. The training given to future schoolteachers consists of interminable classes on child psychology; as in Switzerland and central Europe, the emphasis is placed on education and educational methods. In the universities one is sometimes left with the impression that the authorities are more interested in the buildings, which are indeed splendid, than in learning. Or perhaps nostalgia for things of the spirit will express itself in mysticism. America is a country where religion continues to arouse passionate interest. Formerly the traditional aspect of nonconformist Puritanism was uppermost. This still exists, but it is replaced more and more by other parallel conceptions. Just as mythology had an unprecedented success in German universities under the Hitler regime, courses in religion, but in the broad and nonorthodox sense of the term, are demanded everywhere. This need for emotion, which is mistaken for culture, can produce strange mixtures. The first Kinsey Report on sexual behavior was a best seller, and these problems, far from being considered from the lighthearted angle of Henry of Navarre, are in the end considered with a sort of mysticism. If to such mysticism is grafted a respect for action, one will arrive at a civilization new in its orientation, though not without its ancient traditions.

One has the impression that this country of vast possibilities, of complete good will and intense sincerity, requires dosing with a large portion of classicism. It needed a Montaigne and achieved an Emerson. Dominated by the didactic tendency of the century, it would easily be capable of forgetting that the essential aim of civilization is not technical progress, or output, or equipment, but man himself. Europe remains penetrated by Greco-Latin culture and remembers a civilization prior to the machine age. Russia, which has separated from Europe, worships technical progress and is an industrial disciple, not of Germany or France, but of the United States. From this point of view America and the U.S.S.R., though in violent opposition to each other, incline toward the same technical conception of civilization. On either hand their vast expanses of territory favor standardization and mass production and incite them toward this goal. They are two huge continents which, above the head of little Europe, are imposing on the world a standard different from that of former tradition.

In these circumstances, some may well ask what is to become of our Western civilization if its center deserts Europe and is implanted in the vastness of America. It will preserve under this new leadership its essentials, a conception of science based on objectivity, and a conception of the individual based on the respect of man. But under the pressure of a permanent lever action, science will become more technical and less contemplative, and the ideal man a man of action rather than a man of thought. The classical tradition will still survive, but the American will be a highly developed *Homo faber* rather than the Homo sapiens as conceived by Socrates. The Christian tradition will remain alive, but less exclusively in its Greek form than according to the inspiration of the Old Testament; this will mark the decline of Mediterranean influence and, to quote Amiel, the emphasis will be placed to a greater extent on "this oriental aspect which Christianity represents in our culture." In the spectacular race into which America has drawn it, this civilization inherited from Europe will shed on the way shreds of contemplative spirit, something of the critical spirit of the individual, as it moves toward a new conception of human dignity, which is more social. The essential element will be preserved and it will always remain a Western civilization, but it will no longer be European, and the inhabitant of the Old World thinks in melancholy fashion of the words of Corneille: "A great destiny is ending, a great destiny is beginning." *

* *"Un grand destin finit, un grand destin commence."*